The Transformed Life

Living and Growing in Christ

Father James Rosselli

PASCHA PRESS
Educate Edify Entertain

Father James Rosselli

Bio:

Fr. James is a priest serving in the Western Rite of the Russian Orthodox Church Outside of Russia (ROCOR).

He is Rector of St. Joseph of Arimathea Orthodox Church and House of Prayer in La Porte, Indiana. A convert to Orthodoxy, Fr. James spent seven years in the Catholic Charismatic Renewal, eleven years as a Lutheran minister (AALC), ten years in the non-canonical church, on loan to a Kievan Patriarchate parish from the UAOC, and joined ROCOR in 2011. He spent twenty years as a military chaplain, serving State Guard units in New York, New Mexico and Indiana.

Fr. James is a graduate of Holy Apostles Seminary in Cromwell, CT (BA), the Franciscan University of Steubenville, Ohio (MA), and Holy Resurrection Orthodox Seminary, the former ROCOR Western Rite colloquy program.

Fr. James, his wife, Sue, their daughter, Alyssa, and their cat, Victoria, live and minister in La Porte, IN.

You can access Father's You Tube channel, here:
https://www.youtube.com/channel/UCMZ0iMtv1eoF8jSYAPaG0DQ

© Copyright May, 2016 by Rev. Fr. James Rosselli. All rights, in all media, are reserved throughout the world. Permission is granted to cite passages for purposes of criticism, and acknowledgment is requested.

U.S. Copyright Office File #1-3397079904

First Edition: American Orthodox Institute, e-book, 2018

Pascha Press

Toll-free telephone: 1-844-4-PASCHA mkunch@paschapress.com
http://www.paschapress.com

This publication is designed to provide accurate information, for general purposes only, in regard to the subject matter covered. There are no warranties, expressed or implied.

ISBN: 978-1-5323-7257-5

Dedication

*This is dedicated to my wonderful wife Susan,
and our fantastic daughter, Alyssa:
warmth of my heart, women of God.*

~

*With profound thanks to my Bishop, His Eminence
Metropolitan +HILARION, First Hierarch of ROCOR,
whose suggestions made this a better book; and to
The Very Reverend Hans Jacobse of the American
Orthodox Institute, for his friendship, support and
encouragement; and to Fr. Richard Stoecker, whose
early enthusiasm for the project was a tonic!*

~

*Honorable Mention to our delightful cat, Victoria,
who is seldom late for Chapel.*

*"All you beasts, wild and tame, bless the Lord!"
Daniel 3: 81*

Fr. James Rosselli's book is a pastoral catechesis. His approach is farsighted and even groundbreaking in its own way. As the broader culture increasingly drifts from its Christian moorings, propositions about the Christian faith are no longer understood. Rather, much like the early centuries of Christianity, Christ is first encountered and instruction follows, and if the instruction is sound, communion with Christ can deepen. This is the new and necessary way of teaching through experience where life itself is seen as the sacred enterprise that it is, and the everyday events of life are the places where communion with Christ grows. It will be welcomed by the seeker, the novice, and even the life-long Orthodox Christian. Christians from other traditions with find it enlightening as well.

—The Very Reverend Hans Jacobse, Founder of the American Orthodox Institute

Credits

Original e-book cover by Mat Susan Rosselli

Back cover photograph: Alyssa Rosselli

Book designer and cover artist: Scott Cuzzo, www.scottcuzzo.com

Foreword

By His Eminence Metropolitan +HILARION
First Hierarch of the Russian Orthodox Church Outside of Russia

Fr. James has written a very readable, down-to-earth book. In the tradition of St. John of the Ladder, he "takes the reader by the hand" and leads him or her from very elementary things to the depths of the Faith.

The Transformed Life is on a level with other works of the same type, and I recommend it not only for Eastern Christians, but particularly for Westerners who are pursuing, or who wish to pursue, the richness of Christ's Ancient Church.

+HILARION
Metropolitan of New York and Eastern America
First Hierarch of the Russian Orthodox Church Outside of Russia

Father James Rosselli

Introduction

My spiritual director at seminary was a very holy and perceptive priest who had paid very harsh dues on the South American mission field during the rampaging days of Che Guevara. One of his frequent observations was, "torture hurts." When I was applying to him to take me on, I parroted to him a phrase I had encountered from my reading and which sounded suitably humble: "I will obey you as Christ." He immediately fixed me with a stare I will never forget, and proclaimed, "You will not!"

It's amazing how a good spiritual director will dump you right into reality, and out of the silly and dangerous romantic abstractions to which we tend to fall prey at the beginning of our serious walk with the Lord.

What we need to understand right from the outset is that all this stuff is real. It isn't a pleasing theoretical construction or just one more congenial way of life. It isn't a compendium of learned speculation that's subject to argument between academics. It's Reality. It is in fact the most real thing we have ever encountered, and it is much, much larger.

My first spiritual director, before seminary, was a wise and holy Capuchin friar. I was just beginning my serious adult walk with the Lord, and had a tendency to get over-romantic about it all. At these moments he would say to me, "Jim, don't be a horse's a_ _!"

This is counsel I have tried from time to time, with varying degrees of success, to actually follow. I humbly pass it along to whoever may happen to read this little book.

In some four decades of ministry. I've learned some things about living the transformed life in Christ. I am woefully imperfect in actually applying these things, but for reasons known only to Himself, God put me in a cassock and called me to talk about them, and perhaps make a little progress along the Way, myself.

Whatever is useful about this book, I owe to the marvelous teachers with whom the Lord has blessed me throughout my life in Him, a few of whom you will see on the "Thanks" page at the end. Whatever is not is entirely my own fault.

~ ~ ~

> *Behold I stand at the door and knock. If anyone hears*
> *My voice, and opens the door, I will come in to him and*
> *dine with him, and he with Me.*
> (Revelation 3:20)

This is a book about Jesus: Jesus Christ, the Messiah, King over all kings, Lord over all lords, Son of God and God the Son, sole and only hope of the world and sole and only hope for our personal salvation. It is therefore a book about God: about entering into His Mystery and indeed about becoming part of it. Not just a "participant" in it, but an actual transformed, and forever-transforming, part of His Life and work.

As countercultural as this may seem, God is not a consumer product and He is not a salesman. While He may "stand at our door and knock" (see above), He doesn't do so because He's asking for anything. God is fully sufficient in Himself, and doesn't need anything from us. He stands at our door because that's where to find us, and He knocks to get our attention. He is not asking but offering, and for no other reason than that He loves us.

Somehow, our culture has got this backwards. We have come to view God as some pesky salesman Who somehow needs us to "ask Him into our lives." It's as if He's some cosmic hobo, who wants to come into our house and eat with us because He needs a meal. And when we make any response at all, however meager, we act as if we were doing Him a favor.

In retrospect, this is unsurprising. Back in the 1980's there arose a movement to "use the tools of modern marketing to reach people for the Lord." The intentions may well have been good, but the results have been a disaster. Today we have a church, or something that calls itself a church, on nearly every street-corner, that pushes a "seeker-sensitive service" geared to "identify and meet the felt needs of the people" with almost no emphasis at all on sin and repentance, obedience or commitment. Yet, awareness of sin and repentance, obedience and commitment, are the cornerstones of the Christian life. In far too many "Christian" environments we are invited not to worship God, but ourselves; not to thank God for permitting us into His Presence, but to congratulate ourselves for being gracious enough to permit Him into ours.

In truth, relationship with God is about *His* Grace, not ours. It is not about God "becoming part of our life," it is about us becoming part of His.

We cannot be saved by regarding God as a brand of toothpaste on which we have decided. Still less do we have a shot at Heaven by regarding Him rather like a candy bar being sold door-to-door by a charity, which we in our generosity have graciously bought. That's a worldly perspective, ground into us by a society whose every offer has strings attached and whose every benefit has a price.

Before we can get anywhere in our walk with the Lord, we need to gain a different perspective, one which is not of things but of Him.

The first thing we need to do is discard pop-Christian-culture's portrayal of God as some sort of complacent, benevolent grand-uncle who wants us only to be "happy" and who approves of everything (or almost everything) we do, because we have generously consented to be "saved."

The reality is, God does not approve of almost everything we do. In fact, He doesn't fully approve of anything we do. We are flawed people, and we perform flawed actions. Even when those actions are good and holy, they are imperfect. That's because we, being imperfect, cannot perform a perfect act. The holiest among us have always known this. Abbot Macarius, the towering Fourth-Century Desert Father, complained on his deathbed, "I go to my Lord having barely made a beginning." This same sentiment has been echoed, time and again, down the corridors of the time we inhabit. It has been the end-of-life confession and counsel of the greatest of the Saints throughout history.

So what hope do the likes of us, have?

I will share with you a secret: the greatest saints are sinners, too. All of us are in the same boat, flawed creatures in need of the Grace and Mercy which are freely offered by our gracious and merciful God.

~ ~ ~

Our hope is in Christ-God, and our confidence is reinforced by the fact that He has no "hidden agenda." The invitation is simple: turn away from my fallen, hell-bound life and turn to Him, and He will give me a new, Heaven-bound life.

Our minds are geared to respond, "What's the catch?" It is difficult— actually, it's impossible-- for fallen man to conceive of an utterly selfless action. We have never experienced an utterly selfless moment. We have never observed, despite all the impressively selfless acts we have observed, an utterly selfless act. Yet, that is what we encounter when we encounter God: utter Selflessness. Unconditional Love.

After all, what does God have to be selfish about? Selfishness is born of insecurity, and insecurity is born out of the innate knowledge of our incompleteness. But, God is complete. In fact, He is Completeness, itself.

Selfishness is born out of desire to meet needs. But what does God need? He is the Creator, completely sufficient in and of Himself. He has made, and makes, everything that was or is made. If He did have a need, it would by definition be fulfilled.

Selfishness is born out of a desire to put oneself forward in the eyes of others. But, why should—in fact, how could—God do this? He is already above and beyond all that is. How could He have a desire to advance Himself? Where could He go?

Our limited imaginations lead us to speculate that perhaps God gets bored, so creates the requisite "lack" out of a desire to relieve His boredom. But, how can a fully self-sufficient Being, of infinite variety within Himself, ever get bored?

There is no Earthly logic that can explain the hope we have. It demands Heavenly logic, which begins and ends in the fact that God Loves.

Life in Christ is a journey: an interior, transformative voyage that, if you stick with it, will reveal to you who you are, and equip you with the tools to be that person. It will give you a whole new perspective on "going to church," and indeed on what "Church" actually is. It will, hopefully, give you a whole new insight into the business of being human, particularly of being human in the ever-present Presence of God. It will set you a-sail upon the river that flows into Eternity from Ancient Days.

Table Of Contents

Bio .... a

Dedication c

Credits .... e

Forward .... f

Introduction .... g

Table Of Contents .... m

PART ONE: LIFE AND ITS CHOICES 1

    ONE: The Human Condition 1
        When the Woman Saw... 4
    TWO: Nature 4
    THREE: Human Culture 8
        Life on the Road 12
    FOUR: The Church 14
        The Present Reality of Eternity:
          Religion and the Church 17
    FIVE: Virtue and Vice 18
        VICE 19
        Pride 19
        Envy and Wrath 21
        Sloth 24

>   Greed 27
>   Gluttony 29
>   Lust 30
>   Read Ahead to the End of the Book: We Win 32
>
> VIRTUE 33
> THE VIRTUES 34
> THE CARDINAL VIRTUES 35
>   Temperance 35
>   Prudence 38
>   Justice 43
>   Courage 48
> THE THEOLOGICAL VIRTUES 52
>   Faith 52
>   Hope 56
>   Love 59

PART TWO: THE JOURNEY 66

> SIX: VOCATION 66
>   Our Relationship to Nature 71
>   Our Relationship to God 71
>   The Call of Christ 73
>   Jesus and Reality 75

PART THREE: THE TOOLS 79

>   Real Spirituality 82
>   Humility 85
>   Commitment 89
>   Responsibility 91
>   Gratitude 96
> SEVEN: DIGNITY 101

PART FOUR: FEET UPON THE PATH 109

    Contemplative Prayer..109

    EIGHT: THE PENITENTIAL LIFE...111
        NINE: THE SACRAMENTAL LIFE 116
            Baptism 119
            Chrismation 124
            Anointing (Holy Unction) 125
            Confession...128
            The Holy Eucharist..130
            Matrimony 135
            Ordination...139
            The Sacrament of Nature 144
        TEN: CHURCH LIFE 147
            Getting Into the Church..150
            Getting Out of the Church 151
            The Domestic Church..152
    The Atmosphere of the Home 155
    Getting Out of the House 159
    ELEVEN: THE CONTEMPLATIVE LIFE......................................160
        The Difference Between
            Christian and "Eastern" Mediation...................165
    Defined Exterior Object 165
    Theanthropic Emphasis..167
    Revealed Ontology 167
    On Method 168
    Contemplation and Rule 170

PART FIVE: THE ABCD'S OF CONTEMPLATION.........................173

    TWELVE: ABANDONMENT 173
    Vulnerability..174
    Transparency...179

Trust 182
THIRTEEN: BEREFTNESS 189
Self-Abnegation 189
Poverty of Spirit 192
Balance 196
Guilt 197
Discouragement 198
Enthos 201

FOURTEEN: COMPOSITION OF PLACE 202
The Gift of the Present Moment 202
Holy (and unholy) Fear 204
Doing the Stuff 208
FIFTEEN: DISPONABILITY 208
Disposition 210
Recollection 213
Not just for "meditation" 213
A Listening Ear 215
The Power of Silence 216
"The Rules" and beyond 217
Trust 218
Ego, Ambition, Deception and Availability 219

PART SIX: CONVERSION OF MANNERS 223

SIXTEEN: CUSTODY OF MIND 224
"...for as he thinketh in his heart, so is he" 224
The Phronema 226
Spiritual Ambition 228
SEVENTEEN: CUSTODY OF THE EYES 230
Making Choices 231
The Killjoy 233
The Art of Seeing 233

  False Heroism 235
  The Importance of Grace 236
 EIGHTEEN: CUSTODY OF HEARING 239
  Credulity 239
 NINETEEN: CUSTODY OF SPEECH 243
  Gossip 243
  Vain Speech 247
  Vainglorious Speech 249
 TWENTY: CUSTODY OF SELF 252
  The Error of Quietism
  Co-operation with God 253

PART SEVEN: MARY, THE MOTHER OF GOD 257

  An Important Personage 260
  Mary as Icon 263
  Mary as Intercessor 265
  Mary and Virginity 267

PART EIGHT: A PRACTICAL FAITH 271
  The Anthropic Principle 273
  Intelligent Design 274
  A Life of Faith 276
Thanks 277
Bibliography and Suggested Reading List 279

The Transformed Life

PART ONE: LIFE AND ITS CHOICES

All the ways of a man are pure in his own eyes, but the Lord weighs the spirit.
(Proverbs 16: 2)

~ ~ ~

ONE: THE HUMAN CONDITION

The heart is deceitful above all things, and desperately corrupt; who can understand it?
(Jeremiah 17:9)

We are forever being told, "follow your heart." "Let your heart lead you," and the like. But how reliable is that? To the world, "follow your heart" means "follow your affections." All that advice boils down to is, "do what you really, really, really want to do!" But how does that contribute to a stable life? Our affections change. Much of the time, we don't know what we really—or even really, really, really—want to do.

To a Christian, "follow your heart" means, "let Christ lead you into the very center of your being, and when you get there, listen to Him." The world's "heart," a product of our own immediate and fleeting desires, leads us not to the exaltation of God, but of ourselves.

In a nutshell, our condition is that we are sinners. "So," one might say, with the Pelagians, "let's just stop sinning." The problem is, as pious and God-loving a man as Pelagius was, he had it wrong—which is why Pelagianism is a heresy.

You see, Pelagius thought that we are sinners because we sin. But that's backwards: we sin because we are sinners. And we are sinners because of a fatal flaw we inherit from our first parents: Pride, the Original Sin and our fatal, tragic flaw. Pride is the origin of all sins, because without it we would be unable to arrogate to ourselves permission to commit any of the other sins. We would not be able, when confronted with an act of wrongdoing, however large or small, to assure ourselves that "it's okay."

For instance, who is there among us who has not lifted a pen or two, or some paper, or some paper clips, from the office, without permission? Yet, stealing is wrong. It is a transgression. God tells us not to do it (Exodus 20:15, the Eighth Commandment). That being the case, where do we get permission to steal the pen? When pressed, the usual answer is, "Hey, everybody does it." And indeed, everybody, or almost everybody, does. But what does that say about us? Right there on the surface, it shows us that we as creatures have collectively decided that it is okay to transgress the Commandment of God in this particular instance. Lacking God's permission, we give permission to ourselves—and we have no actual authority to do that.

The two most common justifications for office pilfering are, "everybody does it" and "It's only..." perhaps coupled with, "it's small--nobody'll even notice." None of these statements actually addresses the issue: the fact that we are stealing. All they do is give us an excuse—a self-granted permission--to steal.

Where does the authority to give such permission come from? The collective "everybody?" Does that mean that if all of us make up our minds to disregard what God says, He somehow hasn't said it? or that if enough of us agree about something, we can overrule Him? Is it the size of the object that determines the legitimacy of the act? If what we steal is small enough, is our act no longer a theft? or does its small size imply permission to steal it? Or, if "nobody notices" what we do, does that mean we have permission to do it?

I am using the occasional filching of a box of company paper clips as just one example, because it's a pretty common one. In reality, we tend to try to minimize our sins, whatever they may be, in hopes that if we make them small enough we will "cut them down to our size," to where maybe we can legitimately give ourselves permission to commit them. I remember having spent some time working with a prison ministry. One day, and not atypically, an inmate explained to me that he didn't belong in jail because he had only been dealing "a little" cocaine.

Given God's directives not to do some particular things, we need "permission" from somewhere else if we want to do them. But, there is no legitimate source of such permission. Our act of giving that permission to ourselves—usurping God's prerogative and declaring it somehow "okay" to disobey Him—is the fruit of the original sin. It is the very expression of our fatal flaw.

"But," runs the usual protest, "that's just human nature!"

Yes, it is. And that's the whole point.

The third chapter of Genesis tells the story of a similar "small thing," just a piece of fruit among a whole planet full of pieces of fruit, and the first-ever decision of this type: the one that brought the universe crashing down around our ears. We will be referring to it frequently throughout our discussions.

The salient part is in verse 6a: *So when the woman saw that the tree was good for food, and that it was a delight to the eyes, and that the tree was to be desired to make one wise, she took of its fruit and ate..."*

When the woman saw...

Eve *formed a different opinion* from God's admonition, and thereby separated herself from Him. Choosing her own perception over the Truth, she made the decision to defy God. Then, as miscreants have done ever since, she enticed another, Adam, to join her. Adam—who was supposed to be her protector—assented. And the universe, created to be held in an eternal perfect balance through obedience to the Creator by His creation, lurched.

TWO : NATURE

> When I look at Thy heavens, the work of Thy fingers,
> the moon and the stars which Thou hast established,
> what is man that Thou art mindful of him, and the son
> of man, that You care for him?
> (Psalm 8: 3-4)

God's own iconic creature, having been given sovereignty over nature as God's steward, upset the balance. Having introduced a dynamic contrary to God's Order, he arrogated that sovereignty to himself—and invented Pride: the presumption of self-sufficiency apart from God. In His turn, God, Who had given man sovereignty, honored that sovereignty, saying to him, in effect, "go for it. Sow as you will but know that you will reap what you sow."

The problem is, our first parents couldn't cash the check. They were not God, they were only His stewards. They were given authority over the creation, and the creation was radically intertwined with them. The power behind that authority, however, was their union with God. Once that union was broken, imperfection was introduced. That which was created perfect had become flawed. The flaw was thus engrafted into the universe, and into our DNA. We live—and live in—the result.

The universe certainly doesn't look broken. The Hubble telescope and various other probes have revealed to us an enormous, unfathomably mighty and compellingly beautiful creation. The forces that hold it together are measurable in mathematical terms, but beyond that they are beyond our comprehension. Even here, in even the simplest of back-yards, breathtaking splendor surrounds us, moving us at times to astonishment as we behold its beauty.

Yet, for all its solidity, majesty and beauty, nature, like us, is ever winding down. Everything, regardless of its magnificence, is subject to the inevitability of decay and eventual decease. We grow old, our vital functions begin to fail us and we die. The same process is at work in the mightiest of stars in the farthest reaches of space, and in the most humble grain of sand here at home. It's called, "entropy," and it's the fundamental law of nature.

When we reflect on this, it doesn't seem to make sense. Just to look at them, it is obvious that the things of creation are made to live, not to die; to thrive, not to decay. For ourselves, we see that the body is designed to heal and regenerate itself, and that it does. So, why does this alien process, this absurd condition that insists we and all things must continually wind down, and then eventually stop, exist?

The answer is, because of the Fall. We humans are splendidly more than our fellow creatures, but tragically less than we were designed to be and once were. Nature and the universe remain splendid. but they, too, are subject to the dreadful condition we brought upon them.

You see, it was never God's intention that anything He created should die. Everything looks so permanent—because it was meant to be so. Yet, in order for this permanence to be real and not just apparent it would have to be perfect. And imperfect man could never survive in a perfect world.

C.S. Lewis, in his incredibly perceptive novel, The Great Divorce (Geoffrey Bles, London, 1945), brings us to terms with the fact that we, while appearing handsome and substantial to each other, are merely wraiths: shadows of what was intended for us. We could not lift, let alone eat, a perfect peach.

A nice, gentle, perfect rain would destroy us.

So, in order that we might live, nature had to fall with us.

Astrophysicists tell us that the universe is expanding at an incredible rate, literally flying apart. Some hope for a "boomerang" effect: that there will be a point of critical inertia, and that the universe will "snap back," like a rubber band. This is the "breathing universe" hypothesis, advanced mainly to support the idea that "it has always been so:" the universe eternally expanding and contracting since the Big Bang.

I think they advance this idea mostly as a way of avoiding consideration of the simple and obvious fact that there was a time before the Big Bang, when there was nothing to expand or contract. No matter how many wormholes, alternate universes or new dimensions they postulate or discover, there was a time when none of it was. Howevermuch some mathematicians might parse the "concept" of zero, it remains that there is a concreteness which is not vulnerable to our ameliorating concepts, and simply is what it is. Nothing is—

nothing. Not a concept, position or proposal, but simply a condition: that which was, or rather was not, before there was something.

Yet, here it all is. How? What is the Ultimate upon which it all—and that is to say, quite literally, all depends; without which it would simply not be? The only logical answer to this is the Uncaused Cause: God.

I occasionally speak with a fellow who has a fine mind and a helpful and giving personality. He is truly a fine young man. Yet, he is too caught up in the mechanics of things to see beyond them. He answers my "God talk" by postulating dimensions beyond our comprehension, just now being mathematically outlined by people on the very outer cutting edge of physics. I talk about the Realm of God. He can't see we're talking about the same thing.

Personally, I don't think the universe will snap back. Even if it does, however, energy will be lost in the transaction and sooner or later it won't. Entropy is the fundamental law of physics because it is the fundamental fruit of the Fall. It is what makes the universe we inhabit what it is.

Our hope is not in our vain denial of What Is: the Breathing Universe hypothesis necessarily denies entropy, and arrogates to human logic the power to somehow "redeem" it.

Entropy, however, isn't just the product of our curse, it is also a component of our hope. We are promised new heavens and a new earth (Revelation 21: 1), where the curse, and with it entropy, simply don't exist.

Like a butterfly emerging from a chrysalis, we—who entered the universe looking for all the world like a sort of worm—will be made new and splendid. Nature, its integrity critically wounded, will likewise be healed: like us, returned by God to its intended state.

THREE: HUMAN CULTURE

> *You cannot serve God and mammon.*
> (Matthew 6: 24b)

As fallen creatures inhabiting a fallen universe, it is natural that we would build fallen cultures. Since we are icons of God, and therefore intrinsically magnificent, it is natural that our cultures, throughout history, have been as impressive as we've been able to make them, and have reflected an aspiration to higher things. Since we are marred icons, it is equally natural that our cultures would also reflect our tragic flaw. Moreover, since we continue to be bound under entropy, the trajectory—predictable yet consistent--is that the force of our flaw eventually prevails and our cultures decay.

I am impatient with modern Bible versions that talk about how we "can't serve both God and money." Mammon is far more than money. Mammon is a system—is, in fact, what we call the World System. It does not run on relationship with and obedience to God, but rather relies on man and his ingenuity to give it shape and structure.

Predictably, since our tragic flaw is Pride, the kingdom of mammon is rooted in vanity and the trappings that serve vanity: power, influence and self-exaltation. These things are bought with money, so money and mammon are closely identified; but they are not the same.

God doesn't have anything against money or making money. One of the things the Bible is known (and often dismissed) for is its work ethic. Money's rightful place is not as a master but as a tool. To "serve mammon" is akin to kneeling down and worshiping one's pipe wrench; or thinking oneself superior for having amassed a great collection of pipe wrenches, and stoking that feeling by amassing still more.

There is a comparative example I like to call the juxtaposition of the Rich Fat Guy and the Gracious Landowner.

The Rich Fat Guy is the "rich man clothed in purple" in Luke 16:20-25, whose generosity of spirit was limited to letting the beggar Lazarus eat the crumbs that fell from his table, and letting his dogs do what they could to clean his sores.

Alternatively, we have the parable of the Gracious Landowner in Matthew 20: 1-16, who, seeing men idle and in need of work, hired them. The story is iconic of our salvation, the last to be hired receiving the same wage as the first. It also, however, models to us the personal generosity of the landowner who permits the Grace of God to flow through him.

Obviously, the kingdom of mammon is represented by the Rich Fat Guy, and the Kingdom of God by the generous landowner.

Two different ethical systems are represented here, and they go beyond generosity or the lack of it. The Rich Fat Guy owns his stuff. Since it's his stuff, and he owns it, he can do whatever he wants with it. He epitomizes those spoken of in Psalm 73: 4-10:

> *For they have no pangs, their bodies are sound and sleek. They are not in trouble as other men are, they are not stricken like other men. Therefore pride is their necklace, violence covers them like a garment. Their eyes swell out with fatness, their hearts overflow with follies. They scoff and speak with malice, loftily they threaten oppression. They set their mouths against the heavens, and their tongue struts through the earth. Therefore the people turn and praise them, and find no fault in them.*

It's worth noting (Luke 16:24) that so ingrained is the Rich Fat Guy's worldly pride that even after he has died and been condemned, even in the midst of looking at the heavenly-exalted Lazarus, he still regards Lazarus as a servant: "Send Lazarus to…".

The Gracious Landowner, however, epitomizes the generous man in Psalm 112: 5-9:

> *It is well with the man who deals generously and lends, who conducts his affairs with justice. For the righteous will never be moved; he will be remembered for ever. He is not afraid of evil tidings; his heart is firm, trusting in the Lord. His heart is steady, he will not be afraid, until he sees his desire on his adversaries. He has distributed freely, he has given to the poor; his righteousness endures for ever; his horn is exalted in honor.*

Like the Rich Fat Guy, the Gracious Landowner owns his stuff. He, also, can do what he wants with it. He just wants to do different things.

Like Genesis 3, this juxtaposition of the two kingdoms will be a recurring theme in our discussion,

What we want to do: Morality and its fruits

What we want to do, which of these two role models best fits us, determines the nature of our culture. That's important, because our practical choices in the world have ramifications beyond the practical and worldly.

Remember, we are the crown of God's creation, made in His Image. We are spiritual beings as well as physical, which means that our actions reverberate not just in the physical and immediate, but throughout the spectrum of creation. God created the universe and put us in charge of it, and that didn't change with the Fall. Remember, we spoke about "entropy" earlier, and the same process that applies to natural systems applies to cultures. That's because entropy is principally a spiritual thing. The process of entropy is weakened by a strong morality, and strengthened by a weak morality.

We can easily see this at work in all of history. The world's mighty empires, when they became morally decadent, collapsed. Not from lack of initiative or economic ambition, but simply because they could no longer sustain the weight of their own sin.

Decadence produces disorder, and disorder requires energy to pull things back together. God is the Source of all energy and Godliness is our means of access to it. Just as morality is the expression and fruit of closeness to God, decadence is the expression and fruit of distancing ourselves from Him, of cutting ourselves off from Him. As we do that, disorder overwhelms us and collapse ensues.

As I never tire of repeating, God put us in charge, here. The way we go is the way the creation goes.

God the Holy Spirit holds all of creation together. The closer we draw to Him, the closer we draw the systems that sustain us to Him. The further we drift away from our relationship with God, the more we draw those systems away from Him. The result is diminished coherence: diminished ability of the systems to hold together.

We call it the "judgment of God," because that's the way it looks from our perspective. It really isn't, though. God doesn't "smite" us. God loves us. He sets out for us a way to live happy and stable lives. The real problem is that we insist upon ways that demonstrably do not work! The result isn't that God "smites" us, but that we in fact smite ourselves.

It is not fear of God's "wrath" that should give us pause. It is the power that He grants us, which can be either wonderful or terrible—and the liberty He grants us to determine which of the two it will be.

Life On the Road.

I like to compare living life with driving a car.

A car comes with an owner's manual that was written by the manufacturer. If you read it and follow it, use the recommended oil and change it when indicated, do the outlined maintenance routines etc., the car will run well and last for a good long time. Depart from that and it will run less reliably and last for less time. Disregard the manual entirely and the vehicle will hardly last at all.

What if, for instance, I wanted, instead of gasoline, to use Three-in-One oil in my car's engine? It does sort of make sense, doesn't it? After all, Three-in-One oil is a petroleum product, and so is gasoline.

I might argue, "I'm not at all comfortable with gasoline. I don't like the way it smells. Besides, only hypocrites go to gas stations, and I don't see why I have to fuel my car according to what some book says, anyway."

It's worth noting that those arguments are all about what "I want" and what "I prefer," and what "I think is fair." They don't have anything at all to do with the facts, or the reality of the situation itself, or even with what might be good for the car. The fact is, my car won't run on Three-in-One oil, no matter how superior a product it is when properly used, or how fair it seems that it should, or how loudly I proclaim that Three-in One oil is the petroleum product that "suits me."

The Bible is the owner's manual for our life. It was given us by the Manufacturer. When we follow it, life runs properly. When we do not, there are persistent problems. Eventually, as we see and have seen so many times, there are so many breakdowns and wrecks that the highway itself becomes impassable.

As I write this, in the United States of America, in the middle of the second decade of the twenty-first century, the truth of this is obvious. I live in, and enjoy the privileges of, the greatest and most accomplished nation in the history of the world. I'm writing this on a machine from which I am able to access all of the knowledge stored in all the world's libraries, and speak face-to-face with people anywhere on the planet. I am an unwealthy man, yet I have access to medical care no amount of money would have been able to buy, even twenty years ago. Much of this medicine and expertise is exported to the poorest regions of earth by brave and selfless, brilliant people. Our machines send back pictures and even movies from the farthest reaches of our solar system, and beyond.

We have mapped the human genetic structure. We have discovered what may well be the key particle in the atomic and subatomic structure of the universe.

We dress in wrinkle-free fabrics.

All reason demands that we should be grateful to the God Who has so miraculously gifted us; that we should wish above all else to draw closer to Him than ever, that we might experience in our lives the reality of the multidimensionality that, for the world, is only a set of mathematical hypotheses. We should eagerly explore and follow the Book, God's own revelation to us, that is the key to the fullness of life.

Instead, we have immersed ourselves in our stuff. We have insisted upon worshiping ourselves and our proclivities, even to taking steps to have the Owner's Manual removed from public places because it tells us things we would rather not hear.

As we "progress" along this path, our culture bears the fruit of it: ruined cities, social chaos, poverty in the midst of plenty and economic ruin.

We murder our children and call it "health care."

As a result, we have lost our smile. We have lost our confidence in the future. If we do not turn around, we will lose our nation.

For what? For vanity? Is it worth it? Yet, vanity is all a Godless culture has. The story of Jonah and his mission to Nineveh (See the Book of Jonah) shows us that a culture can turn from vanity and be restored. The story of Sodom and Gomorrah (Genesis 19: 1-29) shows us what can, and does, happen to a culture when it will not.

FOUR: THE CHURCH-

> *And let us consider one another in order to stir up love and good works, not forsaking the assembling of ourselves together, as is the manner of some, but exhorting one another, and so much the more as you see the Day approaching.*
> (Hebrews 10:24-25)

God provides another culture for us, a culture that frees us from the demands of an infantile and demanding Self and provides a context in which we may live life in its fullness, in Him.

The world's culture tries to convince us that self-indulgence will make us happy and successful. Credit card ads picture exotic tropical resorts and glamorous people (one of whom we can presumably be, if only we borrow enough on the card) getting on and off airplanes and yachts and sunning themselves in utter stressless bliss. Real estate gurus offer us the opportunity to make millions, if we will only buy their twenty (marked down from six hundred, just for this offer) dollar wealth-building course. "What would you like to have..." goes the pitch, accompanied by visuals of beautiful, scantily-clad women, handsome men and the usual planes, yachts and fancy cars. These are the things you should want, is the implication, and these are the things we can deliver.

Our "entertainment" consists mainly of watching successful young people find bliss by having heedless and unlimited sexual encounters. Our schools helpfully assure our children from the earliest years that this is the way to personal fulfillment.

Our culture presents us a fairy tale world, without responsibility and without consequences, if only we will become sufficiently self-indulgent.

Then reality breaks in, as it always does. The credit card bill, with a usurious interest rate that will keep us paying off our glamorous vacation for years, comes in the mail. The broken-down house we bought by mortgaging our own home, to "fix up and flip," turns out to cost 'way more to repair than we could ever hope to recoup. The doctor tells us we have a venereal disease that will kill us, cripple us or at least keep us annoyed for the rest of our life.

Or, maybe we're one of the lucky ones. The real estate deals all work out. We have a fancy car, a nice house, a largish boat, maybe a small plane hangared at a local airstrip and a lingerie model for a live-in girlfriend.

Yet, something's missing.

Performer Freddie Prinz, a hugely talented young man, made it to the absolute top of the entertainment heap, and had all this. His suicide note read, "Is this all there is?"

Our culture is built around the ticking of the clock and the inevitability of death. It offers us amusements to distract us while exhorting us to squeeze as much stuff as we can into however many seconds we have left. There is another culture: one that doesn't despise wealth or success, but which doesn't covet them, either: a culture where we find out, and live out, the fact that "this" is not in fact all there is; a culture that stands between Heaven and earth, and measures its movements not in hours or days or years, but in millennia; where death is not an end, but a transition; where we are allowed to be peaceful, simply because peace is better. It is a culture based not on the temporary shakiness of my present mood but upon the reliability and permanence of God Himself. The culture of the world forms me into a burnt-out hedonist who finally dies, debilitated and discarded. The culture of the Kingdom of God forms me into the divinized soul I was created to be. The culture of the Kingdom is found in Church.

If I had a dollar for every time I've heard some poor soul say, "I know the Lord, but I don't need to go to church..." I'd be able to afford dental work. This statement is usually followed by a litany that varies so little from person to person that it sounds pre-recorded and downloaded: "I tried going to church, but it just wasn't for me..." "The people didn't welcome me..." "The pastor wasn't interested in me..." "It was their own club and I didn't feel like there was room for me..." and of course the ever-popular, "The place just wasn't meeting my needs."

The question here is, what do these people see the church as? A place to worship God, or themselves?

We live in a society whose employers have lost their respect for God, and who insist that all their employees must work on Sundays. This provides a new excuse: "I need to work." I tested this one, once, by changing the time of my Service to accommodate an individual who assured me she would be going to church if only she could find one at the right time (a tiny house-church ministry like mine can do things like that). When she hadn't shown up for two weeks in a row, I asked her why and she gave me the real reason: "I sleep on Sunday mornings."

We find the fullness of life in Christ, and we encounter and grow in Christ, in His Church. There are no real alternatives, although there are lots of false ones. Christ is the Author of Life, and the Church is the Theanthropic (Divine / human) institution that God has established. In it, we are nurtured in, and taught the ways of, and come to know the present reality of, eternal life.

The Present Reality of Eternity; Religion and the Church

The "present reality of Eternity" isn't just a saying. The fact about Eternity is that it begins here and now. It began for each of us, in fact, at our conception. We are all eternal beings, and the question is not, "Will we live forever?" but, "How?"

The key to, "How?" is found right here, in this, the briefest part of our life. There is a parallel with our formative years here on earth, which are called "formative" for a reason. Just as they prepare us for adulthood here, so does our life here prepare us for the rest of our life, which begins when we grow up and leave here. Just as our childhood "formative years" require a proper nurturing and teaching environment, so do these "formative years" of earthly life.

Strangely, it has become fashionable in some circles to speak of "religion" and "relationship," as if they were somehow opposed. I say "strangely" because to do so ignores the Bible (try to find somewhere in the Bible where "religion," in and of itself, is used as a bad word). It also ignores the nature of relationships, which are rooted in knowing, and growing in the company of, others. Most relationships are in some way "ritualized," as routines that enhance the relationship are established between the participants. These routines provide a foundation for expanded and expanding scope and growth. Religion is the living out of this same dynamic in our relationship with God.

Relationships are not simply "there." They take place within a context. In lasting and vital relationships, the context provides opportunities to spend time together and to grow in knowledge of each other. Religion is what provides the context for a lasting and vital relationship with God.

The Church provides the context for the relationship, just as the home provides the context for a marriage or an office, farm or factory provides the context for our work.

Both the kingdom of mammon and the Kingdom of God are learning environments, and they teach us the attitudes and skills that are appropriate to their respective cultures. If we live a life inserted in the world, "not needing" the church, we will learn the ways of the world, accept the values of the world and eventually drift away from God in everything but the mistaken conviction we are still Christians. If we live a life inserted in the Church, we will learn the ways of Godliness and will grow in virtue, which will strengthen us in character and in resilience.

FIVE: VIRTUE AND VICE

> *The Cardinal Virtues: Temperance, Prudence, Justice and Courage.*
> *The Theological Virtues: Faith, Hope and Charity.*
> *The Seven Deadly Sins: pride, envy, wrath, sloth, greed, gluttony and lust.*

The secular culture doesn't have much to tell us about virtue and vice. Decades of moral relativism, situation ethics and the "self-esteem movement" have discouraged consideration of right and wrong as objective values and have all but eliminated such discussion in the "official" marketplaces of ideas.

The transformed life, however, requires a firm and objective understanding of what is virtue and what is vice, because these things are not up to us. They are indeed objective values, true for all people at all times and in all circumstances.

Discussion of these things is essential, particularly today, because Christianity engages the realities of Right and Wrong in the midst of a world which has, largely, forgotten the difference.

VICE: pride, envy, wrath, sloth, greed, gluttony and lust.

The kingdom of mammon sets up the historic "Seven Deadly Sins" as cultural norms and encourages us to live our lives by them. When, for instance, did you ever go through an entire day without seeing or hearing at least one of the "seven deadly sins" extolled as desirable, even as virtuous?

Almost every sales pitch we get, from whatever medium, appeals to our vices: counterfeit virtues that seek to corrupt and disarm our spiritual nature and make us slaves to, rather than masters of, our fallen nature.

Pride.

It all starts here. Pride is the vice that lets all the other vices in. It's the Original Sin, the fatal flaw. Without it there would be no other sins.

> *So when the woman saw the tree was good for food,*
> *and that it was a delight to the eyes, and that the tree*

was to be desired to make one wise, she took of its fruit and ate; and she also gave some to her husband, and he ate.
(Genesis 3: 6)

Notice the operative phrase: "(she) saw...". God had said the fruit was poison, yet Eve saw that it was "good for food." The fruit, being the potential engine of her destruction, should have been abhorrent to Eve; yet *she saw* that it was "a delight to the eyes." God's Wisdom concerning the fruit was that it was deadly, something to be avoided. This wisdom—God's Wisdom--was imparted to both Adam and Eve. Yet, She saw that the tree was to be desired "to make one wise."

Through what lens was she seeing? Certainly not the lens of Godliness. It was, rather, the lens of her own opinion, an opinion she had formed in opposition to the admonition of God. It was a distorted lens, that brought distortion into a world that had theretofore only known clarity.

"But she was tempted! What about the serpent?" you might say. Bear in mind: the serpent had no actual power over Eve. All he had was a sales pitch. It was Eve, as Queen of creation, who had the power. A perfect being, she had no genetic compulsion to rebellion. She didn't even have any obligation to continue the conversation. At any time, she could have called upon Adam, or God Himself, for help, or at least for clarification when the conversation began to take a wrong turn. Instead, she allowed herself to be led into an alternative viewpoint: one which, even though she was fully cognizant of the Will of God, differed.

This new, distorted way of seeing, crystallized for Eve *her own way.* Theretofore, there had existed in the universe only God's Way. But now there was another way: an opposing way, a discordant note in a universe where only harmony had existed.

Sin entered a universe where there had been only perfection, and brought it down. There arose in its place a world where sin was the standard. Adam, the last bastion against the breach, proved unreliable.

In fact, where was Adam during all of this? Where was his vigilance? During all the time his wife is under attack by her deadly enemy, Adam isn't mentioned once.

Envy and Wrath

Pride led to Cain's *envy* of Abel, and that envy led to the wrath that drove him to the universe's first homicide. There wasn't any reason for it. God accepted the blood sacrifice of Abel the hunter, to which Abel had been commanded. He rejected the blood-sacrifice of Cain the farmer, mainly, it seems, because he was emulating his brother out of envy. Genesis 4:5 tells us that when God "had no regard" for Cain's offering, "Cain was very angry, and his countenance fell." Hebrews 11:4 speaks only of Abel's offering, that it was the one that was made "in faith."

Note that it was Cain's offering, not Cain himself, that God "had no regard for." This reveals something critical about the pride/envy/wrath dynamic that we should all take note of: Cain's offering reveals itself as not having really been made out of deference to God. If it had been, he would have seen God's disregard of it as a learning experience, and would have sought to join his brother in offering acceptable sacrifice.

Cain's offering turns out to have been made in deference to himself, to the way of his own, "me-too-ist," preference rather than the preference of God..

This reminds me of the fellow who chooses a church to attend, not because "it's where I learn and grow," but because "it's where I'm blessed!" Meaning it's an entertaining place that makes him feel good. Until, that is, the preacher says something he doesn't like, something perhaps that convicts him of sin. Suddenly, his countenance falls. The preacher is "judgmental," having indicated that there might be something in the man's offering of himself that the Lord has no regard for. The following Sunday will find him "getting blessed" somewhere else.

As with Cain, our church-hopping friend has no actual reason to be upset. What was addressed was not aimed as an insult, but offered as instruction:

> *The Lord said to Cain, "Why are you angry, and why has your countenance fallen? If you do well, will you not be accepted? And if you do not do well, sin is couching at the door; its desire is for you, but you must master it.*
> (Genesis 4: 6-7)

What a gentle word! By any logical, reflective standard, this should have worked. Cain should have been mollified, and that should have been the end of it. But sin is illogical and unreflective. It is a simple, brute response to impulse. In fact, in Verse 8, right after God's very reasonable appeal to him, Cain shows no evidence at all of any reflection on what God has said. In fact, he shows no deference to, or even appreciation of, God--God, Who is humbling Himself to try to reason with His creature! Cain's response is simply to lure Abel out into the field and murder him.

Confronted with his crime in verses 9 and 13, Cain is at first surly ("Am I my brother's keeper?") and then self-pitying ("My punishment is greater than I can bear!") In Verse 14, he even remonstrates with God over the condition of his exile! Nowhere in the entire narrative do we see any reference on Cain's part to Abel or to his own crime; no sign of contrition or repentance. Cain does not see past himself, the imagined slight to himself and his umbrage that "his way" might be unacceptable.

This is the way the kingdom of mammon operates. It is self-centered, urging us to see ourselves as the measure of all things.

Let's take a moment to look back at Genesis Three, Verses 17c and 19a: *Cursed is the ground because of you; in toil you shall eat of it…In the sweat of your face you shall eat bread.*

The Kingdom of God accepts this sentence as the condition brought about by our first parents and therefore the condition of the world into which we're born. Those who are part of the Kingdom of God repent of our fallen condition and do the best we can in spite of it. We offer the fruits of what we do to the Lord, as an offering to Him, in celebration of Him and of the gift of life which he gives us.

By contrast, the kingdom of mammon exalts our fallen condition, itself. If I serve mammon, I serve myself: My efforts, My strivings, the achievements I have attained through "the sweat of My face," as if it were not God Who had made these things possible for me in the first place.

Things are not the way they were (or are) designed to be. The Fall diminished us. At our core, realized or unrealized, we are aware of that diminishment, and it creates in us an essential insecurity. The insecurity, in turn, produces a compensatory drive that demands we prove ourselves to ourselves by exalting ourselves over our brother.

With Cain came the establishment of human culture: he was given a mark on his forehead to warn any whom he encountered that he was not to be killed. For all that, he never won the argument over the sacrifice. The firstling of the flock—blood sacrifice--would continue to be the acceptable sacrifice to the Lord. Man, who now bore the mark of Cain, would nevertheless offer the sacrifice of Abel.

The "world system" was now established.

Sloth

Our culture has a new hero: the slacker. He is a product of a society which has abandoned God in favor of self-worship.

Many view the slacker as lazy and without ambition, but this is only true according to historically- civilized standards. In reality, slackers are not at all lazy: they work very hard at getting away with being unproductive. They have their share of ambition and creativity, but these are invested in the satisfaction of their momentary wants and whims.

Many view the slacker as antisocial, but again, he is not. Slackers like to be liked, and they are good at being charming and likeable. They will be boon companions to those whom they view as potential resources, and simply, cheerfully, disregard the rest. So, the slothful are not, as most people would figure it, lazy. Rather, they simply feel no responsibility to contribute to the common good. The slacker is the ultimate end-product, the teleological dénouement, if you will, of the Self-Esteem Movement.

> *To every man, every other man divine.*
> *-Seneca*
>
> *To every man, every other man a wolf.*
> *-Plautus*
>
> *This is not very kind to the wolves.*
> *-Bouchard*

The "self-esteem movement" pervades every dark corner of our intellectual life, from our critically dysfunctional academic establishment to its companion subcultures in the arts and letters and the social sciences. Tragically, it has sloshed over the rails of the self-consciously-intellectual community to poison the whole culture.

The mantra of the self-esteem movement is, "You are perfect just the way you are." This is the devil's own lie: it cuts us of from the awareness that we are fundamentally imperfect just the way we are, and thereby rejects as irrelevant the only wisdom that can save us.

If we are perfect in and of ourselves, we are our own gods. If we are our own gods, we create our own worlds. If we create our own worlds, we are the determiners of what is Right and Wrong, Good and Evil—things that have throughout mankind's history been the province of the Natural Law.

> *However, we speak wisdom among those who are*
> *mature, yet not the wisdom of this age, nor of the rulers*
> *of this age, who are coming to nothing.*
> (1 Corinthians 2:6)

The spirit of our age rejects Natural Law, and in fact, Nature. The self-exaltation movement rejects the idea that there is anything Natural to man. It maintains that what we regard as "natural" is merely cultural, and seems "natural" to us because of culturally embedded values. It refuses to tolerate the suggestion that values are objective, instead insisting that Right and Wrong, Good and Evil are fluid, subjective and self determined concepts. They must be, if each of us is our own sovereign moral arbiter.

So, if I am my own god, creator of my own world, framer of my own laws, ultimate arbiter, within my world, of Right and Wrong, Good and Evil, what am I if I am not entitled?

Whenever we turn around we are confronted with someone assuring us "we are entitled" to something or other. "You deserve..." runs the ad copy; and the ad copy is everywhere: blaring at us from the large-screen propaganda boxes in our living rooms, assaulting our computer screens, stuffing our newspapers (and our mailboxes, just in case we missed the paper) with ad supplements, even yammering at us from our grocery store checkout receipts.

Is it any wonder the slacker is our new cultural hero? He's a nice, pleasant guy who doesn't bother anyone and doesn't allow himself to be bothered. He does what he has to do to take what he needs to take so he can get what he wants to get. Society doesn't ruffle him, because he feels no sense of responsibility to it. He's entitled. He's deserving. He's perfect just the way he is, and his self-esteem couldn't be healthier.

Ultimately, sloth is a form of reversion to infantilism.

An infant, after all, is the center of his world's attention. All behavior is indulged, all needs are met, every gesture is acclaimed as "cute." A baby has no obligation to the world at large, but is entitled to be provided for by virtue of simply being there. There is that within all of us which would like to have this privileged estate back, and self-esteemism assures us that this is not only possible but "deserved."

The worker who shows up late, and occasionally stoned, for just long enough to get fired and get on unemployment; the driver who thinks that stop signs are suggestions, or whose car stereo hammers the walls of your house (and your ears) as he passes; the character who almost knocks you over as he shoves past you to get through a door ahead of you, all have been carefully taught by the institutions of our secular culture that they are the center of their own self-created world, perfect just as they are, "deserving" of deference. They have reverted to infantilism, giving the rest of the world the task of looking out for and indulging them, assuming no responsibility for anything beyond what they want at the moment.

The guy who pushes past you through the door may be in a business suit. The door might be to an elevator, on the way to an important business meeting. His ethic, though, is no different from that of the teen-aged slacker-hero in the movies. He isn't "lazy," as most would have it, but he's slothful.

Greed.

Sloth produces greed. It has to. If I "am entitled," then "I deserve" the stuff that attracts me. If I don't have that stuff, my sense of injustice will drive me to want to get it.

The Free Dictionary (www.thefreedictionary.com) defines greed as "An excessive desire to acquire and possess more than one needs or deserves, especially with regard to material wealth." I would take it a step further. After all, the difference between "excessive desire to acquire" and "admirable drive to succeed" is mostly subjective. And the thought that one person might be able to dictate what another "needs or deserves" is downright scary.

I propose that the definition "greed" kicks in when the line is crossed into a blind acquisitiveness-for-its-own-sake; an acquisitiveness that applies also to things the greedy individual might not even particularly want but is at any rate able to grab. Isaiah 56:11, for instance, tells us that the greedy "never have enough."

Let's return to our infant, now a small toddler. Have you noticed a tendency among toddlers to hoard things, even things they don't play with? Perhaps it's something someone else was playing with, and left. Maybe it's just lying there. But if there's a lot of stuff lying around on the floor, and a toddler is given his own assigned space, chances are that sooner or later, if unchecked, a lot of that stuff will wind up in that space. That's because toddlers are people who are just getting over being babies, and that sense of entitlement, that *the rest of the world* exists for me, is still fresh in their awareness.

The toddler is not "greedy." Given proper home support and absent a pathology of some kind, he will learn to share pretty easily. And, in truth, a toddler is in the process of discovering the world around him and does sort of have a pass when it comes to grabbing and collecting things.

There are adults, however, who have arrogated to themselves the same sort of pass. They expect to be indulged, "understood," even admired, when they grab stuff and hoard it. When they have all the stuff they or their heirs could ever possibly use, and all the social influence and event-shaping power that comes from having lots of stuff, they still crave more.

Having money isn't sinful. Neither is wanting more. A while ago, we compared the Generous Landowner with the Greedy Fat Guy, and saw that the Generous Landowner wasn't sinful, even though he was certainly as well-off as the Greedy Fat Guy. The difference was in their approach. What made the Greedy Fat Guy greedy was not necessarily his desire for wealth. Neither was it his awareness that what he had was his: *"Is it not lawful for me to do what I want with my own things?"* asks the Landowner in Mathew 20:15.

No, it was his graspingness, his holding onto things, in his infantile self-centeredness, not because he needed them or even intended to use them--but simply because he was holding them.

A wise man once, in response to the expression "as easy as taking candy from a baby," observed in a question, "Have you ever *tried* to take candy from a baby?!"

Cute, in a baby. But in an adult?

Gluttony

Gluttony is a particular form of greed that is centered on gastronomic delectation. Most of us associate it with overeating, but it can also reveal itself through things like excessive dieting. Specifically, it is a perversion of the natural need to have sufficient nourishment, and an abuse of the gift of God that enables that nourishment to be enjoyable.

The purpose of food is to nourish us. A healthy appreciation of food approaches it on just that basis. A glutton, however, in effect divorces eating from its purpose and subordinates being nourished to the act of eating, itself. Eating becomes less an act of self-sustainment than one of self-indulgence. Indeed, a gluttonous spirit, like all sinful spirits, removes itself from objective considerations. Nourishment becomes secondary; even the food becomes secondary. The act of eating, itself, becomes primary.

The obverse of this is excessive fasting.

Like eating, the purpose of fasting is to promote health. It can take the form of a diet, where the purpose is to "lighten the load" so the body can work more efficiently; or it can take the form of a spiritual exercise, where the body joins the mind and spirit in prayer. Gluttonous fasting, like its counterpart gluttonous eating, divorces fasting from its purpose and centers not even so much on the act itself as on the fact that *I'm doing it.*

In both cases, what is sought is the particular physical or self-congratulatory sensation that attends the act, rather than fulfilling the purpose of the act.

Gluttony and greed are intimately related, as both are a form of acquisitiveness which has subordinated what is being acquired, and why, beneath the act of acquiring for its own sake.

Lust

> *The heavens are telling the glory of God;*
> *and the firmament proclaims his handiwork.*
> *Day to day pours forth speech,*
> *and night to night declares knowledge.*
> *There is no speech, nor are there words;*
> *their voice is not heard;*
> *yet their voice goes out through all the earth,*
> *and their words to the end of the world.*
> *In them He has set a tent for the sun,*
> *which comes forth like a bridegroom leaving his chamber,*
> *and like a strong man runs its course with joy.*
> *Its rising is from the end of the heavens,*
> *and its circuit to the end of them;*
> *and there is nothing hid from its heat.*
> (Psalm 19: 1-6)

All of creation is an expression of God's Love. The stars and the planets, the galaxies and nebulae, wheel through the universe in a great Dance, an expression of the joy of our Creator and of the work of His creating Hand.

> *The earth is the Lord's and the fullness thereof,*
> *the world and those who dwell therein;*
> *for He has founded it upon the seas,*
> *and established it upon the rivers.*
> (Psalm 24: 1-2)

Take a look at the world that surrounds us, the mighty pulsing of the waters; the stillness of old, deep woods; the promise of a backyard garden, the fierceness of a tiny blade of grass that pushes its way even through concrete. From the breath-taking complexity of the veins of a leaf, to the thunderous simplicity of a great waterfall, God creates. And He creates Life!

And, incredibly, He invites us to join Him in it. He calls us together, man and woman, to commit to each other and to Him—and joyfully frolic with the stars and the planets and the lush things of earth in their ecstatic dance, and join with Him to bring forth creatures made in His Image.

Then there's lust.

Lust is a corruption of love.

Lust is a diminishment of all this, a conversion of greatness into greed. It is a sour note in a symphony, a stagger during a pas-de-deux, a grease-pencil mustache drawn on a masterpiece.

It is a theft of that which is freely offered.

Lust does not cherish its object, but rather reduces him or her to a delicacy to be tasted, a convenience to be used and enjoyed in the moment. It is the reduction of an icon of God to an indecent cartoon.

God gives us love as a means of expressing Himself through us. Sin beckons us to kick Him out of the picture, and settle for a grotesque, fleeting parody.

The great cosmic explosion of God's Love is His expression of Himself, and He is radically committed to its fruit.

> *...in Him we live and move and have our being...*
> (Acts 17: 28a)

The Divine Liturgy of Saint James the Just sings praise in gratitude to God that even after man betrayed God, "You did not despise or forsake him, but did chasten him as a merciful Father."

Look at us, in our sinfulness and apostasy; in the exuberant mockery of God that spills out of our entertainment media, our academic institutions, even some of our churches, like sludge from a sewer pipe. It's a world-wide phenomenon. Yet, the world is still here! God continues to invite us to turn away from all the sludge and let Him make us clean! He continues to hold the universe together, to allow our planet to continue to thrive and to provide us a place to live. We treat this incredible gift, this magnificent sign of the Mercy of the God Who created everything and maintains it all in being—with all the reverence and respect the Vikings had for the British monasteries.

In the fallenness of our lust we even try to seduce God! Read the outpourings of the anti-church, of the "high critics" whose goal is to dismember the Scriptures and remove all objective authority from them. In the first chapters of these blighted works, we are regaled with protestations of how great God is, and how deeply we are to treasure "His Holy Word." Do they seek by this to perhaps convince God that they are, after all, a legitimate part of the Church they are trying so hard to wreck?

Read ahead to the end of the Book: we win.

For all of this, God allows us to keep on living here.

In doing so, He demonstrates His commitment to His creation; and in the process, He offers us a future. This is the great, bright promise that shines through the darkness of our exile here in the world we have made after our own dismal image and likeness: In Christ we have a future! A too-corrupted, worn-out and battle weary Christendom might finally be overrun by the devil's hordes, but there will be those who remain faithful, and they will be the Church of the Eschaton, And when the sun grows dark, and the universe wobbles, and the Son of God returns in His Glory; as all that we hold so ultimate vanishes into vapor and dust, the Church will have a future.

We cannot buy it. We cannot steal it. We cannot compel it, and we certainly cannot seduce it.

But we can wed it. We can be the Bride of Christ, and we can freely receive it. For it is our wedding gift.

You think I'm talking about sex, don't you? In a way I am, if you look at sex as an icon of the incredible, boundless fecundity of God; of the fact that everything that exists is the product of the expression and overflow of His Love. But we can lust after anything: money, power, baseball cards, a star's autograph—the object of our lust makes no difference. We can use money and power to improve the lives of others as well as our own. Collections of baseball cards and autographs can be expressions of admiration for the gifts God bestows. Or they can simply be attempts to satisfy a craving.

It's tempting to say something like, "there's a thin line between love and lust," but the line isn't thin at all. It is the universe-wide chasm between virtue and vice, between gluttony and appetite, greed and productivity, sloth and leisure, wrath and heroism, envy and admiration, God-centeredness and self-centeredness; between creation and destruction, salvation and damnation.

VIRTUE: Temperance, Prudence, Justice, Courage. Faith, Hope and Charity.

So, what of the virtues? It's tempting (if you'll forgive me), at this point, to get all Hegelian and oppose the virtues and the vices, as if they were numerical opposites. After all, there are seven of each, and it wouldn't be difficult to set up an oppositional chart and burn up some pages doing something relatively easy—always an attractive idea for someone who's writing a book. The problem is, vice is not actually the opposite of virtue, To call them opposites would suggest they are equal, and they are not. Vice is a diminution of virtue, a disfigurement of it. Vice would not be able to exist without virtue, just as a parasite would not be able to exist without a host.

Vice corrupts all the virtues, not just selective ones. It would be easy to line up "gluttony" opposite "temperance," and explain their particular qualities and how those qualities oppose each other. The problem with that is that the beauty of temperance as a Divine gift would be reduced to "not overeating." The evil that gluttony is—the raging interior hunger that attempts to fill a God-shaped hole with self-indulgence—the demeaning nastiness of it—would likewise be reduced to "pigging out." Both are minimizations that widely miss the point.

THE VIRTUES

And if any one loves righteousness, her labors are virtues; for she teaches self-control and prudence, justice and courage; nothing in life is more profitable for men than these. Wisdom of Solomon 8:7.

The Kingdom of God is where we find virtue exalted. Take the Cardinal Virtues: Temperance, Prudence, justice and Courage. These things stand in contrast—even opposition—to the recklessness, excess, selfishness and fear of commitment that characterize the kingdom of mammon.

"But doesn't everyone want virtue?" one may ask. The answer is, yes and no. We all like to identify with it, pretend to it, even approve of it. but to actually practice it? To the worldly man, frankly, "all the stuff about virtue" gets in the way. The virtues are fixed references for behavior, as self-evident and unalterable as the stars by which we have historically navigated.

All vice corrupts all virtue, and all virtue matures one away from all vice. This is difficult stuff, in a relativistic world where "keep your options open" and "keep your exits covered," are axiomatic; where expediency rules, and where we delude ourselves into thinking we can decide what is "right for us," as distinct from, simply, "what is Right."

THE CARDINAL VIRTUES

Temperance.

"Temperance" is usually identified with "moderation," but it's more than that.

> ...give me neither poverty nor riches; feed me with the food that is needful for me, lest I be full, and deny Thee, and say, "Who is the Lord?" or lest I be poor, and steal, and profane the Name of my God
> (Proverbs 30: 8b-9)

Temperance has to do with our use of our bodies; with the fact that our interactions with the physical world are no less connected to our life in Christ than is our "spiritual life."

The early Gnostics maintained that there was a dichotomy between matter and spirit that applied also to the body. Matter was evil, because it is as material beings in a material world that we sin. They therefore saw holiness, and salvation, as a business of overcoming matter with spirit, of detaching ourselves from things material (because they are "bad") and cultivating things spiritual (because they are "good"). The Gnostic heresies are not alone in this; they are joined by most of the pagan mystical practices, which is in fact where they got the idea.

The problem with that is that not everything spiritual is helpful, and not everything material is harmful.

In the Creed, we confess that we believe in "One God: the Father Almighty, Creator of Heaven and earth and of all things, visible and invisible…"

…all things, visible and invisible: That which is seen and that which is unseen, that which is matter and that which is spirit is all created by God.

The ancient record of the sayings of the Desert Fathers, From the *Verba Seniorum*, puts this in perspective. It tells us of a young brother who came to a lavrum of anchorites (an anchorite is a solitary monk. A lavrum is a colony of anchoritic dwellings, or *cells*), to visit. He was welcomed by the Elder, who invited him to join in the common work of the colony and then have lunch. "No thank you," responded the brother, "I am told not to work for the bread that perisheth." So, the Elder had books, presumably scrolls of Scripture, brought to him.

Later in the evening, the brother was curious as to why he had not been called for the evening meal. "Have you eaten?" he asked the Elder. "Why, yes," responded the old man, "and it was very good, thank you for asking." "But," asked the brother, "Why was I not called?" The Elder, with a look of surprise, replied, "Why, you are a spiritual man, with no need of the bread that perisheth. We provided for you books, that you might be nourished." At this the young man fell at the old man's feet and did penance, having been edified.

Temperance has nothing to do with opposition to the body. We are body, mind and spirit, and are deliberately created that way by the Living God, Who creates out of Love and loves His creation. It is therefore not a Godly thing for us to despise one part of ourselves and set it up in opposition to the others. That which edifies one part edifies all.

So, temperance is not there to deprive us, but to strengthen us: to *temper* us.

It is not matter which is our enemy, but rather what we impose on matter. The fallenness of nature is an accommodation to our own fallenness, not a cause of it. The material world was given to us for our use. It is we who misuse it, not the other way 'round.

To be temperate, as in its root word, the Latin tempero, is to be "moderate," "self-controlled." Tellingly, the word also means "tempered" in the sense that when we temper iron, it becomes steel.

Temperance is a turning-away from the selfish demand of our fallen nature that we must indulge ourselves at all times, at all costs. As we do this, we turn toward God. Thus, just as we are able to pray with our mind and with our spirit, we find we are able to also pray with our body. Our three parts thus become more unified: less. not more, opposed to each other and therefore more mature in Godliness.

Fasting is a function of temperance. A deliberate self-denial, however minor or major, is not so much a denial of self as it is of selfishness. Selfishness is, of course, a function of Pride, which is the Original Sin and the root of all our problems. Selfishness is normal for us, an ever-present condition of our fallenness. Temperance is the lived experience of the preference we are cultivating for the company of God over the distractions of our selfishness. In this it is the same as spending time in prayer when we could be spending it self-centeredly.

The result? We are *tempered*, the way steel is tempered in fire.

Our fallen nature rages and wheedles, demanding we indulge in this behavior or that amusement; that we turn from God, "just for the moment, mind you," to embrace some self-indulgence or other. To resist is painful. But…

> *The refining pot is for silver, and the furnace for gold, but the Lord tests the hearts.*
> (Proverbs 17: 3)

On the other hand, we are imperfect. If we are serious, we seek to walk the path of perfection, but that's what it is—a path. We do not reach the destination here. So, despite our best efforts and motives, our feet will occasionally slip and we will feel crushed. Even this is a positive thing, because it drives us to prayer and to greater vulnerability before God.

So, we are refined as in a furnace. The furnace of un-indulged temptation (or of the conscience-reaction after an indulged one) does not exist to break us down, or even, particularly, to deny us anything. Temperance exists to temper us, to make us strong for the service of God in a sinful world that would devour us, and those whom we are called to help, if it could.

The bottom line is that Temperance is the bedrock of the serious religious life. All the other virtues contribute to it, and it feeds all of them. Properly tempered steel is a sure servant in the hands of its master. So is a properly tempered Christian.

Prudence.

When we think of "prudence," we ordinarily think of "caution," and we ordinarily equate "caution" with "minimization of risk." The "prudent man rule" that bankers used to follow when investing, comes to mind. Prudence works in a worldly sense insofar as it serves our own interests. We try to invest wisely, to measure our words in the presence of people who can do us some good; to avoid legal liability.

God tells us that wisdom dwells with prudence (Proverbs 8:12).

Now, the wisdom of God is God-referencing rather than self-referencing, and is concerned with "keeping and doing the statutes and ordinances of God" (Deuteronomy 4:6).

The wisdom of the world is self-oriented and deals with how I might advance myself. God's prudent man, however, is concerned with the advancement of the Kingdom of God, both within himself and in the world around him. He is concerned that his words and behavior contribute to this, and so he wishes to form himself and be formed in such a way that such is his "default setting," if you will.

Jesus summed up all of the statutes and ordinances of God in the two admonitions which are called the "New Testament Commandments," or the "Commandments of the Kingdom" by many commentators:

> *You shall love the Lord your God with all your heart, with all your soul and with all your mind. This is the first and great commandment. And the second is like it: you shall love your neighbor as yourself. On these commandments hang all the law and the prophets.*
> (Matthew 22: 37-40)

We see here that the wisdom of God is directed outward rather than inward. Therefore prudence, as it is exercised in the Kingdom, is concerned with the things of love:

> *Love suffers long and is kind; love does not envy; love does not parade itself, is not puffed up; does not behave rudely, does not seek its own, is not provoked, thinks no evil; does not rejoice in iniquity, but rejoices in the truth; bears all things, believes all things, hopes all things, endures all things. Love never fails.*
> (1 Corinthians 13: 4-8a)

The world has a word for people who behave like this: Naïve. Suggest to a group of worldly men that these things are the stuff of "prudence," and you'll be laughed out of the conversation. "Naïve," however, means "innocent," or "childlike," and that's how the Lord tells us to be (Matthew 18:3).

Does that mean we're to just stumble around in the world blindly, defenseless in the face of predators? Certainly not! The Books of Psalms, Proverbs, Wisdom and Sirach are chock full of sage advice on living in the world and dealing with its ways. In Matthew 10:16, the Lord tells us that He is sending us out "as sheep in the midst of wolves," and He tells us what to do about it: "Therefore be wise as serpents and harmless as doves."

We can't help living in the world, but the Lord tells us not to be "of it." In John 13: 15-18, Jesus prays for our protection. He does not pray for us to be taken out of the world, because He has sent us into the world even as the Father has sent Him. So, He prays that we should be kept safe from the devil.

When we look into the Bible, at all the places in, say, Proverbs, where prudence is mentioned, we see prudence in a broader sense. The prudent person has "wisdom" (Pr 8:12, Eph 1:8), emotional stability (Pr 12:16), is modest (12:23), has a teachable spirit (13:16, 15:5), is discerning (14:8, 15), is knowledgeable (14:18) and is not reckless (22:3, 27:12).

The word that comes to my mind when I put all these traits together is, "reliable." This is someone who can be depended upon. He's not the guy who, having discovered something or heard a rumor about you, will blab it all over church, feeling a little thrill as he goes, "You know, in confidence, Bob needs prayer for...". A prudent man, or woman, is someone whose advice is sound, whose word is good (if he says he'll be somewhere, he'll be there; if he says he'll do something, he'll do it), in whose company you won't get into trouble and with whom your personal conversations are safe.

A prudent person is a reliable person.

The Apostles and great Saints of the Church demonstrate to us that a prudent person is not necessarily risk averse. Paul, for instance, may not have rushed headlong into things, but he lived an incredibly daring life. He was a bold man, unafraid to preach to people he knew would arrest him and even have him flogged, beaten and stoned for his trouble (2 Cor 11: 24-25a). Determined to preach even to Caesar himself, Paul got himself arrested, refusing opportunities for release, and appealed to Caesar (as a Roman citizen he had that right) so he'd get free transportation. As a result, Paul spent little time in actual chains, and spent most of his prisoner-time under house arrest, free to receive visitors and even venture out occasionally, rather than in a prison.

Paul was daring, but not reckless. He knew the risks before he ventured out, and made sure it was God who was calling before he responded. He was something which, in our by-turns irresponsible and over-cushioned age, is increasingly rare: a prudent adventurer.

The history of the Church is replete with such people. The Desert Fathers, framers of the mystical (and much of the pastoral) Theology of the Church, left cities, towns and farms, places where their livelihoods, if not abundant, were at least assured, to seek God in the solitude of an arid and unforgiving desert. Many of the Celtic Fathers were nobles—even princes—who abandoned lives of luxury and privilege to beat their way through forest wilderness to preach to hostile, warlike tribes.

These were people whose discernment of God's Will moved them to acquire knowledge and whose stability enabled them to acquire wisdom. Even though the circumstances that surrounded them might have been hazardous, they themselves were, in effect, a safe harbor. As a result, Paul's shipboard captors followed his instructions when a storm brought about shipwreck. In the same way, the great monasteries that nurtured the Church sprouted like a spring garden and the Gospel was preached to the ends of the known world.

None of this could have happened if the confidence of others had not been inspired. The soldiers on shipboard not only followed Paul's instructions to save themselves, they also broke out of their customary pattern and saved the other prisoners instead of leaving them to drown. In the monastic wildernesses, novices entrusted themselves to the wisdom and survival skills of the desert elders and the Western planters of remote communities.

Though less outwardly dramatic, the same dynamic is at work in the modern confessional. Penitents, a wary lot these days, entrust the deepest, most undisclosable secrets of their lives to God, through men whom they perceive to be prudent. Likewise, in the Church's monasteries and houses of prayer, people vulnerably entrust their needs and the desires of their hearts to those on whom they rely to help them live deeper lives before God.

Perhaps this trust of a prudent guide is nowhere more stark than in the simple sharing of the Gospel: in the timorous hopefulness of a worldly man or woman whose trust has been abused and battered by a lifetime of back-stabbing and betrayal, jumping off the spiritual cliff into the arms of the Savior, trusting the word of a Christian who has promised to stick with them.

These are humbling experiences. After all, who exactly am I to have people so entrust their lives to me? I must treat these people, these tender souls, with discernment, with discretion, with such wisdom as I might have: with Prudence.

Prudence ultimately points not to me, but to others. Our cultivation of the good habits that make us a reliable person is not for our sake but for the sake of others. If we are reliable, God will send others to rely on us. They're the ones for whom our maturing into prudence is readying us.

Justice.

All of us encounter, on a frequent if not daily basis, varieties of people and questions about how we should treat them. There are political questions about "social justice," juridical questions that are the business of judges and juries and every-day –personal questions about how we are going to deal with this or that individual. For bishops and abbots, pastors and parish councils there are questions of church discipline. For all of us, there are questions about how we're going to respond to this or that new parishioner, or this or that unbeliever. We view incidents and movements on the world stage, all of which involve people, and we make decisions about them. These questions and decisions are all matters of justice.

Complicating the situation is the fact that we measure almost all of these questions and decisions according to a set of preconceptions in which we are emotionally and intellectually invested.

The question is not whether or not we should have such preconceptions: there's an old saying that wisely counsels, "If you don't stand for something you'll fall for anything." Rather, the question is, what sort of preconceptions should I have? Or, what is the standard by which I should judge? How do I co-operate with God to form my mind after His Will, when there are so many paradigms competing for its attention?

The refining fire rarely burns as hot as when we are called upon to be just.

> *He has showed you, O man, what is good, and what does the Lord require of you but to do justice, and to love kindness, and to walk humbly with your God?*
> (Micah 6:8)

The Word of God tells us that there is something called Justice; that it is not theoretical or amorphous, but real and objective. It is a habit of behavior, a certain sort of virtue that guides how we deal with people.

Leviticus 19:15 tells us,

> *You shall do no injustice in judgment; you shall not be partial to the poor or defer to the great, but in righteousness shall you judge your neighbor.*

This is hard.

It is natural for us to defer to the wealthy, the well-groomed, the socially skilled. We naturally want to "be on the good side" of the powerful and influential, and—face it—we judge those whose company is enjoyable with somewhat more leeway.

On the other hand, if we are God's people we feel an obligation to the poor. We are in fact commanded to help the poor among us, and it's easy to become so involved in this most obvious need that we neglect the less-obvious demands of charity. We might even grow to judge those with needs other than financial, as "less worthy."

God tells us to do neither of these. This passage from Leviticus reminds us that the people we meet and deal with are—people. Each of them is beloved of God and each of them is to be dealt with as God deals with them—as individuals, not as "part of a group."

So, by this standard the virtue of Justice would simply be summed up, "be even-handed."

But is it right to "judge our neighbor" at all?

> *Judge not that you be not judged. For with what judgment you judge you will be judged; and with the measure you use it will be measured back to you. And why do you look at the speck in your brother's eye, and do not consider the plank in your own eye? Or how can you say to your brother, "Let me remove the speck from your eye"; and look, a plank is in your own eye? Hypocrite! First remove the plank from your own eye, and then you will see clearly to remove the speck from your brother's eye.*
> (Matthew 7: 1-5)

We run into a particular problem here. Our post-modern culture has no fixed values. It in fact regards any mention of fixed values as "intolerant." The culture has its own, very elusive way of thinking and its own set of, often contradictory, definitions. Accordingly, denying sin and (often simply automatically and absent a frame of reference) defying God, the worldly reflexively attempt to turn this passage against us. "Hypocrite," they accuse, "Don't judge me! Are you perfect?"

But the passage continues, in verse 6…

> *Do not give what is holy to the dogs; nor cast your pearls before swine, lest they trample them under their feet, and turn and tear you in pieces.*

Here the Lord is warning us to beware of the attitudes and philosophies of mammon. Reflexive response can progress into deliberate hostility and belligerence. The "dogs" are those who would corrupt even the Church; who would introduce the supposedly superior, more "tolerant" mindset of the secular culture into her midst, by way of "correcting" her, of "bringing her up to date."

The "swine" are those worldly men who, having attained to ecclesiastical power, exact deference and demand "dialogue;" who smile and flatter even as they discard the offerings of righteousness, and harshly condemn even as they rebuke the righteous for "judging."

This can be challenging. The philosophy of the secularist anti-church may be amorphous, but it is heavily laden with simple, emotionally-impactful phrases that seductively resemble logical thought. Additionally, its sales pitch is always laced with an appeal to our pride and self-interest. The rich influential guy can get the church its needed new roof. Well-publicized ministry to the poor can win us applause from both the Church and the world, particularly if the preaching of the Gospel is minimized in deference to "the sensibilities of those who may believe differently."

All of this is to say that, as much as we may be rhetorically vulnerable to the world's misuse of passages on "judging," we must resist it.

Specifically, we need to resist mammon's insistence that to faithfully reject their positions is to condemn individuals who may hold them. After all, to warn someone of hell is to attempt to keep him out of it, not to condemn him to it.

As people of God, we are bearers of His Grace and messengers of His Mercy. To "judge as we would be judged" is to apply to others the same standards we apply to ourselves—and the same treatment we hope for from God when we fail to live up to them:

> *Therefore the kingdom of heaven is like a certain king who wanted to settle accounts with his servants. And when he had begun to settle accounts, one was brought to him who owed him ten thousand talents. But as he was not able to pay, his master commanded that he be sold, with his wife and children and all that he had, and that payment be made. the servant therefore fell down before him, saying, 'Master, have patience with me, and I will pay you all.' Then the master of that servant was moved with compassion, released him, and forgave him the debt. "But that servant went out and found one of his fellow servants who owed him a hundred denarii; and he laid hands on him and took him by the throat, saying, 'Pay me what you owe!' So his fellow servant fell down at his feet and begged him, saying, 'Have patience with me, and I will pay you all.' And he would not, but went and threw him into prison till he should pay the debt. So when his fellow servants saw what had been done, they were very grieved, and came and told their master all that had been done. then his master, after he had called him, said to him, 'You wicked servant! I forgave you all that debt because you begged me. Should you not also have had compassion on your fellow servant, just as I had pity on you?' And his master was angry,*

> *and delivered him to the torturers until he should pay all that was due to him. "So My heavenly Father also will do to you if each of you, from his heart, does not forgive his brother his trespasses.*
> (Matthew 18: 23-35)

So, what's the rule of thumb? How do we know if we're judging justly, or even-handedly, when our pride and self-interest are always and inevitably in the way? Jesus, Himself, gives the answer:

> *For with what judgment you judge, you will be judged; and with the measure you use, it will be measured back to you.*
> (Matthew 7:2)

Justice is a virtue, and is therefore personally formative. We are encouraged to even-handedness when we reflect that, before God, the standard by which we judge is the standard to which we are held.

That doesn't mean we should become blind to sin, seeking to keep ourselves off the hook. We are called to clarity of vision, not relativism. We must always be in service to the Truth. At the same time, we must remember that we are at the service of the soul of the person we are called to counsel, and that we must take care to temper justice with prudence, that we might not break an already-bruised reed (cf. Matthew 12: 19- 21).

Courage.

In his book *The Screwtape Letters* (Geoffrey Bles, London, 1942), C.S. Lewis says of courage:

> *Courage is not simply one of the virtues but the form*

> *of every virtue at the testing point, which means at the point of highest reality.*

Living a virtuous life isn't easy. Mainly this is because we live in the world, and the world opposes virtue. How do we overcome the fear of social opprobrium, even of job discrimination or government harassment?

How do you maintain temperance in a world of excess? It seems like every day's mail has an invitation for you to go into debt for some new, shiny toy. You can't turn around, without encountering advertising. It's on the computer, on television and radio, on billboards as you drive down the road, even on your receipts from the supermarket. Pages and airwaves are filled with seductive women, successful men, tropical vistas, fast cars and good restaurants, and they're all assuring you that "you need this" in order to "live the good life."

How do you maintain prudence in a world of reckless role models? Almost everything we encounter is over-the-top and distorted. Our "entertainment" gets cruder and less intelligent by the day, but compensates for that by being louder and lewder. Our politicians make impossible promises they have no way to keep. An out-of-control government places electronic eyes and ears on our e-mails and phone calls, The IRS sells our personal information. How do we learn prudence, when the system itself appears to recognize no boundaries?

And justice? How do you learn about justice in a world that runs on injustice? We can murder our children on whim, as long as we do it before they leave the birth canal; yet a child who has survived long enough to make it to school can be suspended for pointing out that a cloud formation resembles a gun (yes, this actually happened).

Cities freely spend our tax money to support parades that celebrate sexual perversion, in the name of freedom of expression, yet a child can be sent home from school for wearing a T-shirt with an American flag on it. You risk your career in the military for refusing to express approval of "gay marriage" to a homosexual who outranks you or for posting a Bible verse on a whiteboard outside your quarters (again, these specific things actually happened, and there are scores more that aren't as well-publicized).

The unfortunate fact is that we have given hell free rein in our society. Our culture has actually come to the point of calling evil good, and good evil. And evil doesn't tolerate being confronted. It takes courage to stand on your convictions in an all-pervasive socio-cultural environment that demands we abandon them.

Why, you might ask, do we particularly need to confront the culture? Why can't we just stay in our own sub-cultural enclave, and not worry about it?

The answer is that as much as we might try to leave the culture alone, the culture will not leave us alone. Evil tolerates no dissent, and the Church is the only restraint on evil. We are placed in society not just for ourselves, but for everyone: that the culture, already mired in relativistic fantasy, might not be completely swallowed up by the darkness against which it doesn't even know it needs to defend itself.

In conversation, Christians refer to God's revelation of Himself in Scripture and in the Natural Law. We refer to objective reality and to an unchanging moral code. We refer to the intrinsic dignity of human beings and the immutability of right and wrong, good and evil. This is very threatening to a culture that rests its hope on a tissue-thin worldview in which nothing is real or lasting and everything is up for grabs. Mammon has to work very hard to maintain its fairy-tales, and cannot abide the influence of Reality.

Every person is not in fact his or her own moral arbiter, and every opinion is not sacred just because "we're entitled to one." But the secular world has appointed every man his own god—a job for which we are completely unsuited and at which we are consistent, catastrophic failures. The Presence of the real God exposes the shallowness of self-idolatry, and in doing so provokes its adherents to frenzy.

Academic honors, social acceptance and advancement, wealth and influence are the (mostly empty and unkept) promises of the kingdom of mammon. These blandishments are the brambles in the soil of our society, and they can all too readily choke off the nourishing fruit of the Gospel (see Mark 4: 7 and context). To make our way through them to our goal requires courage.

The voices of mammon beckon us with the seductive urgency of Ulysses' sirens, to shipwreck. It takes a stout heart and a strong character to resist them, and these are in desperately short supply in our contemporary culture. In fact, our culture fills our airwaves—and thus our minds—with violent fiction about physical courage, but its heroes are situational pragmatists. Our culture, almost extinguished by the blanket of sin that is smothering it, actively and ruthlessly opposes moral courage. Our schools, and now our laws, forcibly coerce us into the most vulgar and degrading "new norms."

Even a life of simple decency today requires that we march, as the saying goes, to the beat of a different drummer. The issue with that is that it requires us to leave the pack and to become starkly visible, as the rest of the procession sees us walking in the opposite direction.

Our culture offers little or no avenues to moral courage, or even to human dignity. In the Church, however, we can overcome the world, because it is in the Church that we find Christ:

> *For God has given us a spirit of courage, and not of timidity.*
> (2 Timothy 1: 7)

Temperance, Prudence, Justice and courage are what are called the "cardinal virtues" They are the traits we must cultivate in order to have a solid character, whatever our path.. They are essential to a successful Christian life, but they do not of themselves constitute a Christian life. Indeed, they could apply in equal measure to anyone who lives by a defined code of ethics, from a monk to a mobster. Which brings us to...

THE THEOLOGICAL VIRTUES

Faith

When the world speaks of "faith," they mean what amounts to "making a wish." Have faith, they say, and "it," whatever "it" is, will all "work out."

But, faith in what? faith in the future? All the future is, is a period of time. It shapes nothing, it is simply the passive receptacle of whatever we all pour into it. So, when people say things like that, it seems they're saying that if we think positive thoughts we will somehow propel events in the desired direction.

To a limited extent, this is true. Optimism and confidence can make us more convincing in our dealings with others, and can get us through psychologically bleak periods. A conviction that "it will all work out," because "it has so far," can carry us through some tough times.

Optimism grounded in past victories, however, can be harmful as well as helpful. What if "it" doesn't work out? or doesn't work out as well, or even does more damage, this time around?

Confidence grounded in what? In my ability to sell my way into and out of situations? But what if the problem is an earthquake or a flood? a forest fire? an avalanche? a tsunami? In cases like this, my personal resourcefulness is limited or irrelevant and any substantial help may be unavailable. I may be under the avalanche, or in front of the wave, with nowhere to go. What then?

At the point where we have exceeded our limitations, the world's version of "faith" becomes useless. In the burning house, when the floor is giving way under my feet and there's nothing to grab, "it" isn't going to "work out."

The only sensible place to put one's faith is in God.

God is in charge. He created the world and everything in it. He runs everything and everything that runs it. He is Omnipotent, Omniscient and Omnipresent, meaning He can do absolutely anything, knows absolutely everything and is absolutely everywhere, everywhen.

Who better to put faith in?

For all the world blathers at us about "faith in ourselves," our own consistent experience of ourselves indicates we are limited. The best football team loses a few. The smartest people make some of the dumbest mistakes. Our own rock-solid competence in one field of endeavor or another, be it auto mechanics or theoretical physics (to me, not all that different) doesn't keep us from being occasionally embarrassed.

The Theological virtue of Faith involves giving up our faith in the limited and trading it in for faith in the Limitless.

This can be disconcerting, because the Limitless does not play by our rules. His ways are not our ways, nor His thoughts our thoughts

(Isaiah 55: 8-9). We are used to an environment where our opinion shapes much of what we choose to call "reality." The ultimate Reality, however, does not conform to our opinion, nor is He affected by it. The rules we prefer to play by are often not the rules we find in force, and things may go in ways we neither expect nor wish.

The overarching fact is that God is good, and he desires our salvation. God is He Who...*desires all men to be saved and to come to a knowledge of the Truth.* (1 Timothy 2:4) *The Lord ...is not slack concerning His promise, as some count slackness, but is long-suffering toward us, not willing that anyone should perish, but that all should come to repentance.* (2 Peter 3: 9)

I think that what interferes with faith in God the most, is not believing this; not believing in the goodness or the love of God, not believing in His personal concern for us.

Granted, there are some pretty good reasons for this. First of all, the world is a mess. If God loves us so much, why doesn't He do something about it? and how can I entrust my life to an Omnipotent, Omnipresent Being who stands around and lets children die of starvation and whole cities get wiped out by disasters? Wouldn't it be safer to keep as much distance from this Guy as possible?

Those of us who know Christ might find that idea funny. But to someone who doesn't know Him, these are real questions and serious concerns. We draw our conclusions from our experience. How can we believe in a God of Peace, when all around us is conflict and chaos? How can we relate to God as a loving Father, in a world of divorce and promiscuity where huge numbers of people have never even met their fathers and whose mothers may not even know who their fathers are?

How can a sane man place his faith in an all-powerful Being Who would allow all this to happen?

I read a very interesting quote some time back. Can't remember who said it, but he remarked that, *if we really wanted peace on earth, we would have it.*

What an interesting observation! and on reflection, isn't it true? We really don't want peace on earth in any tangible sense, because that would entail a degree of sacrifice we are not prepared to make. What we want is peace in our own life, to pursue our own way. Or, if we have some broader vision, a vision of "peace on earth," it is to our vision—not to peace, itself-- that we commit ourselves. That's because "peace" is something that stands outside of us and involves the co-operation of others, a whole world full of others, who don't think like us; who might even dislike us for no good reason we can think of.

In the world, we eat bread by the sweat of our face (Genesis 3: 19). Very few things are handed to us, and in one way or another we have to fight for the rest. If our ambitions and capacities are very large, and we have the wherewithal to finance them, we can drag a lot of people into our fight, who will in turn have to fight to defend themselves against us. Or maybe my ambition is to live a quiet life, with a simple job that allows me to pay the rent and pursue my interests. I will still have to get up in the morning, be responsible at work and deal with the people I encounter there. Sometimes that can be a struggle. And there are always those times when my comfortable, if sometimes strenuous, routine is interrupted by periods of unemployment, illness and unexpected expense.

The long and short of it is, no matter who we are, how impressively powerful or comfortably anonymous we are, nothing works just as it should all the time.

The world is broken. We're broken. If this were not the case, our desire for, for instance, world peace, would be real and we would bring it about instead of attempting to exploit the conflicts; or, even worse, creating conflicts to exploit.

It makes no sense to blame God. My sin is not His fault. My redemption, however, is His doing. God desires our good. And if we can't have peace in the world, we can have peace within ourselves because God, if we let Him, will give it to us. The key is to let go of our defensiveness and resentment, our excuse-making and second-guessing, and to turn to the Lord in trust that He desires our good: to remove our faith from the world and its ways and from ourselves and our capacities, and place it in Him.

> *Now, faith is the substance of things hoped for, the evidence of things not seen.*
> (Hebrews 11: 1)

Our Unseen God is seen every time we turn around: principally in the fact that we are turning around, and that there is an environment in which to do the turning. It all--we all--came from somewhere—and all the speculations of all the people who (oddly) want to avoid confronting that fact, only push it away, they don't eliminate it.

Those times of peril and distress, when, against all odds, we make it through, are instances of God reaching out to show us He's there. The evidence of our unseen God is everywhere, if we simply look. Reason can confirm to us that He exists (Romans 1:20), but it is faith that enables us to embrace Him. The unseen is still unseen, despite its evidence: after all, we only believe in air because we feel the breeze. What good would that do us, if we didn't inhale?

Hope

Hope is ordinarily thought of in terms of something to be hoped for, as in, "I hope I win the lottery," or "I hope my car can make it through the winter without breaking down," etc. To a Christian, though, hope is more like something to be absorbed into. That's because Jesus is the Blessed Incarnation of God's Hope for His creation. Once we declare that "Christ is my hope," we are caught up into the very dynamic of God, Who is Hope, itself.

Whoa, hold it! Did I just say, "God's Hope for His creation?" How does that work? Doesn't "hope" imply doubt? Yet, God's intention is His action. What need of—indeed, what capacity for—"hope," has the omnipotent Creator and Sustainer of the universe? Isn't there a pretty distinct qualitative difference between, "I hope it happens," and "It will happen!"?

From our earthly perspective, certainly! From a Heavenly perspective, not so much:

> *The Lord is not slack concerning His promise, as some count slackness, but is longsuffering toward us, not wishing that any should perish, but that all should come to repentance.*
> (2 Peter 3:9)

Or how about, the passage in First Timothy 2: 3-4, which tells us of "God our Savior..."

> *...who desires all men to be saved And to come to the knowledge of the truth.*

How can God "wish?" How can He "desire?" Isn't it intrinsic to God's Essence that whatever He wishes or desires must, simply thereby, happen?

That would be a pretty thorny question, if we knew God in His Essence. We don't. We only know Him in His Energies, in terms of how He deals with us—and He deals with us in terms of things like "wishing" and "desiring." In other words, in terms of Hope. He deals with us not in terms of how "contingency" applies to Him, but of how it applies to us.

Hope is an expression of the Divine Love, which

> ....*hopes all things...*
> (1 Corinthians 7: 13c)

This Divine Hope is Incarnate in Christ:

> *Blessed be the God and Father of our Lord Jesus Christ, who according to His abundant mercy has begotten us again to a living hope through the resurrection of Jesus Christ from the dead...*
> (1 Peter 1:3)

and is not rooted in earth but In Heaven:

> *...to an inheritance incorruptible and undefiled and does not fade away, reserved in Heaven for you...*
> (1 Peter 1:4)

Hope, of course, is propelled by Faith:

> *...who are kept by the power of God through faith for salvation ready to be revealed in the last time*
> (1 Peter 1:5)

The Divine Hope is transformative of our character. As we yield to Christ, it becomes part of us: dwelling in us even as we dwell in Him:

> *To them God wished to make known what are the riches of the glory of this mystery among the Gentiles: which is Christ in you, the hope of glory.*
> (Colossians 1: 27)

Love

By answering the invitation posed by Christ the Divine Hope, we are caught up into God's Love.

> *And we have known and believed in the love God has for us. God is Love, and he who abides in love abides in God. and God in him.*
> (1 John 4:16)

To live a life of love is to do nothing less than to share in the nature of the very Essence of God. That isn't easy to do. In fact, it is impossible to do in its fullness, because we can't do it consciously. We can't "push" it, or "engineer" it, the way we are used to doing in most of our activities in the world. It involves, as we have discussed so often, getting myself out of the way and letting the Holy Spirit flow through me.

Curiously, as I do this I become more, not less, engaged. As I surrender my defenses to the activity of God my volition changes, and with it my behavior,

You see, even though Love has its emotional component, it is more than just an emotion. Love is a decision and an act.

Love's emotional component is found in *Eros*, the love that is rooted in physical attraction and emotional affection. It is also found in *Filios*, or "brotherly love," committed companionship and sense of shared mission and/or family feeling.

The decision part of Love is *Agape*. Agape is the fruit of my conscious decision to love, to be a loving person who cares about the salvation and well-being of all people and seeks the condemnation of none.

All of these are put into action in the practice of *Caritas*, or charity, which is the expression of Love to which the verse refers. "Charity" means "giving," which is what God does: He gives. God's giving is a continual outpouring of Himself, in Selfless service to His creatures.

Caritas differs from (eros), the physical love which culminates in interpersonal passion, and from *filios*, the "brotherly (or sisterly) love" of friendship. It differs in that it is what gives them expression; even as *Agape*, flowing from the decision to have concern for the other in the first place, makes the rest possible.

We deal with God in terms of His Energies: of His activity, rather than His Essence. All we see around us is indicative of the creating and sustaining God, and it is very beautiful, whether it's the compelling view from the top of a mountain or the more humble (yet much more complex) network of veins on a leaf. These things, and everything in between, are things God does or has done, but they are not God, Himself. In our Baptism, we receive the Holy Spirit. From then on, to one degree or another, we directly experience the Presence of God.

This can become quite profound when we deliberately dispose ourselves to experience Him, as in prayer and meditation. Also, God's Grace is *prevenient*: it is everywhere. So, as well as those times when we particularly reach out to Him there are always those blessed moments when He reaches out to us; then He puts some particularly timely thing before us, catching us, so to speak, by surprise.

In the midst of all of these moments, what we are experiencing is the fruit of what God has given and is giving us; His Act upon us in response to our having opened ourselves to Him: His Energy.

Now, certainly God's Energy derives from and proceeds from His Essence. It can tell us about, put us in touch with, make us aware of, even experience His Essence—but we are still being acted upon. It is still His Energies with which we are directly in touch, and it is those Energies that put us, in ways we can neither understand nor manage, in touch with the inconceivable Mystery of His Essence.

God *is* Love. And when we abide in Love, we *abide in Him* (see above). We are, in other words, directly in touch with Him and participating in and with Him as we cannot do in any other way.

So, what is Love?

What it is not, is the sort of self-referencing romance that is the "love" of the world's poets and popular songwriters.

One of the most moving and powerful love poems ever written is *How Do I Love Thee? (Sonnet 43)* by Elizabeth Barrett Browning (1806 – 1861). I think most of us have read it, but since we're discussing love it seems right to repeat it, here:

> *How do I love thee? Let me count the ways.*
> *I love thee to the depth and breadth and height*
> *My soul can reach, when feeling out of sight*
> *For the ends of being and ideal grace.*
> *I love thee to the level of every day's*
> *Most quiet need, by sun and candle-light.*
> *I love thee freely, as men strive for right.*
> *I love thee purely, as they turn from praise.*
> *I love thee with the passion put to use*
> *In my old griefs, and with my childhood's faith.*

> *I love thee with a love I seemed to lose*
> *With my lost saints. I love thee with the breath,*
> *smiles, tears, of all my life; and, if God choose,*
> *I shall but love thee better after death.*

What powerful and evocative verse! Yet, on close reading, we see that the poem is less about her beloved than about her: her feelings, her passions. Not about love itself, but about her reactions to it.

Similarly stirring is Sammy Fain's theme from a 1955 movie (produced by Buddy Adler for 20th Century Fox), entitled, *Love is a Many Splendored Thing*:

> *Love is a many-splendored thing,*
> *It's the April rose that only grows in the early spring,*
> *Love is nature's way of giving a reason to be living,*
> *The golden crown that makes a man a king.*
> *Lost on a high and windy hill,*
> *In the morning mist two lovers kissed and the world stood still,*
> *When our fingers touch, my silent heart has taught us how to sing!*
> *Yes, true love's a many-splendored thing.*

Here, Mr. Fain makes a valiant attempt to paean love, itself. In some really quite fine verse, we're led into a glimpse of love, the phenomenon. The end of the piece, however, rather than soaring past itself as one might anticipate, finds its resolution in the personal experience of the poet.

I suggest that this is the best we, of ourselves, can do.

To touch Love is, in the profoundest possible way, to touch God. Remember, God is Love, and we cannot explain God in terms of His Essence, This is why, for all the songs and stories, narratives and poems, we still cannot adequately describe Love. The best we can do is to describe its impact, and hope this will convey the idea.

So what of the virtue of Love? How can we practice it, if we can't describe it?

Fortunately, we don't have to. We can't describe Love, but God can, and He has:

> *Love suffers long and is kind; love does not envy; love does not parade itself, is not puffed up; does not behave rudely, does not seek its own, is not provoked, thinks no evil; does not rejoice in iniquity, but rejoices in the truth; bears all things, believes all things, hopes all things, endures all things.*
>
> *Love never fails. But whether there are prophecies, they will fail; whether there are tongues, they will cease; whether there is knowledge, it will vanish away. For we know in part and we prophesy in part. But when that which is perfect has come, then that which is in part will be done away.*
> (1 Corinthians 13: 4-8)

There is nothing sentimental about this Love, nor anything self-referencing. Neither is there anything temporary about it.

This passage doesn't speak to us of a feeling, but of a Force: a Force so powerful that it will outlast even the ministry gifts of the Holy Spirit, because after the Lord returns they won't be needed, anymore; a Force that will outlast the end of our universe, for it is the very Character of the Perfect, and when the Perfect comes, it will be Love which has finally manifested itself to us in all its unfiltered, magnificent, terrifying fullness.

How can we possibly practice this?

The answer is in two simple exhortations: to love God with all our heart, soul, mind and strength, and to love our neighbor as ourself (Luke 10:27), because the way we treat our neighbor is the way we treat God (cf. Matthew 25:40).

We're used to thinking of love as an emotion, as affection, as something that references us and our emotional preferences. How can we configure our emotions to "love" our neighbor as ourself, though, when our neighbor might be a total stranger, or even an obnoxious pain in the neck?

How can we configure our emotions to "love" God with all our heart, soul, mind and strength, when—being honest--there are so many instances in life when we question whether or not He even knows we're around?

And how can we do both of these at the same time?

The "love" we're used to, can't. So we must be talking about a different kind of love.

The Theological virtue of Love begins with and proceeds from Agape: It is not an emotion or feeling, it's a decision. It is a rational decision, based on facts. It is a fact that God created me, sustains me and desires my well-being, even if that translates into an early death here, so that I can carry on with the rest of my life, with Him. Therefore I will make up my mind that I will trust Him, and that I will serve Him not out of a sense of obligation or fear but out of a determination to return the Love He shows me as He provides my every breath and has "prepared a place for..." my eternal future (cf. John 14:3).

It is also a fact that, since we are created in the image of God, my neighbor is a living icon of Christ. He might be a very flawed icon, indeed, but then, so am I. I must make up my mind to desire his good, even as God unremittingly desires mine: that if he is a bad person, he may overcome whatever has warped him, even as God wants me to mature past the sin that encumbers me; that if he does not know Christ, that he be saved, even as God absolutely desires my salvation; that if there is something that separates or alienates us, it may be eliminated, even as God works tirelessly within me to bring us closer to unity in Him; that if he has sinned against me, I may wholeheartedly forgive him, even as I hope to be forgiven.

These are not easy things to do.

The Lord tells us to bless those who curse us, and to pray for those who despitefully use us (Luke 6:28). How does that work?! Answer: it doesn't, unless we dispose ourselves to live in a condition of love. Not "affection." We don't have to like someone in order to love him.

Of course, this isn't just pie in the sky stuff, either. Ultimately, God's ways serve a purpose. If we pray for our enemy, and he repents and converts, he is a new person. We have succeeded in killing our enemy, and have gained a friend. Love makes me able to see past who he was, and to accept that he has undergone the same character change that I did. In His Love, God has wiped my former enemy's slate clean. His Love working through me, as a virtue, makes me able to join Him in that.

The personal consequence of loving God wholeheartedly is much different than we might think. Love brings joy, and a joyful embrace of the beloved and the things that are of the beloved. When the Beloved is the Creator of everything that is, life becomes a joyful embrace of the whole creation, and of life, itself. We see majesty in the humblest of created things, the Image of God in the "least" of our brothers and sisters, blessing in the humblest of circumstances, life in the midst of death. For when we love God, we open ourselves to the terrifying event of letting His Love engulf us and flow through us.

Daniel 3: 29-68 reveals to us the exuberance with which we embrace God's dynamic and exuberant creation when we are in love with Him. Thrown into a blazing furnace by a jealous king, Daniel the lover of God encountered there a vision of the Holy Trinity. In response, he raised his voice in celebration, and survived unscathed, and was the agent of the conversion of the king to the True God.

The Theological virtue of Love is nothing less than yielding to God Himself, Who is Love, and permitting Him—come what may—to transform us in character unto Christlikeness.

PART TWO: THE JOURNEY

Therefore we also, since we are surrounded by so great a cloud of witnesses, let us lay aside every weight, and the sin which so easily ensnares us, and let us run with endurance the race that is set before us...
(Hebrews 12:1)

~ ~ ~

SIX: VOCATION

To the world, "vocation" is a fancy word for "job." I still (yes, even after all these years), remember my third-grade English teacher defining, a "vocation" as what you do for a living, something for which you get paid, as opposed to an "avocation," which is a hobby.

Now, while this may be useful for the secular world, we mean something quite different in the Church. We recognize that there is a difference between a job, which is something we choose, and a vocation, which is something that chooses us.

Each of us humans is something, you see. God has individually created us, and invested us with a purpose. What we do should, properly, be in service to the fulfillment of that purpose. What we do, therefore, is properly a reflection of what we are. We find our vocation by opening ourselves to the work of God. He will lead us to where and what we are put here to be: it is He Who created us, Who designed us for our purpose, and it is He Who will reveal it to us if we seek it in Him.

Our relationship to nature

On a general level, there is something we all are—an estate we all inherit—simply because we are human. That estate is magnificent, and like anything else we're given, what we do with it is up to us. We can hoard it like the Greedy Fat Guy (See Part One, Chapter 3), or squander it like the Prodigal Son. We can nurture it like the Generous Landowner *(ibid.)* The inheritance is there nevertheless, and it's ours.

We go through a lot in life. Some of it is good, some magnificent. Some is bad, some is horrible. We do things we wish we hadn't done, and don't do things we wish we had. We have moments of high enthusiasm and moments of depression, great triumphs and occasional great defeats. Through all of it, through the highs and the lows, we remain sinners in a sinful world who, regardless of station or fortune, stand before God as paupers begging bread.

This "pauperish" condition is relative. It applies to our relationship with the Creator, but not at all to our relationship with the creation. It is in terms of our relationship with the creation that our magnificent inheritance comes into play, because before the creation we stand not as paupers but as masters. We are the crown of God's creation, and have a frightening ultimacy in our relationship with it.

Now, what do I mean by "ultimacy," and why is it frightening?

As to the first, take a look at us. In our strictly animal aspect, we are predators. God made us that way out of His Mercy, because after we pulled the world down upon our heads in the Fall it was the only way we would be able to survive.

Now, look around at the other predators. Which among them is weaker than we are? Which is slower? How many of us would be able to win a fight against an enraged and maddened house-cat, let alone a lion or a tiger? Our pet dog is descended from wolves. What if, one day, he decided to revert? How would we fare? By strictly pragmatic standards, none of us should even be here—we all should all have been eaten, long ago!

Yet, here we are. Why?

The world chalks it up to superior intelligence, and to an opposable thumb which enables us to make and use tools and to kill at a distance. But that doesn't explain how we were able to establish such a bond of affection and companionship with the wolves that they became pet dogs; or how the famous desert father, Paul the Hermit, was able to win the affection and loyalty of wild lions. It doesn't explain the loyalty and affection of giant elephants, horses, oxen, camels and other beasts of burden, to and for their human masters.

The pragmatic answer is our station at the top of the food chain which enables us to stand above and apart from the animal world, which is very specific and segmented. A rabbit lives in a "rabbit world," a cat in a "cat world," a dog in a "dog world" etc. The animals are all designed to fill a certain slot in the order of creation, and as intelligent and versatile as they may become in that slot, that's where they remain. Only we can move between, and even command, all of these various worlds.

But, again, how? We are slow and weak, unable to live without clothing and shelter. My house cat, a loving and affectionate pet, is by nature an apex predator. She can be sitting in the living room, and actually hear an insect in the kitchen, a hallway and two rooms away. She can see and pursue that insect in a room dark enough to make me bump into things. Her sensory capabilities are simply unimaginable to me, a mere human—and, for all that, her faculties are not as finely-tuned as one of the great cats who hunt in the wild.

All of my intelligence and both of my opposable thumbs would be useless in a fight against someone's gentle pet Labrador who had decided in that moment that he would rather be a wolf, again.

Yet, time after time we see instances on, say, You Tube, of lions in the wild "adopting" humans; of wolves protecting human children; of elephants joyously greeting humans from whom they have been separated for years. Little children control horses. Toddlers playfully pull on the ears of huge dogs with impunity.

How is it that the great beasts regard us this way? That when we get to know each other, it is they who look to us for affirmation and reassurance? Why will a dolphin or an Orca whale risk its life to rescue a stranded human, and carry him hundreds of miles, if necessary, back to land? What kept Grizzly Adams alive?

The answer is that God built it into the natural order. As He is the Lord of all, He made us—for better or for worse--the lords of His creation. Our fall caused the universe to fall, simply so we would be able to live in it. Our pets, accepted into our households as family members, grow beyond their "slot," and become, in their way, through their proximity to us, illumined.

We are less than shadows of the glorious creatures our first parents were before the Fall; yet we retain, even in our fallen state, the vestigial magnificence that comes from being icons of God. So, albeit imperfectly now, nature responds to us as it does.

Our relationship to God

This human condition of ours, in its odd, occasionally frightening, occasionally absurd blend of ugliness and splendor, can either be a doorway or a trap. It's a trap if we permit ourselves to become caged-up in a narrow space that's only defined by our self-centeredness and our immediate four dimensions. It's a doorway when we become attentive to the still, small Voice of God calling us beyond ourselves, even beyond space and time, into the incredible reality of what He has called us to be.

We are called, each of us, to be the intersection between Heaven and earth.

Think about it for a moment: you are a human being, a creature of body, mind and spirit. You are made in the Image of God, and are the crown of His creation. In you, Heaven and earth meet. Through you, God would make Himself especially manifest in this universe He has created. How can that happen if we let ourselves continue to be locked into the four walls of the secular and immediately apparent? How can we partake of the Living Water offered by Christ, if our hearts are stuck in the arid wasteland offered to us by a Godless world and its clueless sages?

Our intended end is in God, as living icons of Christ. This is the estate to which every one of us is predestined (see Titus 2: 11-14).

God has put us on earth for a purpose, and if we are to fulfill our purpose we must first find it. Having found it, we must live it. Both the finding and the living are the product of a remarkable adventure that can only be carried out in Christ, in a living and active relationship with Him.

Our intended destiny is not inevitable. We can deny it. If we do not, we will know the glory of Heaven. Moreover, we will discover--and experience—the incredible fact that our Eternity begins here and now.

There is good news and bad news about free will. The good news is that God has given us sovereignty on the earth. We are made in His Image, and the sovereignty He gives us is a reflection of His own. Our sovereignty, like His, is intended to be selfless. After all, God, Who has need of nothing, has no reason to be selfish. His Character is revealed by the fact that everything around us exists, in the first place. God is totally sufficient within Himself, and has no need of company; no need of possessions, planets, universes; no need of us. He is, however, Love. And the nature of love, even on our own fallen level, is to give: to share selflessly. Our imperfect selflessness is iconic of God's perfect Selflessness. So, our personal sovereignty is meant to be expressed in love of Him Who first loved us (see 1 John 4: 18-20), and therefore to willingly return to God what He first gave us: Sovereignty over our lives.

Not that God doesn't have this, already: We are, after all, contingent beings and totally dependent on Him. Our next heartbeat is not only permitted, but propelled, by Him. He does not need or desire "control," He already has that. What He seeks is our willingness.

We are sinful, limited, temporary creatures, called to mature into a perfect, limitless and eternal life. We can never gain it unless we permit our own sovereignty to be absorbed into God's, to knowingly and actively become part of His Work.

Does this mean losing our identity? becoming mindless zombies? No! not at all! What we're talking about is a process of maturation, not obliteration.

Father James Rosselli

The call of Christ

As we all know just from personal experience here on earth, maturation—growing up—makes us more of who we are, not less. Once, we were children. We had to die to that "self" in order to grow. We didn't stop being "us," we just became a bigger and better "us," an "us" that was capable of living in and navigating a larger world.

We are called by Christ, now, to die to the "self" we are now, so that we can move into the next stage.

> *Most assuredly I say to you, unless a grain of wheat falls into the ground and dies, it remains alone, but if it dies, it produces much grain.*
> (John 12:24)

We are meant to plant ourselves in the fertile field which is the Kingdom of God: to die to our present selves, that we may inherit an abundance, a fruitfulness and scope of life to which we cannot otherwise attain.

The bad news is, we have the terrible power to turn it all down. We can choose simply for the earth and the things of the earth. We can ignore God, and behave in ways that, in our inherently damaged judgment, seem to be in our best interest.

Bluntly, Heaven and hell are real. They are conditions of being, not geographical locations, and the power to choose between them is in our hands:

> *The sinners in Zion are afraid; trembling has seized the Godless: "Who among us can dwell with the devouring fire? Who among us can dwell with everlasting burnings?" He who walks righteously and speaks uprightly, who despises the gain of oppressions, who*

> *shakes his hands, lest they hold a bribe, who stops his ears from hearing of bloodshed and shuts his eyes from looking upon evil, he will dwell on the heights; his place of defense shall be the fortresses of rocks; his bread will be given him, his water is sure.*
> (Isaiah 43: 14-16)

This "everlasting burning" is God. If we have allowed Him to make us beings who are comfortable and joyful in His Presence, this Presence is a comforting warmth. If we have chosen to be people who oppose Him, who are offended or appalled by His Presence, that Presence will be to us a consuming fire (Hebrews 12: 25-29). It's up to us: the transformed life is truly transforming.

Heaven and hell also begin here, now. Compare the lives of those who know Christ and honor Him with the lives of those who do not. Which ones most maintain equanimity in times of trial? Which ones are humble in wealth and dignified in want? In which ones is joy—not simply mirth or fleeting emotional high-points, but real joy—most apparent?

There is obviously something missing from the Godless, who are daily tormented by the demands and stresses of a world they have chosen to face alone. There is a completeness to those who are in Christ, who face the world for what it is: preparation for Eternity, a place where Vocation becomes visible and the service of God normal and practical.

This is what the Lord meant when He said, "whoever desires to save his life will lose it, but whoever loses his life for My sake will find it" (Mt 16:25).

The creation is trapped in entropy. However long a run it may have, it is at the last temporary. The Creator is Eternal and Infinite. In whichever direction we invest our lives, that is the direction in which we will grow. God would have us grow into something unspeakably splendid, with every-day freedom of movement within and between dimensions of being we can only mathematically theorize about, here. He would have us live in an everlasting harmony with Him.

This can't happen without Christ, and real, single-minded commitment to Him.

We can touch God, become aware of God, appreciate God and even to some extent follow God, doing just about anything that takes us out of ourselves into the service of something greater than us, whatever that something might be and however we might define it. After all, we are born to transcend our vanity, and any step in that direction is a step God-ward. But intimacy with God—with the real and living God Who Is—can only be found in and through the Lord Jesus Christ (John 14: 6). He is the means God provided whereby we imperfect beings can gain citizenship in the perfection which is the Kingdom of Heaven.

Jesus and Reality

Many of us take the Name of Jesus lightly. To do that is to deny Reality.

We declare that there are places in our life which are reserved for us, which belong to the "secular world" we have created for the convenience of our vanity. We create artificial barriers, to insulate ourselves from Christ: "separation of Church and State;" "Religion" vs. "Practicality;" The Ancient teaching of the Church vs. "My Rights And My Way Of Doing Things."

We divide reality into "sacred" and "secular," and claim that each has its own rules, its own "place." We even claim that we can invent our own reality, and divide it into "what's right and wrong for you," vs.

"what's right and wrong for me" and even "what's real for you," vs. "what's real for me."

All of this is artificial and only complicates that which is at heart simple.

Why invent multiplicities of make-believe paths, and dispose ourselves to follow them? Is it because we need something to follow, and what we invent looks the most attractive?

This sort of "reality" is vapor. All it does is distract us from the path of our vocation in Christ.

There is only one Reality, and we're living in it whether we want to be or not.

Reality is given to us by God. it was here when we got here and it will still be here when we leave, should the Lord tarry. We can, to an extent, control—or, more properly, manage, what comes into our lives, but Reality will remain what it is, however much we disagree with it or try to shield or distract ourselves from it.

In the same way, there is only one Right and only one Wrong, Neither has anything to do with my wishful thinking unless my wish is to find and do the Will of God.

Consider for a moment just Who this Jesus, Whose Name we use so lightly, actually is.

He is God. He is the Second Person of the Holy Trinity. He is Omnipotent: all-powerful. That means there is actually and absolutely nothing that He cannot do. He is Omnipresent: all-present. That means He is actually and absolutely everywhere, everywhen. There is not a place or a time that He does not inhabit. He is All, in all. He is Omniscient: all-knowing. That means there is actually and absolutely nothing He does not know. Period.

The Creed tells us that everything—everything—was made through Christ; that nothing was made without Him.

This Jesus Whom we take so for granted, Whose Name we use so lightly, and even occasionally as a vulgarity-- Whose company we often feel we can call upon and dismiss at will -- made us. We are His creatures, and we are entirely, personally, dependent on the Holy Trinity, of Whom He is the Second Person, even for our next breath, our next heartbeat, neither of which will happen unless He continues to permit and propel them. He is always present—never not present—where we are, everywhere, all the time. And He knows everything about us. He is present to our most intimate thoughts, our quietest words, our stealthiest deeds.

We are in His Presence, and answerable to Him, whether we want to be or not. There is no way not to be. And we cannot truly know ourselves without knowing Him.

This is disturbing stuff.

It is so disturbing that we erect barriers to try to preserve "our" privacy from God, like Adam and Eve who wove fig leaves together to hide their nakedness from the God Who created it in the first place.

We invent philosophies that would reduce us to the least enlightened part of our nature—the physical, animal part—and make the other two-thirds, the intellectual and spiritual parts, answerable to its demands, which we turn into rules. We call these rules "being natural," and accuse ourselves of violating them whenever one or both of our higher two-thirds should "interfere." We go so far as to pretend we are simply another species of animal, or that even the earth, itself, is somehow superior to us!

To avoid being disturbed, we go to great lengths to deny what makes us who and what we are.

For a human being, living in only a third of our nature is not natural. It is, rather, a violation of our nature. What we are meant to do is to conduct our life in the body in a way that is transformed in the Holy Spirit and informed by an enlightened intellect. To do this, to set foot upon this path, is to become who we are: it is to become the transforming and transformative presence in the world that God created us to be.

It is impossible to become who and what we truly are, without Christ. We, being critically lacking, cannot make ourselves whole. We cannot forgive ourselves of the sin which is the product of our natural, fallen self-centeredness, or heal our damaged spirit of its effects. Becoming whole requires Grace, and it is in Christ that Grace is found.

Only in Christ-God can we be set free from the bondage of a critically flawed human nature whose prime directive is to serve our vanity. Only in Christ-God can we stop being stifled by the world, and be set free to become who we really are: the light of the world, the salt of the earth, living members of His Body, the Church.

In short, to find our vocation is to discover "who we are in Christ." To live our vocation is to grow as that person--a person through whom God Himself works.

PART THREE: THE TOOLS

....that He would grant you, according to the riches of His glory, to be strengthened with might through His Spirit in the inner man, that Christ may dwell in your hearts through faith; that you, being rooted and grounded in love, may be able to comprehend with all the saints what is the width and length and depth and height—to know the love of Christ which passes knowledge; that you may be filled with all the fullness of God.
(Ephesians 3: 16-19)

~ ~ ~

We'll be specifically addressing spiritual formation, disciplines and practices in the next section. This part of the discussion is about building our practical platform.

Spiritual growth and development is a practical matter, applying classic spiritual disciplines. The Church, the Body of Christ, has tools for this: for the integration of our physical. intellectual and spiritual components into one, whole, person. The objective is intimacy with God at the Person-to-person level: the sort of intimacy that catches our life up in

His, and sets us free to be who we are, who He put us here to be,

It can't be done without Christ. Jesus is the key that opens the door to intimacy with God.

The spiritual life goes on forever, but it begins here and now, in the Church. Jesus is the Way, and the Church is our guide.

I am not necessarily talking here about Religion. Religion is a good thing, because it brings order and structure to the practice of our faith. The question is, what sort of faith are we practicing? To what are we devoted?

Anything can be practiced "religiously." A devotional practice can be built around whatever we do. Confessional speech, regular attendance and an altered consciousness can be found in a bar as well as in a church. Corporate policy manuals, journalistic style-books and even organized atheism, all have dogmas. From a simply empirical standpoint, religion follows a pattern that can be applied to almost any organized, focused effort.

That's what humans do. We organize things. We organize everything from globe-spanning enterprises to dinner-and-movie dates; from troop movements to family trips to the beach. This organizing capacity is in fact a reflection of God, the Creator and Grand Organizer, in Whose Image we are made 1 Corinthians 14:33).

We see organization everywhere we look. Birds build nests. Spiders build webs. Animals on the hunt pick likely locations and patiently wait. Even the creatures we call "inanimate" are organized, from quarks, atoms and molecules to galaxies and universes.

The Great Dance proceeds according to the plan and pattern designed by its Choreographer. Its beauty, like that of any earthly ballet, is only enhanced by its organizing principles, its rules, its doctrines.

Organization is what holds things together. Things that are disorganized fall apart. Entropy itself, the great fruit of the Fall, is defined as a process of progressive disorganization.

There are those who strangely say that our walk with the Lord should operate without doctrine, without organization, with my own personal relationship with God and how I choose to define it—and Him—paramount.

What they are saying, without realizing it, is that it is holier to operate according to the rules of entropy than those of the Dance; that it is holier to define God than to be defined by Him; that our flawed and fallen human "reason" is to be enshrined next to—and, as it inevitably works out in practice, above—Scripture and its defining Tradition.

This is not the way of the Transformed Life. We cannot transform ourselves.

God gave us a Way to be intimate with Him. In order to do that, He came to us and inhabited the universe He created, walking around in it in His Second Person, Jesus Christ. Jesus gathered to Himself a number of disciples and taught them the Truth, and prepared them to share it. He sent the Holy Spirit as He promised, that His followers would form themselves into His Church, which would at once carry the Truth to the world and provide a home for those who would accept it.

In the world, we are used to following things we invent, or extrapolate from the workings of nature, or promulgate by way of intellectual discourse. God's Way is none of these. It is not our invention, but comes from Him. It is not the product if our extrapolation, but of His revelation. It is not a creature of our discourse, but rather the Way that He gave and gives us: ourselves, intimately bound up in God Himself, within the context He, Himself provided: the Body of Christ, the Church.

Real Spirituality

Now. our discussion of things like "doctrine" may sometimes seem too "material" for "spiritual," discourse. Reflect, though, that God made us out of matter, and placed us in a world made out of matter. There is nothing intrinsically unholy about matter, just the opposite: God loves what He creates.

At other times things may seem to be getting "too intellectual," too concerned with the mind, and how we think. But God gave us our intellectual capability. He desires it to be honored, used and developed. Essential to the transformed life, after all, is a renewed mind (Romans 12: 2),

The Gnostic heretics taught that matter was cursed and that spirit was pure, and that in the Fall we "fell into" matter. Redemption, they taught, was found in rejecting the material and "transcending" it. The truth is that we fell, body, mind and spirit, and took matter down with us. So our objective should not be to try to float off on some "supernatural" cloud, but to bring all our faculties: physical, intellectual and spiritual, under the saving Love of Christ.

If we are going to accomplish anything in the Christian life it must involve the whole person: politics as well as prayer, morality as well as meditation, obedience as well as oblation, family as well as fasting.

We tend to expect "spiritual" work to be "otherworldly." We expect to be "lifted to heaven" by it. Fair enough. But if we want to lift something we need to first be standing on a solid surface. We are at present here on earth, and here is where our spiritual life needs to be lived.

That's not as difficult as it might sound.

Many people regard "the spiritual life" as a distinct sort of activity, something separate from "normal" life, and Heaven as a distant sort of place "up there," that's only accessible after our earthly death. That's not the case. Heaven is a dimension, not a geographical destination. We interact with Heaven all the time. Life in Christ encompasses the practical and pragmatic as well as the contemplative, meditative and philosophical. Our interior and exterior lives are simply two sides of the same coin, and it's important that they remain in balance.

Christian life isn't "spiritual" as many would understand the word. It isn't disengaged, or "otherworldly." Moreover, our "spirituality" isn't some separate compartment in our life—some particular thing we do in order to become "better people." Rather, it is Life, itself. It is where we touch God—and since God is concerned with, and wishes to be incorporated into, the whole of our life, so must our "spiritual life" be integrated into the totality of our life. Thereby, the totality of our life is integrated into God. The objective is to be a whole person, where body, mind and spirit work together in unity, rather than as separate parts reserved for particular things and times. If we succeed, there will be no such thing as a "spiritual life" as distinct from a "normal life," anymore: our "normal life" will be the product of our transformation in Christ, which integrates us as whole persons.

As for God, He is not distant at all. God is Omnipresent, All-Present. That means He is everywhere, including right here, all the time, and is always present to us in everything we do. The spiritual life is a matter of maturing in the process of abandoning our prideful defenses, and becoming similarly present to Him.

This is very different from trying to drift off into some "supernatural" condition, where we walk around in a trance-like state all the time whilst mumbling profundities. On the contrary, in the Old Testament we encounter the God Who speaks plainly to us out of an unconsumed burning bush; Who unambiguously parts the Red Sea; Who speaks through prophets who are surprised (and sometimes upset) that He would pick them to speak through. In the New Testament we encounter the same God, in Person, who shakes us by the hand and runs laughing through grain fields with us, and to Whom calming storms, healing people and strolling across the odd body of water are all part of normal life—a life in which He invites us to share. In all cases He meets us, and we meet Him, where we are.

The Bible, itself, is a very practical document. It insists that even the creation is a gospel that speaks to us of Eternity (Romans 1:20); that how we live here on earth will determine our Eternity (2 Corinthians 5: 1-10) and that how we form our minds is critical to the earthly life by means of which we will reach Eternity (Romans 12:2, 2 Timothy 1:7). So, the spiritual life begins, just as we ourselves begin, right here.

I don't want to be the guy who is "so Heavenly-minded he's no earthly good." Neither do I want to be the guy who's so concentrated on the earthly road that he's lost sight of its Heavenly destination. That's lopsided. Christian Orthodoxy axiomatically teaches that the Church in Heaven and the Church on earth are one. We are united, The "natural" and the "supernatural" are intertwined, not opposed or separated. They are the "things visible and invisible" of which the Creed speaks, and every act we perform resonates on both levels. Heaven is not some faraway place, it is another dimension. Its nearness is not measured in terms of distance, of time, or of space, but in terms of our attitude. We approach it not as "natural" men nor as "supernatural," but simply as ourselves.

> *A young monk once visited a neighboring lavrum*
> *(cluster of hermit cells). The Elder welcomed him*
> *warmly, and asked if he would like to join them in*

> *their daily tasks. The brother declined with thanks, saying he would rather spend the day reading and praying. The Elder consented, and gave the brother some scrolls of the Scriptures to read. Toward dark, the brother inquired, "Excuse me, Father, but have you not yet eaten?" "Why yes," replied the Elder, "and it was very good, thank you." "But why was I not invited?" asked the junior. "Well," replied the Elder, "You are a spiritual man, who does not labor for the bread that perishes but who feeds on Divine things. So, we gave you privacy and the Scriptures." The junior, edified, repented.*
> (From the Verba Seniorum)

Humility

Of all the things in the spiritual life, there is perhaps none more essential—or more misunderstood--than humility.

There is a widespread impression that to be "humble" is to be self-belittling, that a "humble"person is one who thinks poorly of himself. That's not the case at all.

> *Let nothing be done through selfish ambition or conceit, but in lowliness of mind let each esteem others better than himself.*
> (Philippians 2:3)

Unfortunately, many have interpreted this passage to mean we should grovel our way through life, cultivating the worst possible self-concept and turning into some sort of doormat. This misses the point.

We "esteem others as better than ourselves" not to put ourselves down, but to lift the others up; to be a source of affirmation for them. Moreover, they are—however damaged they may or may not be—icons of Christ. By seeing Christ in them and thus honoring them, we honor Him. Also, and importantly, we help them attain to a healthy sense of self-worth based not on self-affirmation but on the Reality of the limitless value which God places on them. Our affirmation of them may be the first experience they have ever had of God's Love, and is key to helping them come to Christ.

To be "lowly of mind" is not to cultivate a horrible self-concept, but rather to stop worrying about cultivating a self-concept. I am limited, therefore, any "identity" I desire to assume for myself must also necessarily be limited. I am, however, created for Eternity—for Limitlessness—to grow into the identity God gave me.

The only way I can possibly prepare myself for that is to get my eyes off myself and onto Christ. I need to stop fretting about "what I ought to be," and simply let Him form me. In this way, my fallen (and extremely distracting) tendency to exalt myself will be brought into check naturally as I go about the business of exalting God.

The world of mammon is all about selfish ambition and conceit, about propelling myself forward and basking in the congratulations of others and the trappings of status as I advance, about using all of that to reassure myself that I am a powerful, worthwhile person.

Yet, I am made in the Image of God, Himself, Who invites me to call Him, "Father."

What more do I need?

Humility is often called the key to the spiritual life, because it is the direct opposite of Original Sin, which is Pride.

"Humility" was defined by my Moral Theology prof at seminary as "a realistic self- appraisal." I like this definition, and have never encountered a better one. If we have a realistic self-appraisal we know ourselves to be (a) less than God; (b) responsible to God; (c) made in the Image of God, and (d) absolutely beloved of God. This very useful and practical attitude keeps us away from the twin vanities of self-exaltation and self-pitying self-abasement.

Pride, on the other hand, is an—is indeed the foundational—unrealistic self-appraisal.

Pride is the character defect by means of which we give ourselves permission to differ with God. It is the "original sin" because it is the one in which all others have their origin. It is Pride by which we give ourselves permission to do as we will, regardless of the admonitions of God. Pride creates in us a falsely exalted self-image, one which portrays us as sufficient unto ourself and ultimate in our capacity to be our own moral and intellectual arbiter. It confers upon us that which does not belong to us, which it cannot legitimately confer: the "right" to have an opinion that differs from God's proclamations—to, in effect, become our own god.

As we have discussed, but which cannot be too-often revisited, it all started here...

> Then when the woman saw that the tree was good for food, and that it was a delight to the eyes, and that the tree was to be desired to make one wise, she took of its fruit and ate; and she also gave some to her husband, and he ate.
> (Genesis 3:6)

Eve formed an opinion of her own, one which was contrary to the command of God: "the tree was good for food." In choosing that opinion, she rejected God's admonition that, "in the day that you eat of it you shall die." (Gen 2:17b). She established standards of her own to justify her opinion: The tree was good for food; it was a delight to the eyes, and was to be desired to make one wise.

In this act, Eve arrogated to herself the authority to abrogate God's proclamations—to replace His primacy with her own. It is vitally important to note that her presumption to this authority did nothing to actually give the authority to her—so, we wound up in the mess we're in now , all because of an unrealistic self-assessment.

Who knows why Adam ate the fruit? Where was he when his wife was under attack by the devil? Why did he just unreflectively gulp it when it was handed to him?

Whatever his motivations, the plain fact is that Adam had a responsibility toward his wife and he failed to live up to it. Pride does that. By telling us we're our own moral arbiter, it gives us the illusion that we can, with impunity, eschew our responsibilities as long as we are able to subjectively justify doing so (*"The woman whom You gave to be with me...."* Gen 3: 12).

This self- release from any responsibility we do not actually want, is heady stuff. The world calls it "freedom." God calls it "the way to death." (Proverbs 16:25)

Humility most values and desires the three character traits our contemporary culture most despises and avoids: Commitment, Responsibility and Gratitude. These things have been distorted beyond recognition by a Godless world in which the shifting and slippery rules of "tolerance," "political correctness" and "my rights" have fragmented even our capacity to recognize right from wrong.

In their true state, commitment, responsibility and gratitude are much more than commodities or clever means by which I may "get by giving." In fact, while they are guaranteed to enrich and enlarge me, they hardly reference "me," at all.

Commitment

Our culture has deteriorated to the point where virtually everything is tentative. I have had long-standing appointments with people who have called up and said, "are we still on?" the day before, fully expecting that I might have changed plans without telling them. I have had people miss appointments with me, and when we spoke they simply said, "something came up," expecting me to think this was perfectly okay. We have become so dull of perspective in our enslavement to mammon that if a commitment is not in our immediate perceived self-interest, it is not really a commitment.

In fact, not even that is true. I once needed some back-hoe work done at a place where we used to live. The man I hired did this for a living. I was paying him. Showing up on time was in his self-interest, because it would encourage me to see him as reliable, to recommend him and become a repeat customer.

The appointment was for the next Tuesday at nine in the morning. The fellow showed up on the following Thursday at 1:00 PM, unannounced, and just started working. He didn't even come to the door first to let us know he was there.

What is amazing is that we have come to accept this sort of behavior as normal. I ask people, "has this ever happened to you?" and without fail they answer in the affirmative. Often they answer hesitantly, as if it were somehow their fault! Maybe they weren't powerful enough, or commanding enough, or personally charismatic enough! But I have asked powerful, commanding, personally charismatic people if this has happened to them, and they all answer in the affirmative.

At any rate, the virtue of commitment, like any other virtue, is not a matter of whether the other guy is sufficiently powerful, commanding or charismatic enough to compel it, but whether I have sufficient integrity to exercise it.

Interestingly, not many of us will admit to this behavior. Almost all of us insist that our word is our bond, that once we have said something you can take it to the bank.

There has been quite a run on that bank, and it isn't paying out much, anymore.

You can't trust that you will see your doctor at your appointment time, because that time has been triple-and quadruple-booked. That's because the doctor can't trust that his appointments will show up, on time, as promised. You can't trust you will not be bumped from an airplane reservation, because the reservation has been double-booked. Why? because people don't show up when they say they will. So, the doctor's office and the airline have both failed to keep their word, because so many people have failed to keep their word to them that they have felt forced to take defensive measures.

> *Again, you have heard that it was said to those of old, "You shall not swear falsely, but shall perform your oaths to the Lord." But I say to you, do not swear at all, neither by heaven, for it is God's throne, nor by the earth, for it is His footstool; nor by Jerusalem, for it is the city of the great king. Nor shall you swear by your head, for you cannot make one hair white or black. But let your "Yes" be "Yes" and your "No," No. For whatever is more than these is from the evil one.*
> (Matthew 5: 33-37)

The Lord was talking, among other things, about crowding one's word with qualifiers, swearing on things to give weight to a commitment, or trying to be weaselingly tentative, rather than firm, in refusal.

A wishy-washy word is no word at all. If you can't trust my "yes" to be anything more than, "If nothing else comes up in the meantime," or you can't trust my "no" to be anything more than, "If I don't change my mind," what good am I? Jesus doesn't want us to have to bolster what we say by "swearing on" things. He wants our word to be good because we have given it.

What keeps me from honoring, or at least doing my level best to honor, a commitment? Doesn't it amount to a failure to honor the other person? What can this stem from, except from a feeling, at some level, that I don't really have to? And doesn't this cast the other person as somehow inferior to me, and myself as exalted over him?

We minimize such behavior with phrases like, "I had to blow it off," or "something else came up." In reality, we have slipped out of a Christian perspective. We have failed to recognize the person as an icon of Christ, and have missed the opportunity to honor Christ Himself by honoring the Christ in him. My lack of commitment has thus cheated me of an opportunity to grow in God; all because, for this moment, I sacrificed humility to a distorted self-image.

Responsibility

> *If we say that we have no sin, we deceive ourselves,*
> *and the truth is not in us. If we confess our sins, He is*
> *faithful and just to forgive us our sins and to cleanse us*
> *from all unrighteousness.*
> (1 John 1: 8-9)

The classic scenario comes to mind of the little child standing in the middle of the kitchen, the broken cookie jar at his feet, cookies scattered all over the place, responding, "I dunno..." to his mother's, "How did this happen?" Maybe the kid casts a sidelong glance at the dog, hoping he can somehow pin the fiasco on the family pet.

Now fast-forward twenty years to the same fellow explaining, "Gee, officer, I didn't realize I was speeding," perhaps knocking on the speedometer for effect.

Taking responsibility for our actions isn't easy. Nobody likes to be wrong, and when we are, we don't like to admit it. Our entire society, in fact, from the "As Is – No Warranty" sign on the used car we buy to the "I understand the risks involved" waiver at the doctor's office, our society is inundated with paperwork designed specifically to avoid accepting responsibility for our actions.

The problem, though, is that we are responsible for our actions. All the waivers, disclaimers, diversions, protests and denials in the world will not change that.

When we look at the question of taking responsibility we often do it in relation to other people: not so much, "am I responsible for this action?" as, "Will I be held responsible for this action?" I think we tend to ask ourselves these questions more than we ask ourselves the real one: "What is this action turning me into?"

We "liberate" little things, that in all probability nobody will notice, from the workplace. After a while, we develop a sense of entitlement to these things. With this sense of entitlement comes increasing comfort with taking things that don't belong to us. We have become a thief.

"But," we protest, "nobody misses the stuff." Does that change the fact that we have taken it? "But," we protest, "everybody does it." Does that change the fact that we have joined them in it?

We tell "little white lies" to make the day go more smoothly, As we do, our personal definition of "truthfulness" accommodates itself to our behavior. So, having given our habit permission,we become a liar. "But," we protest, "nobody was hurt by it." Does that change the fact that what I said wasn't the truth?

Or, on a larger scale, say I am opposed to the wholesale slaughter of children in the place wherethey should be safest—their mother's womb? Say I march, give money and pray for an end to abortion. These are all good things. Yet, election after election, I vote for candidates who favor abortion.

How can this be? How can I oppose something with one hand, yet bestow the power to perpetuate it with the other?

The phenomenon is called cognitive dissonance, literally the opposition of thought and action,.

If we do not act on what we believe, do we actually believe it? We may think we do. In the above case, we may actually believe that all of our effort will somehow compensate for supporting someone who will use his power against us. This is like believing that, somehow, we above all others will be able to stop a leak by pronouncing over the hole as we enlarge it.

I might protest, "Now, now, Father, you're getting political." But isn't this just a way of "not hearing" that I have made myself an accomplice to some murderously amoral politician, and thus an accessory to the very act I despise?

Our political life is our way of interacting with and contributing to the development and well-being of the culture in which we live, It is as much a part of our life as any other, and just as answerable before God. I use it as an example, because it is one of those "forbidden" topics we aren't "supposed to" discuss, as if there were areas of our life that could be legitimately hidden away in darkness, responsible to neither God nor man.

We protest, "How I vote is my business." And most assuredly, it is. But what sort of business am I about? What sort of culture am I helping to build by my vote?

What I claim as "my business" could be politics, it could be anything. The danger is allowing it to become the kind of dark place that claims a unique freedom from answerability, that drives us into conflict with ourself and distracts us from the ultimacy of our responsibility before God.

Over time, we build up elaborate defenses against facing the reality of our actions. We adopt phrases like, "Don't try to lay that at my door!" in hopes of scaring off anyone who would confront us with our actions, or, "I'm a good person," to reassure ourselves that our behavior need not impact our all-important self-image; that somehow, by declaring this to the universe, the universe will simply shrug, and reply, "sure, if you say so."

The thing is, the universe has no such power. The universe is just another creature, and a non-cognitive one, at that. But even if it had the power to agree with me, that wouldn't change anything. All that happens, as I broaden my definition of "lying" or "stealing" or "enabling" to accommodate my behavior, is that I end up lying to myself and stealing from my own personal integrity.

I must take responsibility for my actions, because that is where my salvation lies.

The most oft-repeated excuse among humans, be we eight or eighty, ten or a hundred and ten, is "everybody does it."

This is absolutely true. Everybody does do it. But, so what? The fact that everybody does it doesn't make each of us right, it just means all of us are wrong.

We protest, "It's just human nature!" and that's the point. It is human nature. That doesn't mean we are justified in following it, it means human nature is flawed.

"So, you see?" we continue, "I can't help it!"

And indeed I can't. So, where does that put me? Here I am, stuck with following along in a misguided herd, inherently flawed in character and unable to help myself. The herd is headed toward a cliff, and if I am without a remedy, I'll go over the edge with them.

What to do?

Once again, it's a lack of humility that's standing in my way. It's the distorted notion that somehow I, unlike all the rest, will find actual, final refuge in my excuses. But I can't. So, is it all lost? Of course not!

Going back to the passage from 1 John, above, we see that pretending we are "okay" will do us no good at all. But if we drop the pretense and take responsibility for out failings, God will forgive us. We have a Savior, and He is our hope. Indeed, He is mankind's only hope.

What a wonderful thing! We have the opportunity to be made spiritually clean, to have the weight that's dragging us down lifted off of us, to refresh us for the next part of our journey, and it's offered freely, simply because God loves us!

Why in the world would we turn down such a gift, just for the momentary, shallow thrill of the illusion that we can make it all okay by declaring it so?

To avoid responsibility for our actions is to cut ourself off from Grace, because we cut ourself off from repentance. After all, why repent if we have (or can convince ourselves we have) nothing to repent of?

To take responsibility is to open ourselves to the healing and transforming power of God. It is a reciprocal process: as we take responsibility we become more aware of, and more courageous in facing, our shortcomings. So, we turn to God and He heals us and brings about ever-deeper growth. Once again we see that humility, far from being a negative thing, is the engine that moves us out of our own way on Eternity's path.

Gratitude

The last (which may well really be the first) component of humility is gratitude.

Our culture has been programmed by the "self-esteem movement" and by the absolute subjectivism of post-modernism. We tend to be blasé about receiving good things, as if they were simply our due. We are, after all (or at least, so we're constantly told) entitled to have good things. Accordingly, we tend to reject that which makes us less than comfortable as being aberrant, "out of sync" with our preferred reality—which is the only reality we recognize. As for the expressing of gratitude, our worldly pride sees it as a weakness, something that diminishes us and makes "our reality" less enforceable.

The catch is, this is not how things actually work. "Our reality" is interrupted and challenged on a regular basis. Our comfort zone is regularly invaded by the unpleasant things of life on earth, whether we "recognize" them or not. Yet, there are lessons in the bad things and there is rejoicing in the good. Gratitude is the appropriate response to both, yet secular man, recognizing only himself as sovereign, has nowhere to direct it.

There are things that move us, even compel us to gratitude. A fragrant, sunny spring day, with its buoyancy and optimism, demands of us that we shout out from our hearts, "Thank you!" How sad, if we recognize no object for it; if our only response is a dry wind blowing over an interior emptiness.

> *Thou hast turned for me my mourning into dancing; thou*
> *hast loosed my sackcloth and girded me with gladness,*
> *that my soul may praise thee and not be silent. O Lord*
> *my God, I will give thanks to thee for ever.*
> (Psalm 30: 11-12)

There is a sizable intermediate space between unbelief and the transformed life. We can have a vague notion of "Something Out There" who or which deserves our acknowledgment; we can have "our way" of relating to God-as-we-see-Him (or Her, or It). We can even be regular churchgoers or even clergy. If we have not become willing to humble ourselves before the God Who is responsible for the things that happen in our lives, we have not embarked upon the transformed life.

> *But he said to her, "You speak as one of the foolish*
> *women would speak. Shall we receive good at the Hand*
> *of God, and shall we not receive evil?" In all these things,*
> *Job did not sin with his lips.*
> (Job 2: 10)

Gratitude is hard. It confronts us with the fact that we are not, finally, the authors of our own successes and achievements. It places earthly life, itself, in its proper context: as a temporary place, a small part of

Eternity, where our proper business is to learn and grow; where the adversities we encounter are not the "evils" that we normally think them, but more like what a soldier undergoes in training: stresses that teach and toughen us to, if you will, broaden our operational capability and make us more resourceful.

In the midst of a lukewarm, people-pleasing "Christianity," we have grown used to protesting, "Oh, no, that trial doesn't come from God, but from the devil!" This comes from a misguided attempt to portray God as "nice," and His Love that of a doting granduncle who would never be responsible for calamity. Proper formation in Gratitude throws a bracing bucket of cold water on this idea…

> *Then Satan answered the Lord, "does Job fear God for nought? Hast Thou not put a hedge about him and his house and all that he has, on every side? Thou hast blessed the work of his hands, and his possessions have increased in the land. But put forth Thy Hand, now, and touch all that he has, and he will curse Thee to Thy Face." And the Lord said to Satan, "Behold, all that he has is in your power; only upon himself put not forth your hand." So Satan went forth from the Presence of the Lord.*
> (Job 1: 9-12)

Things that impact upon us as evil, do indeed come from the devil. God did not take the devil up on his challenge to stretch forth His own Hand upon Job. He did, however, give the devil permission to stretch out his. Had he not given that permission, Job would never have been afflicted.

So why did He do it?

I have heard opinions that would relegate this conversation to the likes of a confrontation between schoolboys…

Satan: "I dare ya!"

God: "Oh, yeah? I'll show you!"

...as if God had need to, or was even compelled to, "prove something" to the devil. This is, of course, how the adversary would have taken it, but it is actually quite absurd. God is God. He has no need to "prove" anything to anyone, least of all the author of lies and disruptions. The devil's challenge, in and of itself, is powerless. In fact, it isn't even the point, The point is Job, and his family, and his friends--and us, thousands of years later, and what we would all learn through, and through exposure to, this experience.

Should we receive good at the Hand of God, and shall we not receive evil? It isn't the evil experience for which we must be grateful, nor is it to the devil for having caused it (notice that the verse differentiates that which "we receive at the Hand of God" from that which "we receive"). It is the good that comes out of it for which we are to be grateful: the lesson learned, the interior growth, the maturity gained.

People point to disasters and tragedies and either rail against God or try to use them as "proof" that (a) He doesn't exist or (b) He is so nasty He isn't worth following or even (c) is less powerful than satan. In response, we who love Him seek to "stand up for Him" by laying it all on the devil and trying to obfuscate the fact that God is the one who permits the devil to operate in the first place.

The fact is, God doesn't need our defense. He operates at a whole different level and from an entirely different perspective. Please burn this fact into your mind and spirit: Life here is only a minuscule part of life in Eternity. God is only concerned about the things of earth insofar as they might lead us, His icons, to greater awareness of Him, and of the things of Heaven.

One example of this is my own experience. Several years ago, I was diagnosed with Chronic Lymphocytic Leukemia, a treatable but (so far) incurable cancer. At that time I had been in ministry, lay and ordained, for over thirty years. I had a close personal relationship with the Lord, regularly preached and studied His Word and the insightful wisdom of the Fathers of the Church, and had what I considered to be an adequate, improving prayer life.

But...now I had cancer. Me! Cancer! You had better believe, my prayer life improved immensely, as did the quality of my reflections. I was forced to stare Eternity in the face—not aspirationally or even, if you will, recreationally—but from the inside, so to speak. You see, God did not move me to pray, necessarily, for healing. Instead, He led me into the depth and silence of the vastness and everlastingness of His Presence, in a way that made my previous contemplative adventures pale by comparison: an explosion of His Grace, and of the sure and certain knowledge—knowledge that I had thought I already had—that All-Mighty God, the King of the Universe, radically and wholeheartedly loves me—even the likes of me!

Am I grateful for the cancer? Certainly not! I wish I didn't have it. Am I grateful to the devil, by whose hand it surely came? Not at all! I am grateful for the experience, for the advancement it precipitated in my spiritual life; for the many hundreds of people who pray for me; for the kind, and highly gifted, doctors, nurses, therapists and medical techs who keep me, in all other respects, healthy and strong. Not least, for the kitchen staff at La Porte Hospital in Indiana, who make the peerless tuna salad sandwiches I enjoy at my monthly infusions.

Mainly I am grateful to the great and wonderful God Who cares enough about me to have brought about the remarkable experiences I have had and the redoubtable people I have met, as a result of what would otherwise be nothing but a negative, awful thing.

And I am grateful for the opportunity to be introduced to the reality of what is perhaps humility's linchpin: gratitude to the God Who gives me growth in all these moments of the beginning time of my Eternity; and for the freedom to not think I need to justify or make excuses for Him, or for the means by which that growth comes. Making such excuses, you see, would be a way for me to take some sort of control of the situation, to exalt myself even to the position of being God's defender and excuse-maker. He doesn't need it, and I wouldn't learn anything by it.

To paraphrase C.S. Lewis's description of Aslan the Lion in the Chronicles of Narnia, God is not always un-fearsome. He is not always gentle, meek or mild. He is not "nice." But He is Good.

God uncompromisingly loves us, and more than anything wants us with Him; to be well-equipped to live in a world unimaginable to us, now. To this end, He will produce in us results. And for this, without being deterred by the means He might find necessary, it is good for us to humble ourselves before Him. Do I pray for healing? Sure! Am I grateful for the many people who are praying for my healing? Absolutely, and I have no intention of asking them to stop. But that isn't the point. I request of God, I do not command Him. In the meantime I trust Him to work in me what is ultimately best for me.

SEVEN: DIGNITY

On Our Proper End and Place, and Our Present Exampling Of It.~

> *Christian, remember your dignity, and now that you share in God's own nature, do not return by sin to your former base condition. Bear in mind Who is your Head and of Whose Body you are a member. Do not forget that you have been rescued from the power of darkness*

> *and brought into the light of God's Kingdom. Through the sacrament of baptism you have become a temple of the Holy Spirit. Do not drive away so great a Guest by evil conduct and become again a slave to the devil, for your liberty was bought by the Blood of Christ.*
>
> *--From the Nativity Sermon of St. Leo the Great, Bishop of Rome, mid-Fifth Century.*

It's a much-used, commonplace analogy, but I'll use it anyway: the difference between someone who has been transformed in Christ and someone who has not, is the difference between a caterpillar and a butterfly.

The proper end of a caterpillar is to become something glorious. Moreover, assuming for it an imagination, it is to become something it could not possibly have imagined while still a caterpillar.

Think of it—one day you're happily crawling along a leaf-stem, firmly anchored to the earth but not unhappy about it because, after all, there's plenty of stuff to eat. And, if you do say so yourself, you don't look bad for a caterpillar.

Then one day you feel a drive toward your destiny. You don't know what it is, but there's this process you somehow know you need to undergo, so you do. And a while later, you break free of the intermediate state, and—you're splendid!

Can you imagine what flight must feel like to someone who has up to now been a sort of worm?

It isn't just a new ability: it's command of an entirely new dimension. The butterfly's perspective is suddenly vast and panoramic, its relationships with the whole of creation utterly transformed. All because as a caterpillar it answered the call of its destiny, of what it was made to be.

> *And Jesus said to them, "I am the bread of life. He who comes to Me shall never hunger, and he who believes in Me shall never thirst. But I said to you that you have seen Me and yet do not believe. All that the Father gives Me will come to Me, and the one who comes to Me I will by no means cast out. For I have come down from heaven, not to do My own will, but the will of Him who sent Me. This is the will of the Father who sent Me, that of all He has given Me I should lose nothing, but should raise it up at the last day. And this is the will of Him who sent Me, that everyone who sees the Son and believes in Him may have everlasting life; and I will raise him up at the last day."*
> (John 6: 35-40)

Caterpillars, of course, don't have any say in the matter. The drive takes them, and they respond. The problem with us is, we're not caterpillars. We can deny our destiny.

The voices of the world insist that we are perfect just the way we are, and that the butterfly business is at best a myth, a fairy tale and a crutch, and at worst a cruel hoax perpetrated by the uppity and intolerant. They point to grandiose caterpillars who claim to be butterflies and so, cynically, amass followings for their own aggrandizement. They use these examples to declare that all butterfly claims (particularly the genuine ones) are false. Or they will claim that butterfly-hood is simply a metaphor for becoming a more "enlightened" (by whatever definition) caterpillar.

"But," we might ask," what abut the butterflies right there in front of their faces? Can't they see them?"

The answer is, yes they can. But they see them not as a promise, but as a threat. They may even deny that what they are seeing is a "butterfly" at all, but something about which "we do not yet know," or even a "mass hallucination."

Pride is empty. It has no actual content. All it has is defensive clamor, set up to distract even itself from the fact that there is nothing to it. Having rejected the Truth, which would provide substance, it carves out a narrative of its own to justify, or at least attempt to explain, its existence. Whatever challenges that narrative, however benign, thus becomes an enemy, a threat to its existence: It is not real because it must not be real.

If I am such a one as this, I do not draw hope, inspiration or comfort from the butterfly. My desire is not to join it, but to shoot it down.

Truth be told, this is how most of us, however immersed in Christ we may now be, at one time lived. Then something happened to show us that we are more than that, that we had not been living up to the reality of who and what we are; that we are made in the image of the Living God, the Creator and Sustainer of all that is; that we have a destiny and a future, and that if we do not reject them we are bound for magnificence.

Christian dignity is, therefore, human dignity, writ large, as it should be. We are born living icons of Christ, and we are heirs of the Kingdom of God, if we will have it.

Dignity is both internal and external. Externally, it is something which is conferred, as in someone who is "raised to the dignity" of a high office. Internally, it is a style of behavior which reflects that which has been conferred.

Dignity-or the lack of it--comes in many forms. The juvenile who wears his pants down around his thighs, showing his underwear to the world, is not behaving with dignity but with defensive rebelliousness. In the process of trying to show what an "in your face" threatening presence he is, he demeans himself and becomes instead a ridiculous figure.

The young (and occasionally not-so-young) woman who attempts to validate herself through immodesty, doesn't validate herself at all. Rather she declares to the world that her eventually-fading flesh is all she has that she can count on. She seeks to be compelling, but instead models a certain desperation.

By demeaning themselves, these demean the Image of God which was conferred upon them at birth. They have the "caterpillar's choice:" to continue crawling upon the ground, content with a handsomeness that only compares to other ground-crawlers, or to consent to the genuine splendor for which they were made. This consent will engender in them a desire to change their behavior. The change will seem curious and even offensive to those who have chosen to continue crawling on the earth, but it will release the transformed into the reality of the freedom to which they were, before, only pretending. The change, after all, is what enables them to fly.

On the other hand, let's consider the homeless vagrant who politely thanks his benefactors and keeps himself as neat as possible. He may not be much to look at from a distance, but has a quality up close, a certain kindness, that exceeds his material condition.

This is a dignified man. In his humility, he expresses gratitude and honors God (even if he is unaware that's what he's doing) by honoring his own humanity and the humanity of those who help him. He is not far from the Kingdom, and will find, if he consents to it, the glory his attitude and behavior anticipate.

> *The Author of life has shattered the bonds of purely mechanical existence. You are an organic part of a Theanthropic mystery. You have a specific task, a small, minute task, which makes you a partaker in the whole. The mystery of life is summed up and worked out in your character. You are an image of God. You are of value not for what you have but for what you are; and you are a brother of the Son. Thus we all enter into the feast of the firstborn. God, who is above all, may be recognized in the very texture of your person, in the structure of your being. You see Him dwelling within you, And you discern traces of Him in your insatiable thirst for life and in your love. The struggle to reach Him is the very vision of His Face. It is the fundamental principle of your being.*
>
> --Archimandrite Vasileios of Athos, Hymn of Entry, St. Vladimir's Seminary Press, 1984.

How do we live up to something like that?! The bad news is, we can't. We are not God. We can never do justice, at least not in this beginning and very limited part of our life, to the dignity which has been given us.

The good news is, we don't have to. Our path is not so much one of striving, but of yielding: first, to the call of our destiny in permitting ourselves to walk forward into the chrysalis from which we are reborn in Christ; second, to the activity of the Holy Spirit within us, which produces the growth and maturity here that prepares us for Eternity—the change that enables us to fly.

Yielding is difficult work for humans. Our pridefulness demands that we remain always in control, always "on top of things." But we cannot be in control of the Holy Spirit, Who is God, because He is greater than we are. We cannot "be on top of" His work within us, for its ways are beyond our abilities. Acknowledging this rankles us, because we do not like to think of anything as being greater than we are, or beyond us. But such is the stuff of a realistic view of ourself, and is thus the stuff of humility. We will never climb a mountain by imagining we are already there, or by seeing it as something other than a mountain. All we will do is stay on the flat-land, deluded, missing out on both the accomplishment and the view.

Reading the Gospels, we see that Jesus—the most powerful man on earth—never tried to "prove anything." He did mighty things, unbelievable things. But He didn't do them for the sake of exalting Himself. Indeed, when He appeared before Herod, who "hoped to see a miracle from Him," the Lord remained silent (Luke 23: 8-11). The text suggests that showing off might have saved His life. However, it would not have saved ours, and saving ours is what He was here to do.

Jesus was not here to call attention to Himself as a powerful man, but to call attention to God and to the salvation that had now come into the world. In His behavior, He acted consistently with Who He was, and with His mission, and therefore He acted with humility and dignity.

When we think of a "dignified person" we think of someone who commands respect, not by force or fortune, but by being solidly grounded in who he (or she) is. They do not make a big deal of themselves. Indeed, because of their interior resources, they simply don't need to. This is the sort of man—perfect and writ large--that Jesus was, and it is the sort of person He calls us all to be; that He in fact made it possible for us to become.

Our worldly condition doesn't matter. The Lord, in Matthew 6: 25-32, counsels us, *Therefore do not worry, saying "What shall we eat?"*

or "What shall we drink?" or "What shall we wear?" for after all these things the Gentiles seek. For your Heavenly Father knows that you need all these things (vss. 31-32).

What cloaks us in dignity, our solid grounding in who we are, comes from our confidence in our Heavenly Father, Whose children we are and of Whose Kingdom we are heirs. Such a person, the bearer of such an estate, can afford not to make a big deal of himself, but to be gracious to others—extending a grace that is not from himself, but which is bestowed by his Father in Heaven.

Dignity, therefore, is not a component of humility, but its fruit. And a fitting introduction to the 'nuts and bolts...'

PART FOUR: FEET UPON THE PATH

I shared in the image of God, but did not keep it safe; the Lord shares in my flesh, so as to save the image and to make the flesh immortal.

St. Gregory Nazianzan

~ ~ ~

The transformed life is not "work," as we would ordinarily think of it. While it requires effort, it isn't a "chore," something that has been imposed on us. Rather, the effort is something we find we want to undertake. The desire to live a holy life grows within us like the caterpillar's drive toward transformation. it's a desire of our heart, a path we must pursue, without which something essential and desirable would be missing. Christ calls us and leads us, and we answer and follow.

Contemplative Prayer

Advancement in the transformed life is advancement in the contemplative life: in the ability to sit quietly with God and relax before Him.

Contemplative prayer is the "prayer of listening," and this is hard for us. God speaks in a still, small Voice (1 Kings 19: 11-12), and we're accustomed to noise. We are so accustomed to noise, we thrive on it. When it is absent, we feel like something is missing. Modern man needs the TV set blaring in the background, the radio blaring in the car, the telephones or the machinery blaring at work. Even "vacations" become a competitive effort to see how much ground can be covered in however long we have to cover it. So, we come back with jangled nerves even from our "down time."

As opposed to this maelstrom of the kingdom of mammon, the Kingdom of God thrives on silence. We practice silence so that the external silence will seep into us and become internal: no longer something we need to create, but something we carry around inside us that the noise can't touch: a sacred space within us which is always attentive to God.

This detaching of ourselves from noise doesn't happen overnight. Like anything truly transformative and worthwhile, it grows slowly.

That doesn't mean "nothing happens." In fact, the merest beginning will feel like a giant leap—and indeed, it is. It pays, though, to be aware that the giant leap—and the exalted feeling that goes with it—is still just the beginning. That feeling can rapidly become just another kind of noise, and it has to be internalized and allowed to become peaceful if it is to do any lasting good.

The next few sections, outlining different sorts of "lives" within the transformed life, are about growing a complete person in Christ, so we don't become "lopsided" in one direction or the other. The personal disciplines have to come before the contemplative disciplines, otherwise we won't be equipped to properly grow in any of them.

As we open up the contemplative dimension of our spirituality, we find that it both is and isn't what we thought it might be. Perhaps we equate "contemplation" with some austere labor wherein we tightly suppress our fidgeting while we struggle to keep quiet for long periods of time. Or maybe we picked up some popular book on contemplative prayer that has all sorts of rules and guidelines, even including some written-out prayers.

While books can be helpful, the essence of contemplation is simple: Just sit still and listen.

"Spiritual exercises" can come later.

Some, when they hear "contemplation," immediately think, "monastery." But you don't need to live in a monastery to sit quietly and listen to God, or just to bask in His healing Presence. Growing the contemplative dimension of our spirit is necessary for spiritual growth, for all of us, whatever our vocation.

We'll be getting into this more deeply later, but for the present suffice it to say that the ability to sit quietly and comfortably with God, letting Him shut down the noise in our heads so that we can hear His still, small Voice, is actually what we long for when the longing for growth surfaces within us.

So begins a life-long process that leads from desire to fulfillment. That process is the transformed life. The transformed life isn't the destination, you see, but the path.

Becoming a butterfly is just the beginning. Then comes learning to fly.

EIGHT: THE PENITENTIAL LIFE

The transformed life is a penitential life. In other words, it's a life wherein repentance is a key component.

Have mercy on me, O God, according to thy steadfast love; according to thy abundant mercy blot out my transgressions. Wash me thoroughly from my iniquity, and cleanse me from my sin! For I know my transgressions, and my sin is ever before me
(Psalm 51: 1-3)

For godly sorrow produces repentance leading to salvation, not to be regretted; but the sorrow of the world produces death.
(2 Corinthians 7: 10)

~ ~ ~

Christians are the most fortunate people in the world, because we're the ones who can afford to admit we're wrong. In fact, we can—and should—celebrate the ability to admit we're wrong!

The world ensnares itself within actually silly philosophies like "situation ethics" and "moral relativism." So desperate are they to absolve themselves of wrong, they deny that "wrong" even exists! Stacks of meaningless phrases, like "don't lay that at my door," and "I'm a good person" pile themselves on top of insistent consciences in an attempt to quiet them. In the meantime, Christians confess their sins, and so create space within ourselves the Holy Spirit can fill so that He might repair us.

Repentance produces forgiveness and healing. Repentance creates empty space where sin had dwelt, space that is subsequently filled with God's forgiving and renewing Grace. If, therefore, "my sin is ever before me," and I am ever in a state of repentance for it , I am ever being forgiven and renewed.

Many see this as a negative thing, as if God wanted us to be always crawling in the dust. But that's the curse He placed on the devil, not on us. Certainly, our awareness of sin will have an impact on us. Our unworthiness and disobedience to God are thrown into sharp relief when we are convicted of sin, and we will, in a word, feel awful. But this is a positive thing: the fruit of an awakened conscience, not a "lightning bolt" from a God Whom we may have annoyed. We may not like that awful feeling, but we're not supposed to: it's a wake-up call, a prompting to flee to the Throne of Grace, for healing and restoration. Face it—we don't like alarm clocks, either, but they're necessary.

Sin is like a bag of rocks tied around our necks. It weighs us down and slows us down, getting in the way of everything we do. Repentance "cuts the rope," letting the bag drop and setting us free. Free is how God wants us.

Once again: repentance leads to forgiveness, which leads to refreshment. That life wherein repentance is a constant element is a life of constant refreshment. Far from being a burdened life, it is a life of having our burdens continually lifted.

It is essential to any serious walk with the Lord that we enter it without illusion or pretense. We are sinners, God knows it and we know it. Our unworthiness is simply a fact. It isn't anything to build a devotional life around or to get theatrical about, because there's nothing we can do about it. Our imperfect state, vulnerable to temptation, is in our DNA, our genetic inheritance from our first parents. The effects that sin has on our lives are horrible. Christ-God came to rescue us from them, not to chastise us for them.

Getting back to the contrast drawn in 2 Corinthians 7:10, above, there are those, even among Christians, who approach the business of repentance after the "sorrow of the world." They envision God as some dreadful cosmic potentate, whose potential for wrath can only be assuaged, if possible, through demonstrations of self-abasement.

This vision imagines God as a bringer of death, not of life. The resulting self-abasing theatrics are thus more a matter of self-preservation than anything else, so they throw our focus right back where it should not be: on ourselves, and whether we're showing sufficient "humility" to avoid retribution.

God Himself, though, through His Word, tells us that "Godly sorrow produces repentance leading to salvation" (See above).

Many quite healthy Christians are given to doing various penances in response to the prodding of conscience: fasts, prostrations, extra hours of prayer etc. Saint Colum Cille (Columba) used to stand in the freezing waters of the North Atlantic to stay awake as he recited the Psalms during his all-night vigils. For fourteen years, his only pillow when he slept was a rock he carried around for the purpose. Many of the desert fathers wore hair shirts. Things like this can be helpful or unhelpful. If, before one can soften one's spirit, he must harden himself to the beckonings of the world that prey upon the weaknesses of the flesh, so be it. If, however, they engender a sort of penitential competitiveness, a spirit of, "look what I can do for Christ," we're right back in the world—just less comfortably.

The nature of "penances" and their value is invested not in the penances themselves, but in the attitude behind them and the purpose toward which they are directed. Saint Columba, for all his personal asceticism, wrote a Rule that, literally, anyone at any stage of spiritual development can follow. In his wisdom, he knew that the Rule would "mature" along with the person. The great Saint Pachomius, founder of common-life monasticism, wore a hair shirt. Yet, famously, when a young brother approached him and proudly showed him his hair shirt, Pachomius' response was, "Take that thing off. It won't do you a bit of good." And it was the redoubtably ascetic Saint Kentigern the

Scot who Advised Columba to let go of his rock.

An awakened conscience will make sin painfully present to us, and we will respond by trying, in some way, to atone for it. One of these ways is to embark upon ascetic practices, which we will all, sooner or later, begin to do. It just happens, and we respond when it's our time to respond. As long as we realize we are doing this for ourselves, to strengthen ourselves against temptation and wrench our attention back to God, all is well and good. When and if we begin to think we're doing it for God, as a way of trying to redeem ourselves before Him, as if our discomfort somehow pleased or assuaged Him, it would be best to immediately cease any attempt at ascetic practice and simply go to Confession on some regular basis.

> *As regards all actual and supposed evils, God has made use of them to the good, for the correction and benefit of ourselves and others.*
>
> --St. Maximus the Confessor, *On the Divine Names*, P.G. 4:305D

As we progress along the Path, sin becomes more real to us. As it becomes more real, we see it more clearly for what it is and it becomes more distasteful to us. Given that we are inherently and unavoidably sinful, we run the risk of becoming distasteful to ourselves. Then, we run the even greater risk of buying into satan's lie that we are distasteful to God. This is the wrong response. Rather, we must flee for refuge into the ever-waiting, ever-forgiving Arms of God.

Luke 5: 1-11 relates the calling of the first four Apostles. The Lord's dramatic gesture, filling their fish-nets to overflowing on a day that was unproductive and essentially over, impacted Peter (then called Simon) dramatically. He was struck with the realization of the Divine Presence, and his own unworthiness before it. So, he fell at Jesus' knees, crying, "Depart from me, for I am a sinful man, O Lord!"

Rather than departing from them, Jesus consoled the four, telling them, "do not be afraid," and declaring to them, "From now on you will catch men." Their response: "So when they had brought their boats to land they forsook all and followed Him." His response: He accepted them, sinfulness and all, and bestowed greatness upon them.

It is not God's desire to bedevil us with our sins (guess who does that!), but rather to bring good out of them. It is essential to remember, throughout, that God is on our side. What more evidence do we need, than the Cross?

The penitential life is a cleansing life, a freeing life, a life of absolute honesty before God and with ourselves, a continual dropping of the bag of rocks the devil keeps trying to tie around our necks. It turns our mourning into dancing; it looses our sackcloth and girds us with gladness (Psalm 30: 11).

NINE: THE SACRAMENTAL LIFE

> *Open, then, your ears, inhale the good savour of eternal life which has been breathed upon you by the grace of the sacraments; which was signified to you by us, when, celebrating the mystery of the opening, we said, "Epphatha," which is, "Be opened," that whosoever was coming in quest of peace might know what he was asked, and be bound to remember what he answered.*
>
> --St. Ambrose of Milan, On the Mysteries, 1:3

Intrinsic to the transformed life is the Sacramental life. The Sacraments bridge the gap between the material and the immaterial, between "things visible and invisible," and without them our development is simply incomplete.

Sadly, this is an area neglected or ignored by large numbers of otherwise fervent lovers of Christ. These see the Sacraments (or "rites" or "ordinances" as they variously call them) as little more than religious rituals. They see them as "Me" -centered, an expression of "My" faith and convictions within a four-dimensional world bounded by length, width, breadth and time, in which Heaven is "out there" somewhere.

Our objective, though, is to grow beyond these four dimensions and to interact with a Heaven that is not "out there," but close at hand; to be intimate with God and involved with Him in His Work.

The thing is, we cannot actually grasp the nature of God's Work until we are intimate with His present work through His creation. And we can't really get a handle on how this translates into how He works in and through us, without a Sacramental life. That's because the Sacraments are the present and vital connecting points between Heaven and earth. They reveal things to us that nothing else can, because they open to us—and deal with us in --a dimension of being that is not constrained or restrained by our four dimensional walls.

The Sacraments are gifts of God, conveyors of Heavenly Grace through earthly means. They are, therefore, bridges between Heaven and earth in a way that spiritual exercises alone cannot replace. Seven are historically thought of as the Church's "official" ones: Baptism, Chrismation, Confession, the Holy Eucharist, Matrimony, Ordination and Anointing. Since these are physical acts they are more than the aforementioned bridge: they are iconic, teaching us to reflect on the relationship, as the Creed states, between "things visible and invisible."

The Sacraments, if you will, decompartmentalize these things, and lead us to see the work of God not as separate and opposed to, but as seamless with and within, His creation.

A non-Sacramental spiritual life tends to oppose the "things visible and invisible," to carve out different places for "corporeal" and "spiritual" practices. This sometimes takes extreme forms, as in resisting it when the Presence of God begins to overwhelm one in worship; or backing away from, and even denying, the Scriptural ministry gifts or the mystagogy of Holy Tradition. There is the "natural" and the "supernatural," and although one may pray for the "supernatural" activity that one occasionally sees "breaking in," the twain never quite meet. The Sacramental life erases the barrier.

While, as we said, the seven Sacraments may be the ones normally thought "official," Orthodoxy does not limit herself to these.

Any blessing is an earthly act that conveys Heavenly Grace. The tonsure of monks and readers, the Epiphany blessing of waters and all the acts of the Church can be called Sacraments, including the reading of the Word of God and the corporal works of mercy (feeding the hungry, clothing the naked, visiting the infirm and imprisoned). We even view the things of nature as sacramental, as we will discuss later.

We must build a contemplative life on the foundation of the Sacramental life, because it is the way we keep in balance: touching Heaven is best done with one's feet planted firmly on the ground.

We begin this life by establishing an intimate relationship with the Seven Sacraments, thus letting ourselves get used to being fed with the Heavenly food while at the same time gaining insight into—and incorporating into our being--the relationship between Heaven and earth.

Baptism

In Baptism we are ontologically changed.

> *We are buried with Him in Baptism, in which (we are) also raised with Him, through faith in the working of God, Who raised Him from the dead. (Colossians 2: 12). Moreover, by one Spirit we were all Baptised into one body...and have all been made to drink into one spirit.*
> (1 Corinthians 12: 13)

Baptism is the Sacrament of incorporation into the Body of Christ. This isn't like joining a club and going through an initiation ceremony. It is an actual transformation of one's basic character through the impartation of the Holy Spirit. We literally, rather than merely figuratively, die to the world of mammon and come alive in the Kingdom of God. It isn't something we do, it's something God does.

So, where does that leave the opinion of many that Baptism is "an outward sign of an inner conviction," simply a ritual, performed in obedience to the God Who told us to perform it?

Actually, this very widespread theologumen is the fruit of a failure to discern Christ's transformation of John's baptismal rite. What these folks are engaging in is not Christ's Baptism at all, but rather, John's: a "baptism of repentance for the forgiveness of sins." (Luke 3:3).

The Baptism Jesus gave us, which He, Himself modeled (see Luke 3: 21-22) was of an entirely different order.

Jesus was (and is) God, from (and before) the moment of His Conception: Son of God and God the Son, second Person of the Holy Trinity, through Whom all things were created. He was an utterly perfect and sinless Man. Why did He need to "repent," or to be "baptised for the forgiveness of sins?" The answer, of course, is that He didn't.

Moreover, Jesus already, not only "had" the Holy Spirit, but was coequal with Him; and He, Himself was the *Logos*, the very Word of God. So why did He need to have these things "imparted" to Him? Again, the answer is that of course He didn't.

Christ's Baptism was a *prophetic gesture*: not a revelatory word, but a revelatory act. In it, He revealed His transformative Presence, that what had heretofore been was now, in Him, something new. We'll see this again, most markedly, in the Eucharist.

Thinking about it, how could it be any different? Uniquely since the beginning of time, God had now incarnated into the universe He had created, as one of its creatures. This was beyond Theophany. This was *Theos*, Himself, allowing Himself to be made truly Man; God walking among us as one of us, a living and Personal revelation of Himself.

Jesus did not undergo Baptism for Himself, but for us: as a witness to what it--and by extension the whole relationship between God and man, and for that matter the whole of creation--now was.

In the baptism of John, repentance is the point of, and therefore must precede, baptism. It's why those who practice his baptism, today, don't baptise infants. But what did Jesus need to repent of? He had never sinned.

Accordingly, the Church baptises infants. Infants haven't sinned, either.

It seems appropriate at this point to go a little further into infant Baptism in particular...

Those who oppose the Church's practice base their argument principally on Mark 16:16: *He who believes and is baptized will be saved, but he who does not believe will be condemned.*

Their exegetical error is in tying Baptism to belief, rather than tying both to salvation.

It is most certainly true that he who believes and is Baptised shall be saved. We need not, however, conclude from this that both have to happen at the same time, or that one need necessarily precede the other. Pressed, antisacramentalists will argue that there is no instance in Scripture of infants being baptised. Acts 16:33, however says of the jailer who was converted by Paul, "...he and all his family were baptized." Opponents will claim that this "must mean" there were no infants in the family, but that is simply applying a personal preference to the reading of the verse. The Church, whose memory extends back to the actual incident, tells us otherwise.

The answer lies in the consistent practice of the Church, and for that we need to turn to the Church Fathers and to the early Councils and Synods of the Undivided catholic (from the Greek, *katholikos*, meaning "universal") Church:

> *He [Jesus] came to save all through himself; all, I say, who through him are reborn in God: infants, and children, and youths, and old men. Therefore he passed through every age, becoming an infant for infants, sanctifying infants; a child for children, sanctifying those who are of that age . . . [so that] he might be the perfect teacher in all things, perfect not only in respect to the setting forth of truth, perfect also in respect to relative age.*
>
> --St. Irenaeus, Against Heresies 2:22:4 189 AD

And [Naaman] dipped himself . . . seven times in the Jordan' [2 Kings. 5:14]. It was not for nothing that Naaman of old, when suffering from leprosy, was purified upon his being baptized, but [this served] as an indication to us. For as we are lepers in sin, we are made clean, by means of the sacred water and the invocation of the Lord, from our old transgressions, being spiritually regenerated as newborn babes, even as the Lord has declared: 'Except a man be born again through water and the Spirit, he shall not enter into the kingdom of heaven' (John 3:5)

-- St. Irenaeus, Fragment 34, 190 AD

Baptize first the children, and if they can speak for themselves let them do so. Otherwise, let their parents or other relatives speak for them.   --St. Hippolytus of Rome, The Apostolic Tradition, 215 AD

As to what pertains to the case of infants: You [Fidus] said that they ought not to be baptized within the second or third day after their birth, that the old law of circumcision must be taken into consideration, and that you did not think that one should be baptized and sanctified within the eighth day after his birth. In our council it seemed to us far otherwise. No one agreed to the course which you thought should be taken. Rather, we all judge that the mercy and grace of God ought to be denied to no man born.

St. Cyprian of Carthage, letters, 253 AD

Do you have an infant child? Allow sin no opportunity; rather, let the infant be sanctified from childhood. From his most tender age let him be consecrated by the Spirit. Do you fear the seal [of baptism] because of the weakness of nature? Oh, what a pusillanimous mother and of how little faith!

St. Gregory Nazianzan, Oration on Holy Baptism, 388 AD

You see how many are the benefits of baptism, and some think its heavenly grace consists only in the remission of sins, but we have enumerated ten honors [it bestows]! For this reason we baptize even infants, though they are not defiled by [personal] sins, so that there may be given to them holiness, righteousness, adoption, inheritance, brotherhood with Christ, and that they may be his [Christ's] members.

St. John Chrysostom, Baptismal Catecheses in Augustine, Against Julian, 388 AD

What the universal Church holds, not as instituted [invented] by councils but as something always held, is most correctly believed to have been handed down by apostolic authority. Since others respond for children, so that the celebration of the sacrament may be complete for them, it is certainly availing to them for their consecration, because they themselves are not able to respond.

St. Augustine of Hippo, On Baptism, Against the Donatists, 400 AD

Chrismation

Baptism flows naturally into the Sacrament of Chrismation. They are two distinct Sacraments; at the same time, they are intrinsic to each other and form a continuum. Chrismation is normally administered right after Baptism (to the previously unbaptised), but can also be administered by itself--usually (with the local bishop's permission), to those who have undergone a Trinitarian Baptism somewhere else and are entering Orthodoxy.

Chrismation is of Apostolic origin and is part of the living continuum of the Church. Tradition tells us (see St. Hippolytus, *The Apostolic Tradition*, c. 120 A.D.) that as the Church grew it became impossible for the Apostles to lay hands on all the new converts, many of whom were won in remote missions. They therefore consecrated oil of myrrh, in the tradition of the Jewish Temple, to distribute to the missions. Since Apostolic times, all newly-consecrated Chrism includes some remaining "old" Chrism in its batch, which imparts its virtue to the new. The result is that every new Orthodox Christian is anointed, by extension, with oil blessed by the Apostles themselves.

While the regenerative power of the Holy Spirit descends upon the person in Baptism, His power for ministry—for the fulfillment of one's individual vocation--is conferred and released in Chrismation. The individual is thus prepared for ministry by anointing into the threefold offices of prophet, priest and king,

The "priesthood of all believers" is a serious thing in Orthodoxy. The Laity participate in the fasts and prayers of the Church and in the Divine Liturgy. The Ambo (or Amvon, or Tripodion) that stands between the nave and the chancel is the "Altar of the Laity," from which their "sacrifice of praise" (Hebrews 13: 15) rises up.

Many Christian bodies administer a separate Sacrament (or for some, "rite" or "ordinance") of "Confirmation." This is seen as a completion of Baptism, and equipage for ministry as the person reaches the "age of reason," variously viewed as anywhere from age eight to thirteen, or whenever he (or she) demonstrates rational ethical thought.

Orthodoxy sees no need for such a separation, because stages of life, as well as the Sacraments, are part of a continuum. Both Baptism and Chrismation are administered only once, and their manifestation in the Christian's life will be appropriate to his stages of development.

Babies, for instance, do baby things. In the process, they serve the Church and humanity by providing both joy and opportunities for service. Their innocent presence in the world is, in and of itself, spiritually critical. It is vital as a leaven and as a counterpoint to our increasingly depraved and decadent world as it continues to descend into plain savagery. So, even the Baptised and Chrismated infant has already embarked upon ministry.

As the child grows to adulthood, the gifts of the Spirit appropriate to his vocation will, if he is properly guided and taught, continue to manifest. As he becomes an adult his growth in and toward virtue will equip him for maturity in ministry, and all the rest of the Sacraments, particularly the Holy Eucharist, will fuel and sustain him.

Anointing (Holy Unction)

We read in James 5:14-15:

> *Is anyone among you sick? Let him call for the elders of the church and let them pray over him, anointing him with oil in the name of the Lord. And the prayer*

> *of faith will save the sick, and the Lord will raise him up. And if he has committed sins he will be forgiven.*

Chrismation is not the only form of anointing in the Church. Some forms are done with oil blessed by the bishop or priest, some with Chrism. We anoint church buildings, Liturgical apparel and trappings, and people.

Holy Unction, or the Anointing of the Sick, is a Sacrament of the Church that imparts a blessing to the sick. The accompanying prayers call upon the Lord for healing.

It isn't just a ritual. I have read lots of treatments of Unction where "comfort" for the ailing and his (or her) family is stressed, or the "virtue of suffering" is invoked. While all of this is more or less true, much of it seems to me to be an excuse for not really expecting much; in other words, for praying with a lack of faith--trying to "make God look good" despite the expected "lack of results."

Why do we do this? Why do we find it necessary to make excuses for God? Life here is just one part of a life that goes on forever, and if the patient "dies," he will be just as—in fact, more—healed of his infirmity than if he had been raised up to continue here!

Unless what we say about the indwelling of the Holy Spirit and the power of prayer is all a sham, there is absolutely no need for hesitation when we go before God on behalf of the sick. What we may view as a "lack of results" may in fact be (and, realistically, surely is) an advancement of God's plan as it has to do with the patient's life.

When we deal with the things of God, we deal with Eternity. We interact with an entirely different. and at present unfathomable to us, dimension of creation. That's why we call the Sacraments

"Mysteries," because we can't understand the world into which we enter when we interact with them. Understood in this light, we have no need to "cover for" God because He isn't appearing to produce "results." We can free ourselves of our doubts and reluctances, and simply pray in faith. When we do this, the "results" that follow will edify and surprise. The "Priesthood of all believers" is a serious thing in Orthodoxy. The Laity participate in the fasts and prayers of the Church and in the Divine Liturgy. The Ambo (or Amvon, or Tripodion) that stands between the nave and the chancel is the "Altar of the Laity," from which their "sacrifice of praise" (Hebrews 13: 15) rises up.

Many Christian bodies administer a separate Sacrament (or for some, "rite" or "ordinance") of "Confirmation." This is seen as a completion of Baptism, and equipage for ministry as the person reaches the "age of reason," variously viewed as anywhere from age eight to thirteen, or whenever he (or she) demonstrates rational ethical thought.

Orthodoxy sees no need for such a separation, because stages of life, as well as the Sacraments, are part of a continuum. Both Baptism and Chrismation are administered only once, and their manifestation in the Christian's life will be appropriate to his stages of development.

Babies, for instance, do baby things. In the process, they serve the Church and humanity by providing both joy and opportunities for service. Their innocent presence in the world is, in and of itself, spiritually critical. It is vital as a leaven and as a counterpoint to our increasingly depraved and decadent world as it continues to descend into plain savagery. So, even the Baptised and Chrismated infant has already embarked upon ministry.

As the child grows to adulthood, the gifts of the Spirit appropriate to his vocation will, if he is properly guided and taught, continue to manifest. As he becomes an adult his growth in and toward virtue will equip him for maturity in ministry, and all the rest of the Sacraments, particularly the Holy Eucharist, will fuel and sustain him.

Confession

There is probably no more concrete example of how the Grace of God flows through the ministry of the Church than in the Sacrament of Confession. In the confessional environment, lives are unburdened and clarity replaces confusion. Christ's Embrace enfolds us, and we are reassured that there is nothing too bad for God to forgive or too big for Him to forget (*As far as the east is from the west, so far does He remove our transgressions from us.* Psalm 103: 12).

We often hear it declared, "I confess my sins only to God!" It's curious that we mainly hear this from those who claim to be "Bible-only Christians," because the explicit admonition in James 5: 16 is to "Confess your trespasses to one another, and pray for one another, that you may be healed. The effective, fervent prayer of a righteous man avails much."

We see, here, that the confession of sin is placed squarely in the midst of the healing ministry of the Church, and as part of her overall ministry of prayer. If, therefore, we wish to participate in the fullness of the Church's ministry of prayer, we need to participate in the Sacrament of Confession.

This is difficult. One of the hardest things for us vain human beings to do is admit to another person that we are wrong about something; not just that we have "made a mistake," or "slipped up," but that we have, deliberately and without excuse, done wrong. We don't even like to admit such a thing to ourselves, let alone someone else! and the idea that we might be "weak" enough to need an embrace, or reassurance, even from God, is a hard one, especially for us in the male half of the population.

When we admit to another person that we are in the wrong about something, we expose ourselves. We reveal weakness. We thus make ourselves vulnerable, and the predator instincts of our "natural man" howl in protest and in warning.

The thing is, the "natural man" is precisely the man we wish to kill off. The Lord says in Matthew 16: 25 *that whoever desires to save his life will lose it, but whoever loses his life for My sake will find it.*

The process of Theosis is a process of putting the "old man" to death, that the new life in Christ may emerge. In Confession we are behaving completely counterintuitively to the most fundamental of the feral instincts of the old man, and thereby advancing in our journey toward holiness.

There are plenty of Heavenly reasons to go to Confession, and there are no earthly ones not to. Are you worried about your reputation? The Seal of the Confessional is absolute. To violate it is to lose one's priesthood. Are you worried about how you might look to your priest? As a priest, I can tell you that the man you're dealing with is another human being, fully aware that he is as sinful as you are if not moreso. Far from losing face with him, your courage in coming to him in the first place will enhance his esteem for you. Are you worried that your sins might offend your priest? Far from being offended, he will be honored and edified by the trust you are placing in him. You don't need to worry about revealing yourself as wrong and weak, to someone who is aware that he, too, is wrong and weak. Welcome to the club.

Again, we need to understand that when it comes to the things of the Church we are dealing with an entirely different world, a much more expansive dimension of being. All the worldly excuses don't apply, because they're all the fruit of vanity. The kingdom of mammon rejoices in vanity and rewards it. The Kingdom of God weeps for vanity and rejoices at every victory over it, however small. Confession is one of the most potent weapons against vanity, and is therefore an essential component of the transformed life.

The Holy Eucharist

The Lord said,

> *Most assuredly I say to you, unless you eat the flesh of the Son of Man, and drink His blood, you have no life in you. Whoever eats my flesh and drinks my blood has eternal life, and I will raise him up on the last day. For My flesh is food indeed and My blood is drink indeed. He who eats My flesh and drinks My blood abides in Me, and I in him.*
> (John 6: 53-56)

You'd think this would be pretty plain, wouldn't you? Yet, astounding numbers of people who are faithful to the Word of God in almost every other respect, go to great lengths, even absurd lengths, to deny what Jesus has—expressly and repeatedly—told us about the Transformed Passover meal:

> *This is My Body...This is My Blood...do this in remembrance of Me.*
> (Matthew 26: 26-28, Mark 14: 22-23)

Words upon words have been piled on top of each other in what appears to be a desperate effort to deflect, and even to defame, Christ's words. I have heard them skirted, ("He said, do this in remembrance, right? So it's just a ceremony..."), even ridiculed ("He also said, I am the door, right? So did He suddenly grow a set of hinges?"). I have heard the Omnipotence and Omnipresence of God challenged ("If He's present there on the communion table, then is He still in Heaven? How can He be on all the communion tables in the world at once?") and have even heard God's Word blasphemed ("Oh, those are the cannibal passages...").

Many of the people who say these things are lovers of God, lovers of Christ, fervent for souls and serious in their worship. Yet, in this one area they look less like Christians than like the quarreling Jews, who complained, "How can this Man give us His flesh to eat?" (John 6: 52b).

Indeed, these are following the way of the fallen-away disciples who, "when they heard this, said, 'this is a hard saying; who can understand it?'" and turned away. (v. 60)

The Lord's answer to them:

> *Does this offend you? What then if you should see the Son of Man ascend where He was before? It is the Spirit who gives life; the flesh profits nothing. The words that I speak to you are spirit, and they are life. But there are some of you who do not believe...Therefore I have said to you that no one can come to Me unless it has been granted to him by My Father." (see vv. 61 – 65).*

Jesus, in referencing His Ascension, spoke to them of miracle; of the inbreaking of a dimension of existence that was, up to now, inaccessible. If they are offended by one miracle, will they be offended at others? Will they decide which miracles of God are offensive and which are acceptable to them? Yet, those who were offended, rather than being edified by the Lord's admonition, became even more offended: "From that time many of His disciples turned back and walked with Him no more." (v. 66)

The Holy Eucharist is the central act of worship of the Christian Faith. Even those who deny it engage in rites that more or less copy its form while striving to express some sort of alternative meaning. They seek to obey the command, "do this in remembrance of Me." The problem is, they stress the "remembrance" part while ignoring what the Lord had to say about what it is they're supposed to do: what the this, in do this, was and is.

In all the history of Christendom, this sort of thing was unheard of until 1525, when the Swiss politico–religious militant Ulrich Zwingli wrote a novel "communion service." His views on what can only be called the "real absence" were rejected even by Luther and Calvin (and later, by the Wesleys). This did not stop the Zwingliite heresy from spreading throughout, and infecting most of, Protestantism, turning the Lord's great uniting Gift to us into an occasion of division. The ever-multiplying thousands of Protestant denominations are its fruit.

By contrast, the Church has always simply taken the Lord at His word...

> *For we do not receive these as common bread and common drink; but just as Jesus Christ our Savior, having been made flesh by the word of God, had both flesh and blood for our salvation, so also we have learned that the food over which thanks has been given by the prayer of the word which comes from him, [see 1 Cor 11: 23-26; Lk 22; 19] and by which are blood and flesh are nourished through a change, is the Flesh and Blood of the same incarnate Jesus.*
>
> --St. Justin Martyr, Apologies, c. 155 AD

> *Be careful to observe [only] one Eucharist; for there is only one Flesh of our Lord Jesus Christ and one cup of*

union with his Blood, one altar of sacrifice, as [there is] one bishop with the presbyters and my fellow-servants the deacons.

--St. Ignatius of Antioch, *Letter to the Philadelphians*, approx. 100 AD

He took from among creation that which is bread, and gave thanks, saying, "This is My Body." The cup likewise, which is from among the creation to which we belong, He confessed to be His Blood.

He taught the new Sacrifice of the New Covenant, of which Malachi, one of the twelve prophets, had signified beforehand: [quotes Mal 1:10-11]. By these words He makes it plain that the former people will cease to make offerings to God; but that in every place the sacrifice will be offered to Him, and indeed, a pure one; for His name is glorified among the Gentiles.

But what consistency is there in those who hold that the bread over which thanks have been given is the Body of their Lord, and the cup His Blood, if they do not acknowledge that He is the Son of the Creator... How can they say that the flesh which has been nourished by the Body of the Lord and by His Blood gives way to corruption and does not partake of life? ...For as the bread from the earth, receiving the invocation of God, is no longer common bread but the Eucharist, consisting of two elements, earthly and heavenly

--St. Ignatius of Lyons (140 – 202 AD),
  Against Heresies 4:17:5)

> *On the Day of the Lord gather together, break bread and give thanks, after confessing your transgressions so that your Sacrifice may be pure. Let no one who has a quarrel with his neighbor join you until he is reconciled by the Lord: "In every place and time let there be offered to me a clean Sacrifice. For I am a Great King," says the Lord, "and My name is wonderful among the Gentiles."*
>
> --The Didache (Teaching of the Apostles), c. 90 AD

There is no doubt about what the Early Church taught. These were people who had been taught by the Apostles themselves, or by their disciples, in whose ears the teachings of Jesus Himself rang fresh and clear. Up until about 106 AD, in fact, the Apostle John was still alive and the first-person teaching of the Apostles still current. There is, therefore, no doubt as to what the Holy Eucharist actually is.

The Eucharist, like all the Sacraments, is iconic as well as actual: it is not only present, but teaches by its Presence.

First, it is iconic of the whole life and purpose of the Church. It is worth noting that at the time the Lord said, "This is My Body, which is broken for you," and "This is My Blood, which is shed for you," His Body had not yet been broken nor His Blood shed. He was offering the fruit of a Sacrifice which had not yet been made.

It takes a few minutes to come to terms with something like that. The Lord didn't say, "will be broken," or "will be shed." He spoke in the present tense about an event that was still a day in the future.

What we learn from this is that the acts of God, and the Church through which they occur, operate beyond the constraints of space and time as we know them. We'll be going into more detail about this in the next section, on "Church Life."

As for the Eucharist's impact upon us, Clement of Alexandria expressed it beautifully in The Instructor (c. 200 AD):

> *For the blood of the grape--that is, the Word--desired to be mixed with water, as His blood is mingled with salvation. And the blood of the Lord is twofold. For there is the blood of His flesh, by which we are redeemed from corruption; and the spiritual, that by which we are anointed. And to drink the blood of Jesus, is to become partaker of the Lord's immortality; the Spirit being the energetic principle of the Word, as blood is of flesh. Accordingly, as wine is blended with water, so is the Spirit with man. And the one, the mixture of wine and water, nourishes to faith; while the other, the Spirit, conducts to immortality. And the mixture of both--of the water and of the Word--is called Eucharist, renowned and glorious grace; and they who by faith partake of it are sanctified both in body and soul.*

Matrimony

God Himself performed the first wedding, and you can read all about it in Genesis 2: 18-25.

It is worth noting that in the putting together of Creation, God's creation of Eve for Adam was His "finishing touch," so to speak. It was the final act of bestowal upon man of our Divine estate. From now on, we would be partners with God in the act of creation. We would in fact be His agents in the creation of beings after His own Image.

The Fall, as unspeakable a disaster as it was, did not diminish the esteem of the marriage bond. Indeed, so sacred is this bond that Jeremiah, speaking for God, (see Jeremiah 3: 8-9) likens Israel's unfaithfulness to God, to adultery.

There is no lack of Biblical witness to the sacredness of the marriage bond. Indeed, all we need to do is compare the adulterous wife of Proverbs 7 with the virtuous wife of Proverbs 31; or to note that, for all his exalted status before God, it was David's lust for a married woman that drove him to murder and which brought a perpetual state of war upon his kingdom (2 Samuel 12).

In 1 Kings 11: 1-13, we see a stark depiction of the relationship between the marriage bond and our bond with God. Solomon, we read, "loved many foreign women" (v. 1). God specifically warned him against entering into marriage with any of them, lest they turn his heart away to the worship of their gods. This in fact happened: disregarding God's admonition, Solomon--rather than bringing them to worship the True God, established places of worship for the demon-gods of his wives' nations. God's response:

> *Since...you have not kept the covenant and My statutes which I have commanded you, I will surely tear the kingdom from you and will give it to your servant. Yet for the sake of David your father I will not do it in your days, but I will tear it out of the hand of your son. However, I will not tear away all the kingdom; but I will give one tribe to your son...*
> (1 Kings 11: 10-13)

Solomon's adultery with the foreign women was in truth adultery against God. Marriage is God's to define, not ours, and he had commanded Solomon to marry only those of his own people. The marriages he contracted with the "foreign women" were, therefore, not marriages at all. They were adulterous relationships, betrayals of the many wives he had been permitted to take from his own nation. His betrayal of them and his betrayal of God were one and the same. We are reaping the fruit of it even now, in our own age, as the prophesied war between Judah (now Israel) and the surrounding nations continues—to the whole world's peril—to rage.

Orthodoxy speaks of the family as the "Domestic Church:" a place blessed by God and ordered by God, wherein a Godly life is taught and practiced. In an Orthodox wedding, the husband is crowned as the priest of the new household, and the wife the prophet. This is illustrated in Ephesians 5:22—6:4, Colossians 3: 18-21, 1 Corinthians 11: 3, 1 Peter 3: 1-7, etc. That this relationship is a living icon of the right ordering of creation, itself, is made clear by the words of Jesus, Himself:

> *And He answered and said to them, "Have you not read that He who made them at the beginning 'made them male and female,' and said, 'For this reason a man shall leave his father and mother and be joined to his wife, and the two shall become one flesh'? So then, they are no longer two but one flesh. Therefore what God has joined together, let not man separate."*
> (Matthew 19: 4-6)

Marriage is actually the first of the Sacraments, having been instituted by God the Father at the very beginning. Alone among all other human institutions, it has survived since before the Fall. The Christian home, blessed with God's Grace and Regeneration, thus ties together within itself the entire work of God and is—despite the violence we have done to it—mankind's central institution.

I would be remiss at this point not to mention the Religious life in the context of matrimony.

Shortly along, in the same conversation, Jesus added (Matthew 19: 11-12):

> *All cannot accept this saying, but only those to whom it has been given: For there are eunuchs who were born thus from their mother's womb, and there are eunuchs who were made eunuchs by men, and there are eunuchs who have made themselves eunuchs for the Kingdom of Heaven's sake. He who is able to accept it, let him accept it.*

The celibate vocation is here spoken of by the Lord in the context of marriage. It is regarded, in fact, as "marriage to the Church." Thus, Paul:

> *But I want you to be without care. He who is unmarried cares for the things of the Lord—how he may please the Lord. But he who is married cares about the things of the world—how he may please his wife.* (1 Corinthians 7: 32-33)

Paul thus saw the celibate life as he, himself experienced it: as freedom from the obligations of wife and family; freedom to follow instantly where the Lord leads, belonging only to Him.

As for what the monks themselves think, I can't help recalling the quote, "If monasticism were only for the monks, it would be wasted." I think it's attributable to Saint Benedict, but I can't be sure. It is also axiomatic within the Church that the monastic life is not intrinsically holier than the married life: that both are vocations that are equally able to selflessly serve God.

I don't think there can be advancement in the life of a Christian family without seeing the family as a sort of monastery: a community of people committed to each other and to working together to serve

God, and others on His behalf, and to grow in intimacy with Him.

I also do not think monasticism can be considered without reference to marriage, for the same reason. Both are icons of the Church, both are schools of virtue gained through selflessness and both participate in the Sacrament which will find its ultimate expression at the end of days:

> *Then he [the angel] said to me, "write: 'Blessed are those who are called to the marriage supper of the Lamb!'" And he said to me, "These are the true sayings of God."*
> (Revelation 19: 9)

Ordination

From the earliest days, God has taken steps to preserve His teachings and to provide for the shepherding of His people. This has persisted from the days of Moses and Aaron (see Numbers 3: 10) and on into the New Testament (Ephesians 4:11).

> *"Papias [A.D. 120], who is now mentioned by us, affirms that he received the sayings of the apostles from those who accompanied them, and he, moreover, asserts that he heard in person Aristion and the presbyter John. Accordingly, he mentions them frequently by name, and in his writings gives their traditions [concerning Jesus]. . . .[There are] other passages of his in which he relates some miraculous deeds, stating that he acquired the knowledge of them from tradition"*
>
> *Fragment in Eusebius, Church History 3:39, (312 AD)*

> "At that time [A.D. 150] there flourished in the Church Hegesippus, whom we know from what has gone before, and Dionysius, bishop of Corinth, and another bishop, Pinytus of Crete, and besides these, Philip, and Apollinarius, and Melito, and Musanus, and Modestus, and, finally, Irenaeus. From them has come down to us in writing, the sound and orthodox faith received from tradition"
>
> Eusebius, Church History, 4:21 (312 AD)

Only over the last hundred years or so has Christianity become regarded as a "belief system" among many belief systems, something designed for individual comfort and to give stability to one's life. This is wrong. It is, in fact, diabolical.

In fact, the Christian Faith, as practiced from the beginning, is the Truth. It is the Truth upon which every other truth in the world rests, and against which it is measured.

This sort of statement does not fall comfortably on the contemporary ear, which is used to making up its own "truth" as it goes along and becomes defensively insulted at the suggestion there is something else that could override it. But this is not the attitude of the faithful in Christ, who know that the Truth is not in them but in God, and who desire to learn it.

The Bible, with its clear moral and ethical teaching, sets out the healthy and productive way to live life. In its religious teaching, it tells us Who God is, Who Jesus is and how we find salvation by the forgiveness of our sins in Him, by God's Grace, through obedient and committed faith in Him. In its anthropology it tells us who we are, and how we got that way, and what we are destined for.

In the Holy Tradition, we find the mindset that brings us into an attitude of being that produces the life-changing point of view which enables us to live and to grow in the Christ-life.

This, the Faith, is held in sacred trust by the Church, for the good of all mankind, that all who are willing might be enlightened and saved.

The ordained ministry is charged with the teaching and safeguarding of that Faith.

There are three major orders: Bishop, Priest and Deacon. There are also minor orders: usually Subdeacon and Reader. There are other historical minor orders, which have been either confined to monasteries, incorporated into the five major and minor orders or become installed offices performed by the Laity. These are Exorcist, Acolyte, Porter, Cellarer, Sacristan and Sexton. Most priests are now automatically ordained Exorcist. An Acolyte can be a young boy serving at the Altar, or an adult layman studying to be a Subdeacon. The Porter is now the Usher who greets us on Sunday mornings. The Cellarer has become the Parish Council's Treasurer, the Sacristan job has in many cases been assumed by Altar Guilds and the Sexton is now the parish Custodian. In one way or another, all of these offices, ordained and installed, are incorporated into and serve the Church's Divine worship, the center of the Christian life.

Where does the authority to preach the Word and administer the Sacraments, to proclaim the Word or serve at the Altar, come from? How is it that "we little ones," As C.S. Lewis was so fond of saying, are entrusted with the things of God, and delegated to share them?

Ultimately, it comes from Jesus Himself, through the Apostles, and then down through the Church. We see how this works in 2 Timothy 2: 1-2:

> *You therefore, my son, be strong in the grace that is in Christ Jesus. And the things that you have heard from me among many witnesses, commit these to faithful men who will be able to teach others also.*

This does not happen apart from a period of sound teaching and being found worthy by those who have gone before. Even the great Apostle Paul, at his conversion, was not an "instant minister." Rather, he spent "some days" in Damascus, studying under Ananias and his house church before finally being sent out by him.

1 and 2 Timothy and Titus are the great treatises on the ordering of the Church, on ordination and the purposes of ordination. One of these purposes is to ensure the faithful handing-on of the Faith as first given. Reliably handing down the doctrines of the Faith is critical, because the Faith is the Truth and the way to salvation. It is not up for grabs, nor must it be represented as such, lest souls be lost. For this reason we are not to "lay hands on anyone hastily" (1 Timothy 5:22), but to examine the lives and doctrine of candidates for ordination (Titus 1: 5-9).

All the ministries of the Church fall under the authority of the bishops. It is bishops who are consecrated to stand in the line of succession from the Apostles, and who are entrusted with the safeguarding and teaching of the Faith as first given. Bishops are the only ones who can administer the Sacrament of Ordination, and are thus said to have the "fullness of the priesthood."

More than simply teachers and administrators, Bishops are living icons of the continuity of the Faith, of the continuing ministry of the Apostles. All the ministries of the Church, lay and ordained, participate in the ministry of the bishop and operate under his Omophorion, meaning under his authority and protection.

In his Epistle to the Smyrneans (c. 110 A.D.), St. Ignatius writes,

> *Wherever the bishop shall appear, there let the multitude of the people also be; even as, wherever Jesus Christ is, there is the catholic Church.*

Orthodoxy sums this up in the axiom, "Wherever the bishop is, there is the Church."

Priests and deacons, Subdeacons and Readers, are their bishop's local representatives, charged with ministering in his name in local situations. Their orders depend on him, for they flow from and participate in his consecration. In turn, the bishop is daily prayed for and regularly encouraged by his clergy, who are his hands out in the parish and on the mission field. Thus is the ministry of the Apostles carried out and continued.

On one level, this would appear to be simply a management chart: the bishop is the boss, the parish priest is his local manager and the deacon, subdeacon and reader various levels of subordinate management, pure and simple.

That is, however, not the level on which the Church functions. The Church is a Theanthropic institution, indwelt and guided by the Holy Spirit, with Christ Himself as her Head. We say in an immediate sense that the ministries of the Church partake in the consecration of the bishop, but the ministry of the bishop (and hence of all the ministers under him) partakes in the ministry of Christ and is empowered by the Holy Spirit. The ordained ministry is therefore not simply a "management system," but an organic unity of vocations put in place by God, Himself. They carry with them a Divine blessing which equips the ordinand for one or more specific service(s), to which he has been called from the day he was born and for which purpose he was put on the earth to begin with.

~ ~ ~

So, where does all that leave us? First and foremost, it leaves us with the awareness that God radically and Personally loves us; that He arranged for us to be able, stranded as we are for the moment in a material world, to interact with Him in terms of material things. He takes the simple and ordinary things of the earth—water, oil, bread and wine, the laying on of our brothers' hands—and infuses them with the magnificence of Heaven. What's more, He permits us to be His partners in the doing of it all!

One of the most valuable things about the Sacramental life is that it brings us to see God and the working of God in the things we see before us. And that brings us to...

The Sacrament of Nature.

To think in terms of the Sacraments, we need to think in terms of holiness. If we are to become, so to speak, familiar with holiness, it is helpful to consider the holiness of all creation: *And God saw everything that He had made, and behold, it was very good...* (Genesis 1: 31).

We are born to grow up into eternal life with God. That we might be equipped for this, we are born into a temporal life in nature. Nature, therefore, is constantly speaking to us of God:

> *For since the creation of the world His invisible attributes are clearly seen, being understood by the things that are made, even His eternal power and Godhead...*
> (Romans 1: 20)

Nature is God's Grace to us being made starkly manifest. Without food, we would starve. Without water we would wither. Without air, we would suffocate. Without all the things defined for us by the laws of physics, we would freeze, burn up, fly off into space or not be here at all.

The beauty that surrounds us reveals the Character of the Creator of those laws, just as the abundance that surrounds us, propelled by the seasons, reveals His Love. Just as air, which we cannot see, is revealed to us by the rustle of leaves, the fact that anything exists in the first place is the "rustle of leaves" that reveals God's Reality.

We misuse and abuse all of these things, all of the time. In our arrogance, we even deny them outright. But that does not change their reality. Beauty itself is not corrupted just because I view it through a corrupt lens, any more than God would cease to exist just because I might choose to ignore Him.

The interaction between spirit and matter is the essential characteristic of the whole universe.

If it were not for God's activity in the Holy Spirit, there would in fact be no universe, because it is the Holy Spirit Who sustains all things in being. On the other hand, if it were not the Father's desire that matter should exist, there would be no universe for the Holy Spirit to hold together.

When we undertake the journey into the deeper life in Christ, the deeper places of prayer, two things are important. The first is to stay free. If we are not free in our spirit, trusting in the Lord as best we can according to where we are along the Way, we cannot touch Heaven.

Most of us tend to think of "Heaven" as a geographical location, somewhere vaguely up in the sky.

Since Heaven's ways are "higher" than ours, this is a natural—and for purposes of artistic depiction, perfectly acceptable—way of looking at it. But in reality, Heaven is a dimension. We do not so much "ascend" to it as interact with it.

There are layers and layers of defensiveness, ego, sin—or, rather, excuse-making for sin, insulating us from God. As we reject and discard these things, the walls drop away and we get freer and freer. As we thus more closely approach the God Who is Love, there is even a certain euphoria that sets in, something like the feeling we get when a much-beloved relative or mentor, whom we haven't seen in years, shows up one day at our house. We'll be talking more about this in the section after next, but for the moment it's sufficient to say that this feeling is entirely appropriate. We can get lost in it, however, and we don't want to do that.

That would be a vanity, an arresting of progress. Once we let the euphoria mellow into a quiet exultation there's better stuff ahead. That quiet exultation, dug in deep within our heart, is the "joy of the Lord" of which the Psalmist sings:

> *But let all who take refuge in thee rejoice, let them ever sing for joy; and do thou defend them, that those who love thy name may exult in thee.*
> (Psalm 5:11)

This brings us to the second important thing: to stay grounded. God has not placed us in the heavenlies, He has placed us here. Heaven is our true home, but it is so in the same way the wide world is a child's true home. In this earthly part of our life we are no more able to navigate the heavenlies than a child is to navigate the adult world. Contemplative discipline, rightly practiced, is Theanthropic: a blend of Heavenly freedom and earthly groundedness.

The Sacraments are means that God provides us through His Church to be, if you will, our personal mediators between the Theos part and the anthropos part. Once we grow to be able to apprehend the Presence of God in them, we will be able to see something of Him in everything—from the most sublime to the most awful. It is the Sacrament of Nature that provides for us the training ground for Eternity: God bringing us to be aware of Him as we are, where we are, so that our faculties will be prepared for emergence from the chrysalis into the rest of our life.

TEN: CHURCH LIFE

We've discussed the Church as God's own institution, as His locus of praise, as the gathering-place of His people, as the place where we encounter the Sacraments—but what is the mystical Church? The Church is the only institution on earth that derives its power not from men, but directly and immediately from God. It is the institution established by God for the teaching and safeguarding of the Truth.

Now, when I say, "Truth," with a capital "T," I'm not referring to some "organizational truth" that defines what "our bunch" is all about. Neither am I referring to some "personal truth" that I have found useful and which this particular organization supports. I don't mean just one of many "truths" that are out there, this having been the one I picked.

I mean, The Truth.

The content of the Christian Faith is not just some things a group of people called "Christians" have decided to live by. It is, among other things, God's revelation to humanity of the best, happiest and most successful way to live this life He has given us. Christian Orthodoxy is the fullness of the Christian Faith, and in it we find the fullness of that revelation, intact and vital since the days of the Apostles and the Fathers, "without accretion or deletion," as the saying goes.

The Church—speaking in terms of the ancient Western Church, the great missionary Church that went forth from the Celtic lands to evangelize the known world—is a Thin Place: a place where the barrier between this world and the next becomes porous; where words like "natural" and "supernatural" become irrelevant in the face of the incredible Totality into which God draws us.

A church building is solid: hard, durable wood, stone, concrete, it stands like a castle—or, more properly, a King's palace—as indeed that is what it is. But step inside, and we are in Heaven's anteroom. The Body and Blood of Christ, miraculously transformed from common bread and wine, reside in the Tabernacle. The icons on the walls inform us that the Saints and angels are in our midst, and that we are standing—right here and right now—in the flow of all of salvation history.

The church building is sacred space not because we have designated it so, but because God Himself has blessed it to be so. It exists neither "here" nor "There," but is a living bridge between here and There. Our footsteps echo on a solid floor, there are walls and a ceiling, heating, air conditioning, lighting and a sound system. All familiar things. Yet, when we step through its doors, we are stepping—literally, not figuratively—into another dimension: into the Borderland between here and There.

The Church teaches us to become sensitive to this, to yield ourself to it and so to be able to experience it. This developed sensitivity eventually perceives that the Borderland is everywhere, that we are indeed able to perceive it and that we can enter upon it in prayer.

The church building is a place where the miraculous becomes part of daily life: bread and wine become the Flesh and Blood of God; the simple waters of Baptism become pools of regeneration; oil becomes fire, imparting the Holy Spirit. By means of these things we come to see that miracle is everywhere, and that in fact "everywhere," itself, is a miracle.

Icons surround us in the church building. Their purpose is to teach us a certain way of seeing: a way in which our mind sees not only things, but the implications of things. Icons are, in their two-dimensional simplicity, beautiful: ergo, beauty exists, and moreover it can be found in simple things. An icon is two-dimensional, the face of its subject peaceful and undemonstrative. It draws us in, inviting us to engage with it and "fill in the blanks:" ergo, we discover a wordless language of actual engagement with silent things that, suddenly, are no longer "silent." An icon is a handiwork that speaks to us of God, leading us to the fact that all of His creation is His handiwork, and all of it can speak to us of Him.

Actually, the purpose of an icon is to teach us to no longer need icons. Once our minds are formed to be able to engage with them, we find we can meditate on virtually anything we encounter and it will lead us back to God. The result is that we truly see--and so appreciate, our Omnipresent God Whose pleasure it is to be available to us.

Most importantly, in the church building we pray. We invest all the beauty we can muster in the worship of the Lord God, freeing ourselves of the world's burdens and permitting Him to lift our hearts and minds to Heaven.

Through this, the Church teaches us how to become free in Him. Her orderly, Liturgical prayers become the mechanism that frees us in our private, spontaneous prayer life and individual meditation. We also learn the value of praying together with the whole Church, and are guided toward practicing her common devotions at home. What an amazing thing, sitting in our favorite "prayer place," to be lifted beyond where we are into the perpetual prayer of the gathered Church, whose payers constantly resound within the dimension we have just entered.

We learn the value of praying together, period. Scripture doesn't speak of a Church full of "lone rangers." The Lord sent the Apostles out two by two, not one by one (Mark 6: 7). He tells us He is where "two or three are gathered" in His Name (Matthew 18:20). We are admonished in Hebrews 10: 25 not to "[forsake] the assembling of ourselves together, as is the manner of some...", and we are time and again reminded that the Church is a body and each of us a member (Romans 12:5, etc.).

Getting into the church

Psalm 22 is a lament written by David, a warrior-king who was often beset by would-be invaders. In this psalm he cries out to God, in great distress as the current enemy closes in and he feels alone and outnumbered. Yet, for all of this, David exults in verse three: *Yet Thou art holy; enthroned on the praises of Israel.*

Even in the midst of the Psalmist's distress, he is aware that God inhabits the praises of His people. We who are of the New Israel are aware that it is in the Church that His people praise Him. That indicates to us that the activity of praise is not just a one-way street. As we praise Him, God comes to us. In fact, He delights in the praises of His people not because He somehow needs His self-esteem built up (!), but because in praising Him we open ourselves to Him and so remove roadblocks from the avenue where He comes to meet us. So, it is for our good, to build us up, fill us up and bring us closer to Him, that we worship Him.

We can, of course, worship God anywhere. It is even technically true that, if we actually do so, we can worship Him, as so many have flippantly said, on the golf course.

We can fellowship with other Christians at the local after-church watering hole, and build each other up with psalms and prayers and spiritual songs (see Ephesians 5: 19); we can receive the Sacraments at home or in a hospital on a pastoral visit. We can meditate on icons at home. But the one thing we cannot do, is do all of these things at once anywhere but in a church building. The fullness of prayer, of praise, of worship and fellowship can only be found in church, with other believers.

Getting out of the church

The parish church is the center of our worship, and to tell the truth, it ought to be the center of our life. It is where we are equipped and empowered to carry our ministry, whatever it is, outside the building into the world. And it is where we are taught how to personally engage with God.

We hear the Word of God there, and so learn to share it. We are ministered to, and so learn to minister. We are edified, and so learn to edify.

This all happens for a purpose, because the Church is not just for Christians. It is for everybody.

We live in a broken world, a world wallowing in the misery of sin, and seeing no way out but to multiply sins in the vain hope that lots of temporary distractions will somehow add up to some sort of ongoing relief. The world indulges every fancy, encourages every perversion. It calls anything right that is labeled "sincere" or "tolerant," while at the same time immersing itself in lies and in the systematic rejection of any idea that might actually lead it to the peace it claims to seek.

A broken world produces broken people, and broken people need healing. This can only come from Christ, Who acts through His people. This means we need to get out of the building, and apply what we have learned inside of it out in the world.

It's amazing, the effect one new Christian can have. God's activity is very strong in His "babes in Christ," because they are so open to Him. Their level of enthusiasm and eagerness to learn just light up the room and edify everyone around them. They refresh all of us who are so often in need of refreshment, and strengthen the work of the Body of Christ. It is doubly important that these precious, newly-transformed souls be firmly anchored in the Church, that they may grow healthy and strong in the Lord.

The Domestic Church

The "Domestic Church" ordinarily refers to the family. Orthodoxy refers to the family as "the church of the home," ordered in the Godly manner the Lord set up in the Garden, that was unfortunately unrealized:

> *Wives, submit to your own husbands, as to the Lord. For the husband is head of the wife, as also Christ is head of the church; and He is the Savior of the body. Therefore, just as the church is subject to Christ, so let the wives be to their own husbands in everything.*
>
> *Husbands, love your wives, just as Christ also loved the church and gave Himself for her, that He might sanctify and cleanse her with the washing of water by the word, that He might present her to Himself a glorious church, not having spot or wrinkle or any such thing, but that she should be holy and without blemish. So husbands ought to love their own wives as their own bodies; he who loves his wife loves himself. For no one ever hated his own flesh, but nourishes and cherishes it, just as the Lord does the church. For we are members of His body, of His flesh and of His bones. "For this reason a man shall leave his father and mother and be*

> *joined to his wife, and the two shall become one flesh." This is a great mystery, but I speak concerning Christ and the church. Nevertheless let each one of you in particular so love his own wife as himself, and let the wife see that she respects her husband.*
> (Ephesians 5: 22-33)

The world actually despises this passage. In our time, hell has successfully, and cruelly, manipulated souls beloved of God into going to actually pathological lengths to defy it.

The result has been a chaos of meaningless intimacy leading to broken lives, incurable diseases, pandemic loneliness even in the midst of crowds of "merry-makers," a desperate turning to "recreational" drugs, an epidemic of suicide among young people and a general, all-pervasive devaluation of the human person.

"Marriages" have become contractual partnerships, focused on the extrinsic values of sex, money and continued high emotion, dissolvable at will, rather then sacred unions that produce one person in two parts. This union, iconic of the Hypostatic Union itself, is intrinsically holy. It is meant to last for life, not because of a contractual deal or an impossibly romantic version of "love," but because only a madman seeks to cleave himself in half.

In Genesis 1: 28, we see God's intention for man: to fill the world with icons of Himself, who will have the care of and dominion over a perfect world. It didn't work out that way. We do, however, continue to be icons of God, if imperfect ones, and God still desires for us to conduct ourselves according to His original plan. We are to "Train up a child in the way he should go," so that "when he is old he will not depart from it." (Proverbs 22:6)

Children are beloved of God. Jesus, famously, at one point placed a child in the midst of a crowd he was teaching, and declared, *Truly I say to you that unless you are converted and become as little children you will by no means enter the Kingdom of Heaven. Therefore whoever humbles himself as this little child is the greatest in the Kingdom of Heaven.* (Matthew 18: 2-4)

Children are two things above all others: formable and innocent. Their "sins" are born of emotions they have not yet learned to control and frustrations from which they have no experience to keep them from being bewildered. This gives them humility before a world in which they need to learn to function, and a teachable spirit that is only hindered by impulses they can't understand, born of an inherently sinful nature that no-one has yet explained to them. These two qualities, teachability and innocence, are iconic of humanity as God originally intended it.

The world hates teachability and innocence, because it hates mankind.

"How can that be," we might well ask, "when those who are of the world are also human?"

To be "of the world" is to be "not of God." Yet, there is a God-ward drive even in the soul of a worldly man, which creates desires and expectations in him that he can never see fulfilled. He expects friendship, and instead gets competition and mockery. He expects loyalty, and gets betrayal. He expects fulfillment, only to find frustration. So, despite the social networks he collects for his comfort and advancement, there is a place within the worldly man that despises humanity. Since his philosophies deny the explanation, which is a Divine character marred by an inherent flaw, he has at the root of his perception only the flaw, which he takes to be the whole thing. He therefore becomes, in the words of Plotinus, a wolf among wolves. He must find his satisfactions where he will, and deny the legitimacy of anything that would interfere with them. He hates teachability, because he must regard his will as sovereign. He hates innocence because he equates it with ignorance and sees it as a trap.

The fruit of this is a stripping away of the notion that human life is sacred: sacred to what, if there is no sovereign God—if the "Divine" is simply what we make it, subject to the sovereignty of our own will?

So, in our age, we abort our babies and, "for their own good," deprave the children whom we have permitted to survive. We make grotesqueries of our bodies, trying in vain to become a gender we will never be able to be. We make wastelands of our minds, denying objective reality and the natural law, and surround ourselves with noise to drown out our God-ward drive.

The Christian home is the institution that stands against this. It is actually an extension of the parish church, a "thin place" that lives with the parish church in another dimension.

While standing against the kingdom of mammon, it stands for its victims. The Christian household is a place of hospitality. It offers the sort of friendship that will, hopefully, make the worldling aware of what is possible, and will perhaps reach him in the Godly place he has been trying so hard to silence.

In military terms, the home is the force that penetrates "outside the wire," where the enemy is; an enemy it confronts with weapons that are "...not carnal, but mighty in God for the pulling down of strongholds". (2 Corinthians 10: 4)

The atmosphere of the home

Married or single, the Christian home is meant to be a place of prayer and peace, the one flowing from the other. It is also a place of healthy—if occasionally anguished—confrontation with ourself as the reality of our sinfulness surfaces and as we face the fact that sometimes we struggle to get out of the way of the Holy Spirit, Who is working within us to help us overcome.

Step one is to order one's private prayer life. It does us little good to go to church every Sunday, if the chaos and turmoil of the world are waiting for us at home.

Our life may consist of spending our days living up to the demands of office or factory, then tying our stomach up in knots from the noise and turmoil of the highway or the bus or subway. If we then come home and immediately fill the house with the noise of the world from the TV set or stereo, we deny ourself the Godly peace that is so necessary to growth in our spiritual life.

It is essential to realize that the worship of God is not, or should not be, reduced to an "activity" we engage in once a week and/or during Advent and Lent, much as we would engage in any other activity of life. Rather, it should be the central focus of our life, around which all the rest of our life is built and to which all the things of it are dedicated. This includes everything: work, school, entertainment, marriage or dating relationships, the works. A Godly home environment is an essential support for a Godly life.

There are a few simple steps to this. First, establish a place in the house to worship. Maybe just a small shelf or table on the east wall of a room, with a couple of icons and a Bible on it, maybe a couple of candles. Keep it simple. Invite your priest to come over and bless it, together with the rest of your house.

Second, use the space. If you're married, have a simple daily devotional time with your family. If you're single, spend a little time in your prayer space every day. Get into the Bible. With the rest of the

Scriptures, Families should particularly study and take to heart the passages dealing with husbands, wives and children. Single people should steep themselves in the passages that have to do with honor and morality. Yield yourselves in prayer, and let the Holy Spirit bring forth fruit from the seeds your studies plant.

Actually, this is a critical thing. The devil is running a full-court press against the family in our day. The infernal strategy is to set husbands and wives against each other in a competitive, easily-offended relationship. To the devil, the best way for husbands and wives to regard each other is as "equal partners in a relationship" rather than as two people made one flesh in Christ. Strife and stress always proceed from a self-centered, secularized relationship and this suits the purposes of hell, not of Heaven.

The devil is always trying to lead single people, whether never married, divorced or widowed, into relationships that defy, rather than follow, God's Plan. We "see that the fruit is good, and is to be desired..." so we take and eat. We feel entitled to do this—if we are young, because of our natural drives; if we are older, because we have "paid our dues." We seek intimacy to overcome the loneliness that is always in the background of the single life. It is with deceptive and even surprising ease that friendship, or delighted attraction, can be turned away from God to serve the purposes of the enemy.

Proverbs 7:10-27 and John 4:16-18 show us how easy it is for even people who wholeheartedly seek goodness to fall prey to the need for security, recognition and plain physical release. Saint Patrick, in his famous "Breastplate," invokes the power of God against "the natural lusts that war within: the hostile ones that mar my course."

The world is forever propagandizing us that we have no control over these things, that we might as well give in to them because they are bound to overwhelm us, anyway. Our defense against this sort of propaganda is the Christian home.

"But," the single person may ask, "what about the 'family' part?"

Saint Paul writes,

> *He who is unmarried cares for the things of the Lord—how he may please the Lord. But he who is married cares about the things of the world, how he may please his wife. There is a difference between a wife and a virgin. The unmarried woman cares about the things of the Lord, that she may be holy in both body and spirit. But she who is married cares about the things of the world—how she may please her husband.*
> (1 Corinthians 7: 38-34)

Lest this be taken as a command of God, it must be noted that Paul begins this entire narrative with the disclaimer, in Verse 25: *Now concerning virgins: I have no commandment from the Lord; yet I give judgment as one whom the Lord has made trustworthy.*

The passage also needs to be read in light of the extensive treatment of marriage and its holiness in the passage from Ephesians that opened this discussion. So, the Church therefore teaches that the single state and the married state are equally sanctified, and that each has the potential for holiness.

Therefore, whatever our state of life...

> *Let him who is taught the word share in all good things with him who teaches. Do not be deceived, God is not mocked; for whatever a man sows, that he will also reap. For he who sows to his flesh will of the flesh reap corruption, but he who sows to the Spirit*

> *will of the Spirit reap everlasting life. And let us not grow weary while doing good, for in due season we shall reap if we do not lose heart.*
>
> *Therefore, as we have opportunity, let us do good to all, especially to those who are of the household of faith.* (Galatians 6: 6-10)

The answer to the question, of course, is that the family of the single Christian is the Church, the "household of faith."

We are in the Church and of the Church. Our home must be a place of refuge, itself a church.

Getting out of the house

Lay and ordained, we are all "priests" by virtue of our Baptism and Chrismation. The Laity are not simply observers of the Divine Liturgy, but active participants. The Amvon (or Ambo, or Tripodion), situated between the nave and the chancel, is the Altar of the Laity, whereupon they offer the sacrifice of praise (Hebrews 13: 15) that is an integral part of the dynamic of the Sacrifice of the Eucharist.

There are many installed ministries by which the Laity advance the worship and life of the parish. There are lay readers and Altar servers, these latter often on the way to being ordained into the minor orders of Subdeacon and Reader; there are ushers and greeters, sextons (caretakers), cellarers (treasurers), and sacristans (those who care for the Altar appointments). There are Parish Council members.

These ministries are not for us, but operate through us for others. Accordingly, we don't confine our ministry to the inside of the building.

God equips us with actual spiritual charisms, gifts, that some would call "supernatural" but which we call simply part of the Church's ministry. These operate inside the Church, for the upbuilding of our brothers and sisters, and outside, that we may bring the Love of God to a hurting world. God can incorporate these into the ministry and life of any of us. Only one of them—Pastor / Teacher—is reserved to the ordained priesthood. The rest are open to, and very beautifully manifest themselves through, the Royal Priesthood, the Laity.

At this point, I would ask you to read Ephesians 4: 11-13 and 1 Corinthians 12: 7-11 and 27-31.

Ask the Lord for wisdom as you read, and let the Spiritual Gifts and their various purposes form in your heart and in your mind. Then discuss your perceptions with your priest or spiritual director / counselor. We are beginning to journey into places where we must not venture alone, now, so it is essential to have a relationship with a trusted, mature Orthodox Christian who can reliably counsel you. Needless to say—but I'll say it anyway—the places which we are about to explore cannot be properly or productively entered without a faithful parish relationship and a prepared home.

ELEVEN: THE CONTEMPLATIVE LIFE

The thing about a deepening relationship with the Lord is that the closer we get to Him, the closer we want to get. So, sooner or later, the transformed life develops into, at one level or another, a contemplative life.

Now, when I say "at one level or another," I mean the contemplative life takes on a variety of exterior forms: from simply having a daily "quiet time" with the Lord, to following St. Benedict's famous admonition that "work is prayer," and so consecrating one's daily activities; to moving into a cave and being a hermit, and everything in between.

> *Now when He was asked by the Pharisees when the kingdom of God would come, He answered them and said, "The kingdom of God does not come by observation; nor will they say, 'see here!' or 'see there!' For indeed, the kingdom of God is within you."*
> (Luke 17: 20-21)

The external form varies according to one's vocation. The important thing is the interior practice that will permit God to build an outpost of His Kingdom: an outpost into which we can then move.

For example, back in the Fourth Century there was a gigantic renewal movement in the Church. Thousands upon thousands of men and women, seeking an undistracted relationship with God, moved out into the Egyptian desert, into the regions of Scetis, Nitria and Kellia along the Nile Delta.

The desert monks lived in "cells:" huts fashioned from adobe, with spaces for sleeping and for prayer. They sought the Lord in silence and solitude, and gathered together for common work and, in some communities of cells, common prayer. But the essence of their practice, monasticism, stressed the *monos*, or one-ness of their life: one person, seeking God in solitude, living with Him in Person as the hinge upon which their life turned.

Thus, to revisit:

> *A certain brother went to Abbot Moses in Scete, and asked him for a good word. And the elder said to him: Go, sit in your cell, and your cell will teach you everything.*
>
> --From the *Verba Seniorum*

Now, what can an adobe hut teach you, apart from how to build and maintain an adobe hut?

The cell is an icon of the Kingdom of God within. We build our cell as we build an interior peace in our lives, a stillness at the center of our being wherein we meet God Personally and dwell in His Company. We maintain our cell as we maintain this relationship, even in the midst of the noise and turmoil that surrounds us.

The transformed life is a life that is serious about God. The good news is that if we are serious about Him, He will be serious about us. He will lead us, at our own pace, into a life wherein every fiber of our being and every moment of our sleep and wakefulness is permeated with and by Him.

Eventually, your walk with Christ, whatever your work in the world might be, will be your life's principal desire and undertaking

Don't let this daunt you, it isn't something you "need to and had better go for," some obligation that's attended by a lot of work (as if we didn't have enough to do already!). It's something which God will form in you naturally—which is in fact being formed in you even now—which will develop and mature according to His place and plan for you.

Simply, a deepening prayer life is nothing more (or less) than an increasing ability to relax before God. It is not like "swimming upstream against sin," or something. It is more like relaxing in a heated swimming pool and ceasing to resist the work of Grace. To repeat what bears repeating, God is on our side. He loves us, and desires our good, not our harm.

What resists God is not what goes on in the depths of our being. The moral law, the natural law, exists within each of us and creates in us a longing for a moral and orderly life. Our fallen nature, rooted in pride, drags us into vanity and acquisitiveness. It wars against this deepest center of our being, and creates around it an animal, sensual crust. As a result, we are thrown into confusion: our sensuality, attached to the contingent, and our noetic longing, our longing for the Absolute, war against each other.

Only God can make the peace. Not by eradicating our sensuality—after all, it was He Who put it there, in the first place—but by converting it: bringing it into line with our best self, so that we are brought to Him as whole persons.

Many people call this the "ascetic battle," but it is not the sort of "battle" we are accustomed to imagining. It is more like a surrender, where we allow God to do battle for us and then occupy the ground He has gained within us. This is very different from, and in fact much more difficult than, trying to run the battle ourselves.

Our worst self, our fallen nature, resists Grace. The father of lies whispers to us that we should feel offended at God's explanation that we are unable to set things right by ourselves, and that we should feel patronized by His free gift of forgiveness. That may sound odd, but our vanity is where the enemy reaches us and it always wants to be in charge. At a certain point in our spiritual life, it even wants to be in charge of how we develop selflessness!

Many if not all of us of us begin our serious quest for the transformed life by praying, "God, help me become better." Sooner or later, this changes—as it must—to, "God, enable me to co-operate with You as You make me better." In the first instance, it is I who am assuming the task and asking for God to help me with it: I am sovereign. In the second instance, I am acknowledging that the task can only be accomplished by God; that it is I who need to be co-operating with His work, not He Who needs to be helping me with mine. He is Sovereign.

There is a well-known story in this regard concerning one Colonel Robert L. Scott, a devoted Christian who was a pilot with World War Two's Flying Tigers. He wrote an inspiring book about his experiences, entitled "God is my Co-Pilot" (Charles Scribner's Sons, New York, 1944). It became popular once again in 1976, when it came out in paperback from Ballantine Books. It didn't take long for wags to point out that "if God is your co-pilot, you're in the wrong seat."

We keep fighting this battle, centered around the fact that, in our spiritual life as in everywhere else, we would prefer to do the driving. The thing is, in a serious spiritual life, there really is nothing else. Our goal is that we, and everything about us, should become God's.

The most widely-favored Orthodox approach to this is called "Hesychasm," after a monk, Hesychius, who had a vision of death which transformed him from laxity to repentance and deep contemplation. Its best-known champions include St. Gregory Palamas, St. John Climacus, St. Theophan the Recluse and the ancient teacher known as Pseudo-Symeon. I won't go into the works of and about these, for your most profitable approach is to read them for yourself. This is deep and personal reading. It brings you into places that reveal things to yourself about yourself, and I don't want to get in your way. You can find their writings on the Internet, at www.ccel.org. You can also punch up "Hesychasm" on your search engine.

Briefly, the point to Hesychasm is "inner peace." God tells us in Luke 17: 21 that His Kingdom is within us.

The point to Hesychasm is to move into that inner space, where God will "build His Kingdom" within us as our home, from which all the actions of the rest of our life will proceed.

There are different points of view regarding Hesychastic practice. All revolve around repeating the Jesus Prayer: "Lord Jesus Christ, Son of

God, have mercy on me, a sinner," or some personal variation of it.

Whether we go out into the desert and build an adobe dwelling, or live in a crowded city and take a subway to an office every day, the objective is to build a cell in our heart. It is this "interior cell" of which any exterior cell we may build for ourself is an icon.

The difference between Christian and "Eastern" meditation

Before going any further, it's necessary to point out the differences—and the similarities—between Christian meditation and contemplation and some of the "Eastern" techniques to which most of us have been exposed.

First, God made us to function physically in certain ways, and all meditation techniques will produce the same physical reactions: there will be sensations of tranquility and peace, due to the alpha waves and endorphins that meditation produces. Over time the brain functions more efficiently and there is a healing effect on the body. And, importantly, one's spiritual capacity opens up. The resemblance ends here. The difference is found in the objective, in where one's meditation is, if you will, pointed, and in the directions given to get one there.

Christian meditation differs from, for example, yogic meditation, in that it has a defined exterior object, a Theanthropic emphasis and a revealed ontology.

Defined exterior object

The objective of "Eastern" meditation is to empty the mind and make contact with "the ineffable;" to become "one with the universe." There is awareness that the power that controls the universe is spiritual, but this power is undefined and indefinable. So, the emphasis is on the Self, with a capital "S." Eastern (and Western pagan) religions believe in reincarnation. So, it is felt there is a duty to one's "Atman," or the Self that will be reincarnated into a better or worse life. The more "spiritual" the person, the better the next life. The Ultimacy toward which one points is a matter of indifference. If you want to "believe in God," or in gods, or no God or gods, or in "nature," it's all good. Whatever helps "build up the Self."

The objective of Christian meditation is God. Christian meditation is focused outward, not inward. Where a yogi, say, would dive into his interior in order to diffuse himself into "the universe," a Christian focuses outward and allows Christ to lead him inward, to build him up interiorly.

We need to remember that, because of our Baptism, the Holy Spirit dwells within us already. There is no need for us to "create" or "accept" some sort of spiritual "power" into our being: God, Himself, is already there. The problem is, life on earth being what it is, our realization of His Presence is often buried beneath a lot of worldly detritus. Thus, we reach out to God, and as we do He clears the detritus away that we may become free in the Spirit:

> *Abbot Lot came to Abbot Joseph and said: Father, according as I am able, I keep my little rule, and my little fast, my prayer, meditation and contemplative silence, and according as I am able I strive to cleanse my heart of thoughts: Now what more should I do? The elder rose up in reply and stretched out his hands to heaven, and his fingers became like ten lamps of fire. He said: Why not be totally changed into fire?*
>
> –From the *Verba Seniorum*

Such "catching fire" does not happen by striving, but by yielding.

The Christian knows to Whom he is yielding, and through reaching outward to Christ the fire of the Holy Spirit is enkindled afresh.

Theanthropic emphasis

"Eastern," and Western pagan meditation is what we would call Gnostic. It sees matter as something within which we are trapped, which one hopes, through a succession of lives on earth, to escape. It seeks, therefore, to "transcend" matter, to leave it behind and to journey in "spiritual realms," perhaps with the aid of a "spirit guide."

Christian meditation is totally different. We see matter as God's creation, an icon of the Father and of His creating Hand. We see our bodies, and our earthly life, as gifts that give us the wonderful opportunity of growing in the Christ-life here and growing in the realization that this gift He has given us is the beginning of the Eternity in which we already live. So, we seek in our meditations to convert, not discard, the body; to renew, not cancel, the mind; to live a life in Christ that consists of balance between body, mind and spirit.

Christ became Man. He took on a body. He, in His mortality, thought human thoughts, expressed human needs, had human friendships and conversations and expressed Himself intellectually in human terms. He didn't do this to tell us that our mind and body were things to be despised. The aim of Christian meditation is a life infused with Christ, in the power of the Holy Spirit, to the glory of God the Father, Who made us to be coherent and holy.

Revealed Ontology

As mentioned, the Jesus Prayer is at the center of Hesychastic practice. It is not a "mantra" in the yogic sense.

A yogi will chant "Om…" or some other mantra, over and over. It is a meaningless sound, its sole purpose being to forestall logical thought, empty the mind and focus on "interior pathways." The yogi's objective is undefined, beyond his personal growth in his ability to do what he is doing.

A Christian repeats "Lord Jesus Christ, have mercy upon me, a sinner." This engages, rather than forestalls, logical thought. As well as a prayer, it is an ontological statement: Jesus is Lord; He is the Christ, the Messiah, He Who is to come; He is Son of God and God the Son; He is the Source of Mercy, of which I am in need because, appraising myself realistically, I am a sinner.

We thus fill our minds with God, focusing on Him as He enlivens us in the Holy Spirit and leads us into a dynamic interior life which is solidly connected with God the Creator and Sustainer of all things. We abandon ourselves to Him, and simply become fire.

On method

So, what are the rules for this? Are there breathing exercises? postures? numbers of repetitions? Yes, and no. Famously, a young brother once approached a great Hesychast and asked him, "Father, how many times a day must I repeat the Jesus Prayer in order to do it correctly?" The response was , "You must limit yourself to no more than five thousand repetitions."

Now, if you do the math, you'll realize that it is impossible to repeat the Jesus Prayer five thousand times within twenty-four hours. It can't be done.

> *A brother asked one of the elders: What good thing shall I do, and have life thereby? The old man replied: God alone knows what is good. However I have heard it said That someone inquired of Father Abbot Nisteros the great,*

> *the friend of Abbot Anthony, asking: What good work shall I do? and that he replied: not all works are alike. For Scripture says that Abraham was hospitable, and God was with him. Elias loved solitary prayer, and God was with him. Therefore, whatever you see your soul to desire according to God, do that thing and you shall keep your heart safe.*

--From the *Verba Seniorum*

Pseudo-Symeon had an elaborate formula for praying the Jesus Prayer:

> *Sit down in a quiet cell, in a corner by yourself...Close the door and withdraw your intellect from everything transient and worthless. Rest your beard on your chest and focus your physical gaze, together with your whole intellect, upon the center of your belly or navel. Restrain the drawing in of breath through your nostrils, so as not to breathe easily, and search inside yourself for the place of the heart, where all the powers of the soul reside. To start with, you will find there darkness and impenetrable density. Later, when you persist and practice this task day and night, you will find, as though miraculously, an unceasing joy.*

> *For as soon as the intellect attains the place of the heart, at once it sees things of which previously it knew nothing. It sees the open space within the heart and it beholds itself entirely luminous and full of discrimination. From then on, from whatever side a distracting thought may appear, before it...has assumed a form, the intellect immediately drives it away and destroys it with the invocation of Jesus Christ...The rest you will learn by yourself, with God's help, by keeping guard over your*

> *intellect and by retaining Jesus in your heart...As the saying goes, [and here he is quoting the Desert Fathers] 'Sit in your cell and it will teach you everything.' (From "Voices from St. Vladymir's Seminary," Lecture by H.G. Bishop Alexander of the Bulgarian Diocese, OCA, 17 September 2014).*

On the other hand, St. Theophan the Recluse once famously related: "Body postures and breathing techniques were virtually forbidden in my youth, since, instead of gaining the Spirit of God, people only succeeded in ruining their lungs." (See http://orthodoxwiki.org/Hesychasm)

The long and the short of it is that your method of contemplation will be just that: yours. Developing depth in prayer is absolutely essential to every other part of your life, and like everything else, it is a growth process. Your "method" will probably change over the years, but the stability it will produce, given the efficaciousness of the Jesus Prayer, should not.

As always, and there is no overemphasizing this, stay firmly situated in the Church and in your relationship with your anam chara / staretz / spiritual director / confessor.

Contemplation and Rule

Speaking of stability, as we grow in the contemplative life we tend to seek more stability in life. As well, we come to know who we are in Christ, and thus discover our vocation. Out of this, our Rule of life emerges. It may be, while informed, pretty much exclusive to us, or we may adopt an already-formulated ancient Rule, such as those of St. Pachomius, St. Basil, St. Benedict, St. Aidan, St. Columba or any, or some variety of, the great prescribed Rules that have done so much for so many. Whichever way it occurs, yours or an established one, you will realize a personalized ownership of it as a gift that God has given you.

You are embarking upon the business of formulating your Rule of Life: the way you, personally, live the transformed life. This is a search that goes on beyond the scope of this little book, whose purpose is to equip you with the basics: the tools you will need to formulate that Rule reliably.

As you grow, you will change. Your personal Rule, or the way you practice it, will, accordingly, also change. Your personal contemplative practice will both produce and follow these changes, as you begin to more clearly communicate with the Lord: that is to say, as your "interior ears" grow and sharpen.

It is essential at this point to remind you—still again--that all true spiritual progress takes place within, and as part of, the Church. The most solitary of hermits pursues his (or her) vocation as part of the Church, and as an integral part of the Church's life and witness.

When we open ourselves to spiritual things, we open ourselves to, and actually enter, a whole new dimension of being. Not at all to be melodramatic, but not all the inhabitants of this dimension are our friends. Deception to the point of being led astray is easy, and our "own personal confidence in our salvation," as many rely on, will not suffice. Our own personal confidence has to be in Jesus Christ, and so instead of going it alone we entrust ourselves to the Theanthropic institution that He established, wherein we will find reliable guidance and all the considerable support we have already discussed.

It is within this context that you will find what the Western Church calls an *anam chara,* a wise and trustworthy spiritual friend, or what the Eastern Church calls a *staretz,* or wise father confessor and spiritual guide: what is commonly called a spiritual director or advisor. It could be your parish priest, a member of a religious community or a mature and Godly member of your congregation.

Whoever it is, it will be someone whom you can trust, whom you recognize as being more advanced along the Path than yourself.

At all accounts, you should let your parish priest know what you're doing. God has put him there for you. Remember that whatever your ministry turns out to be, it is an extension of the ministry of your priest and your parish, even as your priest's ministry is an extension of the ministry of the bishop and the diocese.

When you're ready, you will feel in your very bones the call to the chrysalis. Just go with it. God knows what He's doing. Trust Him.

You will also feel a gigantic temptation to "go it alone." Don't.

PART FIVE: THE ABCD'S OF CONTEMPLATION

Abandonment, Bereftness, Composition of Place, Disponability.

~ ~ ~

TWELVE: ABANDONMENT:

Vulnerability, Transparency and Trust

> *Behold, God is my salvation; I will trust, and will not be afraid; for the Lord God is my strength and my song, and He has become my salvation.*
> (Isaiah 12: 2)

~ ~ ~

Life and prayer intersect and combine at the point of abandonment. Abandoning ourselves into the arms of God is the necessary first—and continuing--step in a life of transformative prayer.

Vulnerability: Don't be defensive.

The prayer of abandonment entails vulnerability. We are, after all, looking to God to transform us into a different person. In order to do that, we have to let Him: we have to become vulnerable to His activity.

I'm reminded of the illustration in the previous chapter of Abbot Joseph advising Abbot Lot to "simply become fire." Joseph began by stretching his hands out toward Heaven. There is nothing defensive, nothing self-protective, about such a posture. He was simply open to the activity of God. In the same way,` we need to cast off our own defensiveness. We need to let go of the habits of years, ingrained in us by everything from bullies at school to competitors in the marketplace; from unfaithful friends to malicious co-workers and insecure bosses, or just from the multitude of little annoyances that interfere with our day. Life on earth can be a rough business, and we spend much of it acquiring defensive attitudes.

In the worldly life, these attitudes are attributes. In the transformed life, they're excess baggage.

God wants to turn us into someone who can live in His Eternal Presence and thrive in a world without the limitations that hem us in, here. In order for Him to be able to work on us to accomplish this, we cannot be closed off. We must be vulnerable to His activity.

I liken the product He wants to produce in us to a desert rose. A number of years ago, I found myself out in the dunes of the great American Southwestern Desert. What a remarkable place! Nothing, as far as the eye could see, but sand: rolling sand, an ocean of sand, with swells mounting up sometimes hundreds of feet, only to be flattened out in the next high wind and pushed elsewhere. The sun was a wild animal, relentless and ruthless. It seemed to come after the unprepared personally, literally sucking the moisture right out of the skin.

Sitting on one of these dunes, I came upon something I will never forget: a red flower, sitting in a nest of green leaves, its petals open to the sun, basking.

I approached this flower, and stroked it. It was soft! Then I grabbed it, and it became all spiky, like an especially dangerous variety of sandpaper. I tugged on it a little, and felt a massive strength anchoring this remarkable creature. Its leaves and petals were plump! That's when it occurred to me that this flower must have roots that reach an inordinate depth into the earth, digging down until they tapped into water. In that moment, it occurred to me that that's what God wants us to be.

That sun was a ruthless killer. Yet, to the desert rose, it was a companionable warmth. It was not folded in upon itself, but completely open. It flourished not because it had somehow found a way to hide from the sunlight, but because it didn't need to: it was deeply rooted, connected into the water source.

God wants us to be desert roses: deeply rooted and connected into the Source of Living Water; soft to the touch, yet bold when attacked. That rose was simply itself. It didn't need to be anything else. It lived peaceful and unafraid in a place of voracious insects, hungry predators and blasting heat, its very vulnerability its strength.

God will turn us into that, if we let Him.

Straining and striving at God is fruitless. We're never going to blast open the Gates of Heaven by our effort, mainly because we don't need to: they're already open. We can't drag God into our presence by the main force of spiritual striving, but we don't have to: He's already here.

So, what's the big deal? If all we need to do is relax, where's the "spiritual battle" we keep hearing about?

Well, have you ever seriously tried to relax? To just sit there, with no fear of being interrupted? No anticipation of the phone ringing and disturbing you?

Most of us "relax" by engaging in some activity or other. We go out to some entertainment or we play some music or work out or go fishing, or something. But this isn't relaxing, really, it's just distracting ourselves. To truly relax is to be able to sit peacefully and let our tensions and distractions go. The thing is, they don't want to. Moreover, we don't really want them to, because the stuff with which we're preoccupied is the stuff of our life. We are used to using those rare moments of quietness and solitude to think these things over and make plans around them, not to let go of them. Letting go of them is not normal for us, and not easy. So there's a battle. It's a different sort of battle: a quiet, even a gentle sort of battle. But our stuff will rage within us, demanding our attention. Before we get the knack of gently turning from it, we will try to push it away or shove it down or shout over it, and so will only succeed in replacing one distraction with another. So, relaxing is a battle.

The battle is interior. If we engage it and have patience, we will change from one kind of person into another.

The person we have been is used to being on his own, "eating his bread by the sweat of his face" (cf. Genesis 3:19), so to speak. All sorts of defensive barriers are thrown up in the process, both to defend us from the sins of others and to protect the sins we, ourselves, prefer. Our spiritual nature becomes heavy with the various aggressions, philosophizings and excuses we need in order to sustain the old life, and layer upon defensive layer is the result.

The similes about removing the leaves from an artichoke to get to the heart, or peeling back the layers of an onion to get to the pearl, are all about this. Just like the artichoke or the onion, we have no power to do the task ourselves. Our part—and it is not an easy part—is to permit the Holy Spirit to do it for us.

> *And we have known and believed the love that God has for us. God is love, and he who abides in love abides in God, and God in him.*
> (1 John 4:16)

It's something like standing on the edge of a cliff, preparing to jump out into the void into the waiting arms of God, of Whose promise I am sure but Whom I cannot see.

The critical question at that moment is not, "have I studied a lot of theology?" It is not, "have I done my best to do what I'm supposed to do?" It's not even, "have I been to church regularly?"

It's "Do I trust God?" Do I trust in His Love for me, and His clearly expressed desire to do me good and not harm? (cf. Jeremiah 29: 11)

Without God's Love, there would be no universe. It would never have been created. It is God's Love that *expresses*, and which holds together everything it has expressed, giving it life at every level. Without God's Love to give it vitality, even stone would crumble to dust. Without God's Love to give it existence, there would not even be dust.

As for us, the crown of His creation, God has permitted us to share in His Love. He has given us an innate capacity to love after a manner that resembles His own Love, and it is to this capacity that the Light reaches out when we confront, as we must, our moment of uncertainty.

If we allow it to, that Love will quicken within us, and we will realize that we do indeed love God. Loving Him, we will trust Him—even to trusting Him to guide us, and then light the way, as we step forward into the darkness of the spiritual unknown.

That's abandonment.

We need to let the Holy Spirit cultivate the trait of abandonment to God in us, because this is not the only dark moment we will encounter.

There was a story told by a lover of God named Keith Green, back in the days of the Jesus Movement. He spoke of a man who had given his whole house to the Lord, except for one closet that he wanted to keep for himself. "Lord," he said, "I have given You my whole house. Please just let me keep this one little closet." Receiving only silence in reply, he supposed he had permission. One day, as he was sitting in his closet, he heard a knock at the door.

"Who is it?" he asked.
"It's the Lord," came the answer.
"What do You want, Lord?"
"I want the closet."

You have doubtless heard the analogy about the artichoke: that the spiritual life is like picking the leaves off an artichoke; one leaf, one layer at a time, on the way to the heart. The thing is, each one of our leaves, of our layers, is stubborn. We can't pick them off by ourselves.

I recently (at least as of this writing) had a total hip replacement. The hip was shot, beyond anything I could do to deal with it. If I could have chopped the thing off and jammed the ceramic replacement into place by myself, I would have done so. But I couldn't. I had to abandon myself into the hands of a surgeon.

Now, the surgeon in question was, and is, one of the best orthopedists around, a superbly skilled man with loads of hip replacements to his credit. But he was going to, literally, separate my leg from my body and put me back together! And I was going to be out cold, unaware of anything, completely vulnerable. My doctor was the best around. The hospital was world-class, with scores of awards. I was in the best possible hands. But still...

Of course I went through with it. The "but still..." was a normal natural reaction, but it needed to be overcome if I expected to be able to continue to walk. I had to trust the doctor and the hospital—and, mainly, trust God, Who had led me to them.

In like manner, we have to continually abandon ourselves, ever more completely, into the Hands of God. Once begun, it's something we will be doing for the rest of this earthly part of our life, if we expect to be able to continue to walk with Him.

Transparency: Be an honest person.

Transparency is the school of vulnerability, and we learn to be transparent before God by becoming transparent with other people. This is completely counterintuitive, because we grow up hearing things like, "Never reveal what you're thinking;" "Never show your emotions except as a tool;" "Keep an appropriate face before the world;" "Blend in but don't be caught out."

What a terribly closed-off way to live! Yet, this is the world's conventional wisdom. One is tempted to say, "They should just be themselves." But, what is "myself," if one of my major concerns is that I must wear various faces in order to be acceptable?

Companionship is one of the four basic human needs, right up there with food, clothing and shelter. The world coldly manipulates this need to the point where all someone has to say is, "that offends me," and everyone cringes in fear and guilt.

So, we learn the tricks of manipulation, ourselves, and project a persona out in front of us for public consumption: an "image" by which we wish to be known; a shell to keep what's underneath protected.

The thing is, that image, that shell, is a wild vine.

In John 15: 1-8, the Lord likens our walk with Him to a pruning process. There's a reason for this: a wild vine puts most of its energy into the vine, itself. So, the vine flourishes but the fruit never develops. When the vine is pruned back, however, the vine's nutrient intake is directed toward the fruit, and the vine, having been pruned, becomes fruitful.

In the same way, the energy we pour into our "image" is energy that we could be using to cultivate ourselves in Christ, to become who He means us to be. The shell we put up, which we think protects us, actually weakens us by deflecting the experiences which will make us strong. It's as if the desert rose found a way to put an umbrella up over itself: handy, until the next windstorm, when the umbrella blows away and the rose discovers that it is now ill-equipped to deal with the sun.

We are made for the desert: for a life with a grand view and all the room imaginable, free of distractions from God, free to be who we are in and before Him. This can be done just as effectively in the life of a commuting office worker or factory tradesman as in a monastery. It's a matter of relaxing before the Lord, and permitting Him to develop in us a certain way of seeing things, so that when we look at people and things we see icons of God.

Who we are and how we are is not something that should be dependent on other people. We are not here to please other people, but to please God. It is He, not our fellow fallen human beings, Who should form us in who we are.

That having been said—while we're not here to please others, we are here to love them. There is only one reason we remain here in this hurting world, and that is to bring Christ to it. We are the Church: the Body of Christ. That means that we are called not just to bring Christ to the world, but to be Christ in the world! In order to do that, we need to be available. We need to be a ready, and sound, healing and teaching presence for others, and in order to do that we need to share with them as who we are, not as some simulacrum we have contrived to project.

Our fellow humans are accessible. They're right here. As we practice transparency with them, we will grow in transparency, period. This will make us more transparent before God, more fearless before Him as we come before Him with our failures and shortcomings, trusting Him to forgive us and clean us out, filling the empty space with more of Himself

We will grow into ourselves and become strong in who we are in Christ. Like the desert flower, our ease with being ourselves will become something permanent and not just there when we're comfortable.

> *O Lord, who shall sojourn in thy tent?*
> *Who shall dwell on thy holy hill?*
> *He who walks blamelessly, and does what is right,*
> *and speaks truth from his heart;*
> *who does not slander with his tongue,*

> *and does no evil to his friend,*
> *nor takes up a reproach against his neighbor;*
> *in whose eyes a reprobate is despised,*
> *but who honors those who fear the Lord;*
> *who swears to his own hurt and does not change;*
> *who does not put out his money at interest,*
> *and does not take a bribe against the innocent.*
> *He who does these things shall never be moved.*
> (Psalm 15: 1-5)

This passage describes a transparent person, someone who acts without guile or artifice and does not change faces to suit different situations.

In order to grow into such a person, we must want the Lord to make us aware of the little defensive artifices we employ throughout the day, so that when we employ them we will catch ourselves at it. Sure, this will be momentarily uncomfortable, but it will enable us to reflect on how we might have handled a given situation more confidently, more charitably and less defensively. That momentary discomfort will turn into permanent progress along the Path of the transformed life.

Trust: God is on your side. Rely on that, regardless of how it may look at the moment.

Just as transparency is the school of vulnerability, trust is the key to the whole business of abandonment. In fact, it's essential to life in Christ. After all, our entire life as Christians is based on placing ourselves in God's care and at His disposal. This is impossible unless we trust Him.

There's an old joke you've probably heard, about a famous tightrope walker who has stretched a cable over Niagara Falls and is performing before a gathered audience of thousands. First he walks across forward. Then he walks across backward. He performs similar tricks, all of them escalating in difficulty, and then he walks across with a wheelbarrow.

Finally, he has the wheelbarrow loaded with two hundred pounds of cement, and walks across a couple more times. Arriving at the cliff-edge once again, he turns to one of the onlookers:

"How are you enjoying the show?"
"A lot! It's fabulous!"
"Did you like the bit with the cement?"
"Yes, I did!"
"Think I could do it again?
"Yes, I'm sure you could!"
"Think I could do it with a person?"
"You know, I'd bet you could."
"Okay, climb on in…"

It's easy to be a spectator. Being part of the crowd allows us to share in the excitement of the event, and even makes us feel like we're part of it, without risk or commitment. If we're part of the crowd, all we need to do is conform in order to be approved of and accepted. To step out of the crowd—to reveal myself as an individual—and enter the event, is a different matter. Now, I'm exposed not only to the obvious hazard, but to public view: how will I handle it? will I back out? panic? upset the wheelbarrow in mid-cable?

Separating myself from the pack and climbing into the wheelbarrow is an act of radical and critical trust, as I put my life in the hands of someone else.

This is how we need to put our life in the Hands of God.

Once again, as is everything in the Christ-life, this is simply a recognition of reality. Our life is in God's Hands, anyway, whether we put it there or not. He put us here, He'll take us out, and what happens in the meantime and afterward ultimately depends on Him, anyway. So, why not trust Him with the parts He's given us? What do we gain by not trusting Him?

This just seems like simple common sense, doesn't it? After all, who is more trustworthy than God? If we don't trust Him, one thing it indicates is that there is someone or something we trust more.

The world would have us believe that that someone or something is, or should be, ourself.

If we trust God, we admit Him into the areas we reserve to ourself: the areas of control and sovereignty. The enemy's sales pitch in Genesis 3: 5 hasn't changed: *You can be like God.* It has been the siren call to our vanity since the beginning. The problem with it is and always has been the same: It demands that we invest the trust that properly belongs to God in those least able to deliver on it: us.

What, after all, was the fruit of our first parents' response? It was to cover themselves and to make excuses, not trusting God to understand and forgive, but relying on themselves to make an effective sales pitch to Him, even to try to manipulate Him: "The woman You gave me..." (Genesis 3: 12). *There, God, You see, it's all Your fault! It wasn't like I was derelict in my duty to protect her, or anything...*

This interaction was lots of things, but one thing it was not, was trusting. To trust in God would have been to simply come clean, and ask for the forgiveness that surely would have been forthcoming. This was our last chance, and Adam chose to trust in his rhetorical ability rather than in the mercy of God. So, here we are—being trained by the world to carry on in the same way.

Adam's lack of trust was rooted in a new onset of doubt over God's all-encompassing Love. Such doubt had never existed before, in either of our first parents. They traded sovereignty over the planet and an unhindered relationship with God, for a state so diminished it was not even a shadow of what they had had: a shallow and self-centered "personal sovereignty" rooted in nothing more than vanity. With this diminished state came a diminished, equally self-centered perceptive capacity that led them to question even the Goodness of God!

By contrast, what God Himself has to say about it, is...

> *For I know the plans I have for you, says the Lord, plans for welfare and not for evil, to give you a future and a hope.*
> (Jeremiah 29: 11)

Trust in God is rooted in confidence in the Goodness of God. It is born of facing up to the fact that He is perfect and we are not; that regardless of how and for what reason it may seem otherwise, His way is superior to ours.

This is not easy. Being creatures afflicted at our very core with the original sin of pride, we are inescapably self-centered. When push comes to shove we call what is in our interests "good" and what might conflict with our interests "bad." Even the character traits we value most highly reflect this: "self-motivated;" "self-directed;" "self-starting."

> *Whoever confesses that Jesus is the Son of God, God abides in him, and he in God. And we have known and believed the love that God has for us. God is love, and he who abides in love abides in God, and God in him.*
>
> *Love has been perfected among us in this: that we may have boldness in the day of judgment; because as He is, so are we in this world.*
> (1 John 4: 15-1)

This is not a self-motivated, self-directed, self-starting statement. It is a Christ-motivated, Christ-started, Christ-directed statement. It is an expression of utter confidence in God based upon one fact: He loves us.

The statement is summed up in verse 16a: "And we have *known and believed in* the love that God has for us." (Italics mine).

God will enable in us such knowledge and belief if we open ourselves to it and to Him. ...*do you love Me?*...(cf. John 21: 15-17)

First I must ask myself, do I love God?

Our first parents dwelled in the Love of God. They shared radically and directly in the love He had for them. Its reciprocal flow between them was just part of their normal life. This changed when the enemy sowed the seed of suspicion into Eve's consciousness: *He doesn't want you doing that. He knows you'll be like Him, and He wants to keep you down.* (cf. Genesis 3: 5)

To give Eve the benefit of the doubt, she may have just heard the "you can be like God" part, which she might have told herself would be pleasing to Him. The thing is, she was already like God! She was a perfect creation, a clear mirror of Him, an undamaged icon. What the devil actually had to offer was a vastly reduced state, a condition of striving to be what she already was. The difference was that, instead of simply living and being herself in her perfect state, she would be able to lay personal, self-conscious claim to the imperfect one. The Love in which she had lived and moved naturally and effortlessly was corrupted by vanity. In that moment she supplanted love of God with love of self.

The key, and final, factor was trust. If you think about it, trust as such had not at this point been individuated: it was not an issue. God's Love, and His creatures' response in kind, was a given: just part of daily life. For that matter, "love" had not yet become a concept in and of itself, because it was simply the condition in which they lived. The statement, "I trust in God because I am confident of His Love" would have had no more meaning to Adam and Eve than, "I trust in water because I am confident of its wetness" would have to a fish.

So, at the last, when they were confronted with the necessity to trust God because of confidence in His Love, our first parents failed to rise to the occasion. Their new-found self-consciousness issued not in "wisdom," after all, but in fear and doubt.

So, fast-forward to today. To us, the Lord asks the question He asked of Peter: "Do you love Me?"

> *So when they had eaten breakfast, Jesus said to Simon Peter, "Simon, son of Jonah, do you love Me more than these?" He said to Him, "Yes, Lord; You know that I love You. "He said to him, "Feed My lambs." He said to him again a second time, "Simon, son of Jonah,[do you love Me? He said to Him, "Yes, Lord; You know that I love You." He said to him, "Tend My sheep." He said to him the third time, "Simon, son of Jonah, do you love Me?" Peter was grieved because He said to him the third time, "Do you love Me?" And he said to Him, "Lord, You know all things; You know that I love You." Jesus said to him, "Feed My sheep."*
> (John 21: 15-17)

The context in which the Lord asked this is the same context in which we find ourselves here and now. "Feed My sheep" is a call to ministry, to be concerned for the concerns of others, to love them because we love God, and are therefore open to letting His Love flow through us to them. It is a call to set out on a selfless path of service.

If that isn't challenging enough, what follows in verses 18-19 is downright scary:

> *Most assuredly, I say to you, when you were younger,*
> *you girded yourself and walked where you wished;*
> *but when you are old, you will stretch out your hands,*
> *and another will gird you and carry you where you*
> *do not wish." This He spoke, signifying by what death*
> *he would glorify God. And when He had spoken this,*
> *He said to him, "Follow Me."*

Peter is here faced with the demand to let his love issue in trust of the most radical sort: literally, to trust the Lord with his life, a life he is told at the outset will be sacrificed for the sake of the ministry to which he is called. He must trust the Lord unreservedly, for his life, his vocation and his Eternity. This unreservedness is underscored in verses 20-22:

> *Then Peter, turning around, saw the disciple whom*
> *Jesus loved following, who also had leaned on His*
> *breast at the supper, and said, "Lord, who is the one*
> *who betrays You?" Peter, seeing him, said to Jesus, "But*
> *Lord, what about this man?" Jesus said to him, "If I*
> *will that he remain till I come, what is that to you? You*
> *follow Me."*

Of course, John was alive—and so was Peter, for that matter—at the Lord's return at His Resurrection. But at the time, Peter is exhorted to a loving trust that has faith in the Lord's word to him and not in speculation over what He meant by it. Because he loves Jesus, Peter is called to invest his total trust in His judgment.

This underscores the difference between worldly "love" and Divine Love. Worldly love expects, or at least hopes for, reciprocity. It makes demands.

It wants explanations. Divine Love simply *is*. It exists not for the sake of some sort of return or condition, but exists for its own sake.

Once Peter assured the Lord of his love, Jesus admonished him to give that love expression: "Feed My sheep." Peter's (and our) consent permits the Divine Love to flow through us, and to replace love of self with Love of God, a Love that issues in radical Trust. Thus, the dynamic that was established in the Garden is reversed.

Love of God is what enables us to trust in God, so that we may be transparent before Him and abandon ourselves into His Hands.

Achieving this is both simple and difficult. Relaxing before God, simply ask Him, "Lord, let me love You." The Holy Spirit will respond, and begin the work that will clear the way for the Divine Love to flow through you. All you need to do, then, is place yourself in His Hands and let Him work in you. In this, you will be practicing Abandonment.

THIRTEEN: BEREFTNESS:

Self-abnegation, Poverty of Spirit, Balance

To be "bereft" of something is to be "without" it.

The transformed life gives us, and can give us, many things. We need to make room for them, and that means there are things we would be better off getting rid of. The things of which we need to be bereft are the baggage and trappings of our carnal, untransformed life; or, as many of my friends call it, "the life B.C."

Self-abnegation: Don't make a big deal of yourself.

> *Also He spoke this parable to some who trusted in themselves that they were righteous, and despised*

> others: "Two men went up to the temple to pray, one a Pharisee and the other a tax collector. The Pharisee stood and prayed thus with himself, 'God, I thank You that I am not like other men—extortioners, unjust, adulterers, or even as this tax collector. I fast twice a week; I give tithes of all that I possess.' And the tax collector, standing afar off, would not so much as raise his eyes to heaven, but beat his breast, saying, 'God, be merciful to me a sinner!' I tell you, this man went down to his house justified rather than the other; for everyone who exalts himself will be humbled, and he who humbles himself will be exalted."
> (Luke 18:9-14)

There is a tendency, I think because of the unfortunate "new age" influence on our culture, to confuse self-abnegation with self-obliteration. While this may be the teleology of some Eastern religions, it is not Christian and it is inimical to the transformed life. God put us here deliberately. He equipped each of us to serve Him in a unique individual way, and we can—and should-- celebrate that. The Lord is equipping us for Eternity, for a life much vaster than the one we now know, and He wants us built up, not torn down.

The thing is, He wants us to be built up in a certain way, a way that cannot flourish in an atmosphere of vanity or by our limited prowess in a damaged world.

As in everything else we have discussed, it is humility that defeats vanity and the key to going forward is a realistic self-appraisal. One of my favorite passages for putting things into perspective is Job 38: 4-7:

> *Where were you when I laid the foundations of the earth? Tell Me if you have understanding. Who determined its measurements—surely you know! Or who*

> *stretched the line upon it? On what were its bases sunk, or who laid its cornerstone, when the morning stars sang together, and all the sons of God shouted for joy?*

The world addresses God from the perspective of its own wisdom, which is self-centered.. Like the devil in Matthew 4: 3-6, who challenged Jesus, "If You are the Son of God… ," mammon continually cries, "if there is a God, then why…" and goes on to enumerate the worldly sufferings we bring upon ourselves through sin. To do this is, like satan in the wilderness, to exalt oneself over God, the creature demanding that the Creator justify Himself to him. This is vanity carried to the point of madness, but we hear it every day from, for instance, apologists for atheism or for what oxymoronically calls itself "Liberal Christianity."

Contrast this with the Baptizer's, "He must increase, but I must decrease" (John 3:30), or St. Paul's, "…the life I now live in the flesh I live by faith in the Son of God, who loved me and gave Himself for me." (Galatians 2: 20c)

The Lord tells us that we are like grains of wheat, that must fall into the ground and die in order to be fruitful (cf. John 12:24). This is not a one time process, but a life-long journey.

As we advance upon the Path of the transformed life, we begin to notice we are thinking less and less about what "we want" and more and more about what God wants from us. We find ourselves making fewer and fewer excuses for sin, instead seeking God's forgiveness and healing. We find ourselves hiding from God less and less, and opening up to Him more and more. A dynamic develops: as we become more forthcoming with God, we empty ourselves before Him. He then proceeds to fill the empty space, and we are changed, improved—not diminished, but made larger!

This is the business of "dying to self."

When we first hear about "death to self," we envision dragging ourselves through the mud, weeping and wailing, berating ourselves and fasting to the point of starvation.

Indeed, there have been great Saints who have done such things. The Saintly, however, don't do these things out of some negative impulse to, if you will, "bludgeon themselves into humility." The impulse is positive, born of a naturally-diminishing concentration on the things of the world as their spiritual vision sharpens and their spiritual life becomes more all-pervasive. When we see the saintly person who fasts, the extent to which he does it may seem alarming to us. But, to him, he just doesn't have the impulse to stuff himself. We, seeing his effort, may try to emulate it. We may, moreover, succeed for a time until we realize that this isn't where we are, yet, and that we'd be better off, for now, being wary of striving out of vanity.

All the dramatic stuff amounts to things we do. We do them to test ourselves, and that's a good thing. But as we grow in Him, we become less dramatic and more surrendered to what God does. We let go of the baggage we brought into the Kingdom with us, like our own definitions of what is proper to a successful life, or even what "success" is. We drop our skepticism and our cynicism, all the defenses and definitions that served us in our worldly life. We become bereft of them. It is at that point that real balance develops, and our vocation pushes through into everything, and we truly begin to become who we are. As with the grain of wheat, dying to self actually brings us to life.

Poverty of Spirit: Remember that God owns everything. He's just letting us use it.

What do I have, that God did not create? What do I "own," but that which He has permitted me?

My prayer must be one of renunciation of the idea that I can, apart from God, hold onto anything I think of as "mine." It must be one of gratitude that, through effort, inheritance or "luck," He's letting me use it. We might refer to the stuff we have as "ours," but in reality it's His: it's just on loan to us, temporarily, while we're here.

That's not to say that having things—or that having more things—is in and of itself bad. What will get in the way of our spiritual progress is a perspective that becomes attached to those things in a way that affects our self-identity.

If we are to advance in the transformed life, we must allow our prayer to lead us out of a sense of "ownership;" of the sense that we have anything that doesn't already belong to God. Should we believe that any such attitude is justified, or even rational, God's great soliloquy in Job, chapters 38—39, will quickly set us straight. I would recommend putting this book down, for a minute, and going to it.

The world, the kingdom of mammon, is all about trying to find fulfillment in stuff. "I own that" is a phrase that is supposed to produce happiness. Worldly power and prestige are measured in terms of possessions. So, we are enculturated into a craving for stuff.

This, of course, produces no end of people who want to sell us stuff. The world screams at us from every doorway, corner and rooftop that, somehow, "we deserve" whatever our whims may dictate, The "good life" flashes before our eyes in visions of tropical vacations, private planes, exclusive clubs and the adulation of the sleek, well-groomed people who gather around us.

Certainly—at least, until the novelty wears off—such a life is fun, but how "good" is it? I'm going to die, one day. When I do, I will enter a dimension of being that's very different from this one: a world of virtual limitlessness. How "good" will all this distraction from prayer, from the things of God that are meant to prepare me for Eternity with Him, seem then? Vacations are a good thing, as long as we don't confuse them with life.

The world tells me that the more stuff I have, the better a person I am. It also tells me that, as far as it's concerned, when I leave I'll simply be gone—done—over with...

> *Their graves are their homes forever, their dwelling places to all generations, though they named lands their own.*
> (Psalm 49: 11)

In Christ, however, we have eternal life. And when this world disappears, we who are in Christ will find ourselves in a newly-made Heaven and earth. (Revelation 21:1)

Once more, the story of the Pharisee and the Publican, in Luke 18: 9-14, seems appropriate:

> *Also He spoke this parable to some who trusted in themselves that they were righteous, and despised others: "Two men went up to the temple to pray, one a Pharisee and the other a tax collector. The Pharisee stood and prayed thus with himself, 'God, I thank You that I am not like other men—extortioners, unjust, adulterers, or even as this tax collector. I fast twice a week; I give tithes of all that I possess.' And the tax collector, standing afar off, would not so much as raise his eyes to heaven, but beat his breast, saying, 'God, be merciful to me a sinner!' I tell you, this man went down to his house justified rather than the other; for*

everyone who exalts himself will be humbled, and he who humbles himself will be exalted."

What was the Pharisee's possession, in all of this? Who was it Who gave him the Law in the first place, that he would be able to so exalt himself for the keeping of it? For that matter, Who granted him the ability to study, and to become an interpreter of the Law? And Who gave him his life, to begin with?

The Pharisee stood before God as someone who claimed ownership of his righteousness and his life. Standing in God's own House, he worshiped not God but himself.

The Publican, on the other hand, demonstrated an Eternal perspective. He realized he was not, and could not be, perfect under the Law; that he was a contingent being, whose life and fortune, and such righteousness as he might have, were in God's Hands.

While the publican, operating from a clear perspective, came to the Temple seeking Grace, the Pharisee acted as if God should somehow be grateful to have him there.

When's the last time we felt that way? Sunday mornings can be tough. The devil is good at keeping us up late on Saturday nights, making Sunday morning a tired, irritable business. This makes it easy for him to get us to quarrel with each other, so that by the time we make it into the car our mood is good and sour. We've probably calmed down by the time we get to church, but isn't there a hint of self-satisfaction about that, as we shake hands with the usher and smile?

For that matter, how many times have I, as a priest, dragged my sorry carcass into the sacristy of a morning, lamenting the hour and the extra movie I watched the night before, almost dropping the censer as I censed the church, rushing through the book of Intercessions and the Office and just blinking awake as I hit the Altar?

Boy, isn't God lucky to have me, His faithful servant, brave overcomer of tribulation that I am, there on the job!

None of us is really immune to this. You have of course heard the old joke, "I'm humble—and proud of it!" Funny, yes--but also, all too often, the frustrating condition of serious seekers along the Path. Our inherent pride is so deeply embedded that even at our best moments we reflect it and thus trip over our own feet on our way forward.

The good news is that God is here, to pick us up, again and again and again, out of sheer love for us.

As we grow in Christ we grow away from a sense of ownership over the things we have. Pride gives way to gratitude. Closed-fistedness gives way to charity. Self-direction gives way to a sense of mission as we seek Him for guidance as to how to use what He has given us. Our world, once closed-in around our stuff, becomes expanded, and then vast, as we allow God to give us the great privilege of becoming icons of Divine Selflessness.

Balance: God works with you and within you, where He has put you. Begin where you are.

There's an old axiom that runs, "You'll never be able to lay your life down unless you have one in the first place."

A serious walk with the Lord begins with discarding the "old life," and setting foot on the road to being built up in the new one.

Naturally, we want to do the best we can, and the tendency is to just plain do too much. All the good intentions and faithfully-practiced spiritual exercises in the world will be to no avail unless they help you structure your personal Rule of life to be consistent with your emerging vocation and with where you are along the Path.

> *Yet another elder said: If you see a young monk by his own will climbing up into heaven, take him by the foot and throw him to the ground, because what he is doing is not good for him.*
>
> --From the *Verba Seniorum*

The three things you want to avoid in your development of balance are guilt, discouragement and enthos.

Guilt

The enemy will always try to convince you that you "aren't doing enough for the Lord." Back in the early Charismatic Renewal, there was a couplet that made the rounds, that went: "Mary had a little lamb, that never became a sheep. It joined the Charismatics, and died from lack of sleep."

The devil delights in pointing out all sorts of "good stuff" that needs to be done, and insisting to us that, if we don't join in the doing if it, we are somehow falling down on the job. Of course, this runs us ragged, ruins our peace and distracts us from the things God actually wants us to be doing.

The devil will also whisper in our ear about every little fault and "failure" (real or exaggerated), to try to convince us we "aren't a Real Christian," because "how could a real Christian possibly behave like that?!"

I'm not talking, here, about convictedness. Convictedness is the good fruit of an awakened conscience. Personal sin is real, and we become more sharply aware of it the more we grow in Christ. This is a good thing because it enables us to unburden ourself in Confession and thus create more space for the Holy Spirit to occupy. Guilt drags us down and makes us sluggish. Convictedness is uncomfortable, sometimes even painful—but it is also enlivening, engendering in us a determination to clear the air with someone we may have offended, or go to Confession and unload, or both.

Sometimes it's difficult to tell the difference. Not a problem. If you're aware of sin, go to Confession. Your confessor will know the difference, and will help you.

Critical point: When you honestly come before the Lord with your sins, He takes them from you and unburdens you. The devil, who wants you burdened, will try to get you to immediately grab them back. Don't. Remember what we discussed above about the penitential life. It isn't about dragging one's sins around and lamenting over them: it's about having a basic awareness of our imperfection and bringing it before the Lord, thus enabling us to live in a continual state, not of condemnation and discouragement, but of forgiveness and refreshment.

Discouragement

Sometimes we try and try, and no matter what we do it doesn't work. So, we begin to feel incompetent and even useless. If we continue along that trajectory, we just give up. And hell rejoices.

If we get trapped into this, it may be (and in fact probably is) that all that effort was being poured into the wrong thing.

God affirms His work. That doesn't mean He's necessarily going to affirm mine. If I'm in the wrong place, doing the wrong thing, God will not support it. Why? Because He wants me somewhere else, doing what I'm supposed to be doing. That doesn't mean it will necessarily be all rosy (or maybe it does—roses have thorns)...

> *From the Jews five times I received forty stripes minus one. Three times I was beaten with rods; once I was stoned; three times I was shipwrecked; a night and a day I have been in the deep; in journeys often, in perils of waters, in perils of robbers, in perils of my own countrymen, in perils of the Gentiles, in perils in the city, in perils in the wilderness, in perils in the sea, in perils among false brethren; in weariness and toil, in sleeplessness often, in hunger and thirst, in fastings often, in cold and nakedness—besides the other things, what comes upon me daily: my deep concern for all the churches. Who is weak, and I am not weak? Who is made to stumble, and I do not burn with indignation?*
> (2 Corinthians 11: 24-29)

So here we have St. Paul, one of the holiest men in history, to whom God entrusted the writing of almost half the New Testament, unquestionably a man who followed his vocation faithfully. Note that through all of his trials he was sometimes wearied, but not discouraged. His ministry was turbulent and difficult, but it was never stalled.

For all the interruptions St. Paul sometimes encountered, he never lost confidence. That's because his confidence was in God, not in himself. None of his hardships drove him to complain, "I just can't do this." Of course, he couldn't do it! But God could.

Or maybe I am doing God's work, but, as above, I've been trapped into doing too much of it: I've gone beyond doing what God wants me to be doing, into what I think I ought to be doing. So, I use up my personal reserves of energy and collapse, and get discouraged that I can't keep up with what I'm not supposed to be doing in the first place.

Or maybe I'm doing what I'm supposed to be doing. Ministry is tough. We come into contact with people in desperation, in grief, in recalcitrant sin. We ride to the rescue, only to be turned away by someone who doesn't want to be rescued. We share Christ over and over again, only to have our words fall on self-deafened ears.

God may have us there because what we are doing will bear fruit years from now. Unfortunately, we will never get to see that fruit. Our job might in fact be as a planter, not a reaper. So we don't get to see our effort "pay off." The (deceptive) appearance is that I'm just not any good at this thing God has called me to do, and discouragement is easy under these circumstances.

I need at times like this to remember the words of 1 Corinthians 3:5-8:

> *Who then is Paul, and who is Apollos, but ministers through whom you believed, as the Lord gave to each one? I planted, Apollos watered, but God gave the increase. So then neither he who plants is anything, nor he who waters, but God who gives the increase. Now he who plants and he who waters are one, and each one will receive his own reward according to his own labor.*

"Neither he who plants is anything, nor he who waters..." If I am to remain in a balanced life, I need to remember that God has the responsibility as well as the authority.

All too often, we acknowledge God's authority in our ministry, but grab the responsibility to make it all work back into our own hands.

This is a formula for disaster, because I will be continually trying to lift a weight that's too heavy for me. You have doubtless heard the expression, "Let God be God." If I try to take His place, whatever I'm doing is guaranteed not to work out. The work is thrown out of balance, and therefore stalled. The result: discouragement.

If I am doing what I'm called to do, and am not "seeing results," it's because the "results" phase isn't my job. "He who plants and he who waters are one." Our reward is that we have been honored by God to join Him in His work in the first place.

A balanced life is a life which is at peace with one's vocation and with one's part in God's work. Interrupting it by pushing my own plans farther than it takes to see that they're indeed my plans and not God's, throws me out of balance.

Enthos

Enthusiasm is a good thing in and if itself, but it has its not-so-good side. In the vocabulary of the spiritual life, enthos is the not-so-good side of enthusiasm. Enthos is what makes us run in our eagerness to greet a returned loved one, and not look where we're going, so we trip over something and fall. Enthos is what causes us to hoist a heavier weight than we should at the gym, so instead of getting stronger we get injured. In short, enthos is the drive to run ahead of ourselves in our eagerness to accomplish something good.

> *Yet another elder said: If you see a young monk by his own will climbing up into heaven, take him by he foot and throw him to the ground, because what he is doing is not good for him.*
>
> (From the *Verba Seniorum*)

We are where we are, and if we act with humility we will accept where we are. That doesn't mean we need to be stuck there, by any means: in our advance along the Path, where we are at the moment is always a starting point. But it won't be a very useful starting point if, while we are there, we behave as if we were somewhere else.

We all want to be spiritual giants, we all want to be like Peter or Paul or Columba; like Brigid or Mary of the Desert—and, in our own way, according to the vocation God has given us, we can be. But we will never grow properly into that vocation if we are always running ahead of ourselves and getting stalled. If we are still in the crawling stage, our job is not to run: it is to learn to crawl strongly in preparation for walking. So progresses the balanced life.

FOURTEEN: COMPOSITION OF PLACE

The gift of the present moment, Holy (and unholy) fear, Being here and now

In prayer, we wish to touch Eternity. This shouldn't be difficult, because we're already living in Eternity. As we have discussed, this earthly part of our life, while only the beginning of our Eternal life, is still fully part of it.

So, why does Eternity seem so elusive? I think it's because we're striving after something we already have. Most of us think of "Eternity" as something "out there," in the "future." But it isn't: It's right here, right now. As the advertising slogan goes, we are "made to last forever—" and our time here on earth is part of forever.

For instance, have you ever looked all over the house for the pair of sunglasses that was sitting right there on top of your head? or asked a store clerk where to find something you were already staring at? It seems we look hardest for the things we already have, and just don't see. So, when it comes to things like Eternity, we're confronted—even inundated—with this or that system, this or that philosophy—when all we need to do is just be where we already are.

The objective is not to *have* an Eternity, because we already have it. One way or the other we are going to live forever, and it starts here. The objective is to get in touch with Eternity.

The gift of the present moment

The only contact we have with Eternity is *right now*. I'm not in the past, anymore. The past is gone. I am no longer when I was when I wrote the beginning of this paragraph, or for that matter, when I wrote that last word. As for the future, it's as close as a fraction of a second away--but it hasn't happened yet.

What I have is the present moment: the Now. This moment is part of the flow of Eternity. To enter it is to step into that flow.

When we undertake to become peaceful and silent, our mind tends to seek to occupy itself. It carries us into the future, to plan future tasks; or it carries us into the past, reviewing various triumphs and tragedies, or just petty details. All these things happened or will happen at a different time, in a different place. They carry us away from when we are.

When we settle ourselves into prayer, we must free ourself from these distractions, and let ourself become still, joining God in His Eternal *Now*.

"But," you might say, "the *when* always changes. How do I stop it?" The answer is, we don't need to. We're already there, all the time. The clock may tick along, but if we immerse ourself in the moment we "tick" right along with it. Whenever we are, is "now."

The present moment is always present to us. The objective is to be present to it.

Remember the A and the B that precede Composition of place. We need to (a) abandon ourselves and (b) become bereft: turn over all the baggage we brought into the room, to the Lord. Then, we dispose ourself to be *where* we are, *when* we are, and we will experience our eternity.

Holy (and unholy) Fear

Detaching ourselves from our ordinary musings as we sit silently, may unnerve us. After all, when there is "nothing going on" we tend to let our mind latch onto what's familiar. The thing is, the "borderland" of which we spoke earlier, the dimension we enter in deep prayer, is not familiar.

As the barrier between "here" and "There" becomes thinner, there are some things that can unnerve us.

First, there is simple boredom. We're doing everything right! Why isn't anything happening?! Sooner or later we realize we need to get past considerations of "doing it right" and "something happening," and simply Be, in the Presence of the Omnipresent God Who is there, even if I don't "feel anything." If I trust in the fact that He is, indeed, there, and if I then abandon myself to His Presence, my awareness will grow on its own. This will bring with it unfamiliar sensations.

Second, our heightened awareness of the Presence of God may produce in us a great hunger and longing to propel ourself ever further "out" from terra firma. This can produce in us the same apprehension we might feel when, going swimming in the ocean, we approach the point when we have swum farther out than we ought. In both cases, the wise course is to turn around and head back.

Third, as our interior vision sharpens, we behold the sheer vastness of

God and His "neighborhood." It is, by definition, too much to take in, and we have not yet learned that we don't have to try.

> *A certain brother inquired of Abbot Pastor, saying: What shall I do? I lose my nerve when I am sitting alone at prayer in my cell. The elder said to him: Despise no one, condemn no one, rebuke no one, God will give you peace and your meditation will be undisturbed.*
>
> --From the Verba Seniorum.

Heaven and Earth are connected. In like manner, our behavior and attitudes as physical people affect our condition as spiritual people. So, our physical life and spiritual life should become consistent.

Our life "in the world" revolves around our interactions with people. These interactions produce most of our stress, and hence most of our distraction in prayer. After all, what workday stress would we have if it weren't for deadlines, policies and planning disagreements—all of which are generated by people: bosses, clients and co-workers? What domestic stress would there be without our spouses, children, neighbors and creditors? What personal stress would there be without apprehension, anticipation, animosity or regret?

These things, unsurprisingly, drive us to try to repair the past or organize the future. And we wind up doing it in the quiet time we've reserved for sitting with the Lord.

Freeing ourself from this sort of distraction is not as difficult as it seems. Most of the battle is won when we simply forgive.

There is incredible power in forgiveness. We don't need a reason to forgive. The other person doesn't need to earn or deserve it, and we don't need to wait until he does.

We are told to forgive others as God forgives us (see Ephesians 4: 32); not as some sort of quid pro quo, but as our response to God's example of how to live a victorious life in Him. After all, we don't deserve to be forgiven, and there is no justification we could make before God as to why He should forgive us. He just does, out of sheer Grace propelled by Love. When we follow His example and do the same, we are flooded with peace. The anger and resentment we were carrying around, leaves. And Love, God's own Love, fills the now-empty space; and love casts out fear (cf. 1 John 4: 18a).

As the elder advised the young brother, this dynamic will free the spirit, enable peace and place us in the way of God, Who will lead us into undisturbed meditation.

Psalm 100: 4 tells us we should enter God's gates with thanksgiving, and His courts with praise. No wonder! Entering the Presence of the Lord is a joyful, exhilarating experience. Even when we're convicted of sin, and go before Him in contrition, He is quick to reassure us and cleanse us. When we, in turn, forgive, we draw ever more proximate to Him, thus being filled with joy, released from the distraction that interior discomfort brings and becoming free to join Him in the Now.

Fear and apprehension are distractions. They disturb our peace and fragment us. They take us out of the *Now* into the "what happened then," or the "what might happen, if..." What we want to be is composed and peaceful. So, we need to allow ourselves to abandon all the stuff that's clamoring for our attention and become composed in the place where we are.

Being Here and Now

As we have discussed, we need to *be where* we are, *when* we are. We've spoken of inhabiting the when, the present moment, but it is also true that at any given moment we are *somewhere*.

Often, the two don't connect. Certainly they're objective facts, but just like being truly present in the when, we need at the same time, in the same moment, to be present in the *where*.

How often, when we sit quietly somewhere, do we think about being somewhere else? Our mind fills with images of places we have been, will be or would rather be. Objectively, we are where we are—but subjectively, we are not present to it.

This may in fact not even occur to us. After all, "I am where I am" is not something we ordinarily go around repeating to ourselves. It is not a momentous concept. It is, in fact, so un-momentous, so commonplace, we may have actually missed it; never looked at it; never been aware of any impact it may have had on us.

For instance, are you sitting still as you read this? Actually, you're not. Like all of us, you're clipping along through space at a brisk 67,000 miles per hour. As if that weren't enough, you're doing it while sitting on a big ball that is, itself, spinning you around at about four thousand miles per hour.

Yet, there you are, sitting "still," not having to do a thing as the universe propels you from place to place at enormous speeds. Does any of this affect your daily life? No. That's because you are gravitationally attached to the planet in such a way that its headlong flight through space does not consciously affect you. Wherever the planet goes, you are where you are, when you are.

If you stop to think about it, this is aptly iconic of composition of place. We already are *where* we are, and we are here, now. It simply remains for us to be still and be in the moment.

Doing the stuff

First, get comfortable. Sit in your favorite place, in your favorite chair, and relax.

You want to clear the stresses and tensions of the day away, and you can do this by breathing deeply, from the diaphragm, filling your lungs from the bottom up, relaxing your back and shoulders, the way singers do. Exhale the same way, from the bottom up. If you've ever been in a choir or taken voice lessons, this will already be familiar to you. As you exhale, you'll find the tension leaving you and you'll settle even more comfortably into your chair. Your mind should be relaxed but attentive, without tension or strain. You should find your breathing lengthening and slowing down. Don't push anything, don't make yourself hyperventilate, for instance. Just keep everything relaxed and natural.

Whenever your mind feels like it's becoming unfocused or distracted, just say the Lord's Name, "Jesus," relaxing into the present place and moment. As the Presence of the Lord grows more apparent to you, and you discover the surprising truth that the Name of Jesus will, actually, dispel the day's tension and anxiety, you will be prepared to pray.

We've already touched on the Jesus Prayer, but for further exploration, Fr. Archimandrite Jonah Mourtos, a monk of Mount Athos, has written an excellent essay on the subject. You can find it at: http://www.orthodox.cn/catechesis/20051216prayerheart_en.htm

FIFTEEN: DISPONABILITY

Disposition, Recollection, a Listening Ear

The whole point of this discussion has been to bring us to a place of *being at God's disposal*, which is what being *disponable* is all about.

For most of us, the word "prayer" means, in one way or another, "talking to God." If we are composed and attentive, this is largely a matter of "flow-through."

For instance, In the Liturgy we say things to Him that are printed out in front of us. Hopefully, we are not just "reading aloud," or "making the proper response at the proper time." If we are properly engaged, we will become part of the Liturgy and it will become part of us. Our words will join with the priest's words. They will *flow through* us, in an ebb-and-flow between nave and chancel, between Altar and Throne, Heaven and earth.

At home, we're usually asking Him for things. When we aren't asking, when things are going well, when our spirit is particularly buoyant, we may break into praise and thanksgiving: the Holy Spirit will *flow through us.*

Or, when we're alone and just feel the need to talk to someone, we may go over our day with the Lord, or even call out our step-by-step to Him as we tinker with an engine or a carpentry project or a recipe. People who don't know any better would look at us and say we're "talking to ourselves." But we're not. We're talking to God. And why not? It isn't like God isn't here, or isn't listening.

It hardly ever occurs to us, though, that He might talk back; or that if He did, that we'd be able to hear Him; that here, in our late age, in our climate-controlled house or apartment with the clocks on the wall and lunch in the microwave, our own "speak Lord, your servant is listening" (1 Samuel 3:9), would actually receive a response. Yet, why not? "Jesus Christ is the same yesterday, today and forever" (Hebrews 13: 8). God is as available today as He has ever been. What we want to do is to enter the dynamic of that availability, and let Him make us similarly available to Him.

Disposition: "It's all in your attitude..."

Whatever we hope to accomplish, we first need to want it. Do we want God? Do we want Him above everything else? Are we willing to walk a different path than those around us? to risk being thought of as unconventional?

> Now great multitudes went with Him. And He turned and said to them, "If anyone comes to Me and does not hate his father and mother, wife and children, brothers and sisters, yes, and his own life also, he cannot be My disciple. And whoever does not bear his cross and come after Me cannot be My disciple. For which of you, intending to build a tower, does not sit down first and count the cost, whether he has enough to finish it— lest, after he has laid the foundation, and is not able to finish, all who see it begin to mock him, saying, 'This man began to build and was not able to finish'? Or what king, going to make war against another king, does not sit down first and consider whether he is able with ten thousand to meet him who comes against him with twenty thousand? Or else, while the other is still a great way off, he sends a delegation and asks conditions of peace. So likewise, whoever of you does not forsake all that he has cannot be My disciple.
> (Luke 14: 25-33)

Are we, when push comes to shove, prepared to see even that which and those whom we love most as obstacles to our salvation?

Remember the young man who approached the Lord. telling Him he wanted to follow Him, but first he had to bury his father? Here was the Lord's answer:

> *Then He said to another, "Follow Me." But he said, "Lord, let me first go and bury my father." Jesus said to him, "Let the dead bury their own dead, but you go and preach the kingdom of God."*
> (Luke 9: 59-60)

This falls harshly on the ears of us, who live in a society where those without God glumly reassure each other that their departed loved ones are "in a better place." No such pretense for Jesus. The young man is challenged to hate the ways of his Godless family for the sake of the Kingdom of God.

The Lord tells us we must "count the cost." The cost is precisely this:

> *Again, the kingdom of heaven is like a merchant seeking beautiful pearls, who, when he had found one pearl of great price, went and sold all that he had and bought it.*
> (Matthew 13: 45-46)

All throughout our lives we have been taught to hang onto things. We are taught that "what's mine is mine," and that "what's mine" determines what I'm worth as a person.

Jesus presents a completely different life to us. Notice, I didn't say, "way of life." Our contemporaries adopt and discard "ways of life" as if they were simply changing clothes. What the Lord is talking about is a complete change of attitude—a change of disposition—to a sacrificial life that is willing to abandon everything else for His sake.

Actually, this isn't as traumatic as it sounds. As we progress along the Path of the transformed life we find our attitude and tastes changing. We find ourselves no longer liking some of the things we used to like; no longer admiring some people whom we used to admire; even actually despising things we used to covet. At the same time we find ourselves loving, and even spending time in the company of, people we used to think of as inconsequential. In fact, with our newfound attitude, we might even find that, in the society we used to inhabit, we ourselves might now be thought of as inconsequential....

> *Now behold, one came and said to Him, "Good Teacher, what good thing shall I do that I may have eternal life? "So He said to him, "Why do you call Me good?[b] No one is good but One, that is, God. But if you want to enter into life, keep the commandments" He said to Him, "Which ones?" Jesus said, "'You shall not murder,' 'You shall not commit adultery,' 'You shall not steal,' 'You shall not bear false witness,' 'Honor your father and your mother,' and, 'You shall love your neighbor as yourself.' The young man said to Him, "All these things I have kept from my youth. What do I still lack?" Jesus said to him, "If you want to be perfect, go, sell what you have and give to the poor, and you will have treasure in heaven; and come, follow Me." But when the young man heard that saying, he went away sorrowful, for he had great possessions.*
> (Matthew 19:16-22)

Turning away from an old life to a new one, however rewarding that new one might be, is a critical step. If we decide to follow the Lord, He will turn us into an entirely new person. We need to count the cost.

Having counted the cost, if we're still asking, "Where do I sign up?" the answer is that we sign up interiorly. We *dispose ourself* to set foot upon the Path and follow the Lord where it leads.

Father James Rosselli

Recollection: Building and living the inner life

An essential element of disponability is interiority. Remember the Kingdom of God within, and building our "cell" inside of it?

If we are "recollected," we are "recalled" to that interior cell, to that condition of prayerful peace that's so essential to our contemplation. Another advantage: that interior cell is portable.

> *A certain elder said: Apply yourself to silence, have no vain thoughts, and be intent in your meditation, whether you sit at prayer, or whether you rise up to work in the fear of God. If you do these things, you will not have to fear the attacks of the evil ones.*
>
> --From the *Verba Seniorum*

Recollection is not some distant, other-worldly business where we're lost to everything around us. To the contrary, a lack of interior distraction brings the things around us into sharper focus, and makes us more effective at the exterior things we have to do.

Not just for "meditation"

Recollectedness does more than simply reinforce our interior prayer: it reinforces our ability to carry our prayer life out into "the world," to carry our interior cell around with us into varieties of not-otherwise-prayerful situations.

The approach of many of the Desert Fathers is illustrative. Having woven their baskets, they would go into the busy marketplace in Alexandria to sell them. The place was crowded, with all the noise, clamor and smells of a place full of busy commercial stalls and the traffic of animals and people through the narrow streets. Nevertheless, the monks were able to maintain their attitude of prayer. Their interior cell remained unbreached.

There are "practical" advantages to this: when we are interiorly at peace we are better equipped to think before we speak and to take a closer, sharper look before we act. Our speech and actions thus become more efficient, and so more helpful to the people around us.

Spiritual disciplines aren't just "spiritual." They pervade and elevate everything we do. Things get done faster when we're not rushing. The less tense we are, the more actually focused we are—so more gets accomplished.

A stable interior life produces interior calm. This calmness directs our effort to the thing at hand rather than to all the normal, empty and useless "stress reactions" we might otherwise have. This is the principal behind the famous "work is prayer, prayer is work" ethic of the Benedictines. We are told in Colossians 3: 23,

> *And whatever you do, do it heartily, as to the Lord, and not to men.*

God has put us where we are that we might be useful to those around us. Entrepreneur, management or labor, educator or entertainer, public servant or private philanthropist, (or, for that matter, monk or cleric). He has arranged for us to be able to contribute to the stability and prosperity of the society around us. He wants us to be reliable and competent, credible ambassadors of His Kingdom.

A recollected character enables us to, as we become absorbed in our work, become thereby absorbed in the Lord; and as we offer the tasks at hand to God, we find that they become more than simply, "tasks." They become movements of Grace.

Once I'm recollected, then I can listen.

A Listening Ear: Getting past the noise

We live in a very noisy age. Booming sound systems in passing cars rattle our windows. TV sets upset our homes. Rock bands fill what used to be our meditative moments at church. I've even stopped for gas and found a video screen at the pump, blaring advertising at me while I was filling the tank!

God is here, and as always He is speaking to us. It almost seems, though, that the society in which we live is dedicated to drowning Him out..

> *And he said, "Go forth, and stand upon the mount before the Lord." And behold, the Lord passed by, and a great and strong wind rent the mountains, and broke in pieces the rocks before the Lord, but the Lord was not in the wind; and after the wind an earthquake, but the Lord was not in the earthquake; and after the earthquake a fire, but the Lord was not in the fire; and after the fire a still small voice.*
> (1 Kings 19: 11-12)

The noise of our clamorous world isn't going to go away, any time soon. Like the monks in the Alexandrian marketplace, we need to learn an alternative way of listening, an interior way, with what I have heard called "the ears of the heart."

The difficulty with this is that we have trained ourselves to deal with noise in ways that discourage the development of this essential interior faculty. For one thing, we spend lots of time creating it. Almost everyone has a TV set, and almost all of these TV sets are on and blaring whether anyone is watching them or not. When we're not watching TV, we're plugged into a portable radio or MP3 player, or blasting away at some video game.

We do these things specifically to distract ourselves, because a society that operates at toxic stress levels drives us to do what we can to distance ourselves from it. The problem is, usually it's just a matter of trading one kind of stress for another: most of television alternates between aggressive advertising and dehumanizing program content. Much of what passes for "music" in our culture is little more than shouting backed up by loud background noise. Even what we've been conditioned to think of as "comedy" is mostly just one vulgarity piled on another.

The transformed life involves developing a whole different lifestyle: one that finds peace in silence.

The power of silence

There are, broadly, two kinds of thinking: exterior and interior. Exterior thinking is concerned with the pragmatic matters of home and work. Interior thinking draws me inside myself.

This latter interiority takes a bit of getting used to, because for most of us, the world's noise and clamor has made "myself" a study in defensiveness. We equate silence with "nothing going on," and become uneasy. The untransformed mind soon comes under attack by the enemy, getting filled with images it doesn't want to see and thoughts it doesn't want to think.

Yet, to the transformed mind, a mind whose habit is to dwell on God and the things of God, silence is a blessing. We welcome being thrown back on ourselves, because it gives us an opportunity for introspection and for conversation with God. It develops our interior ear, our capacity to hear God whispering in the stillness.

"The Rules," and beyond

But do I really want to hear that still, small Voice? It is one thing to want to serve God, and quite another to hear how He wants us to serve Him.

For many, if not most of us, serving God is a matter of doing our best at what we do and following "the rules." We know, broadly, the sort of life God wants us to lead, we know we're supposed to go to church, give to the poor and live up to bunches of other "supposed to's," and as best we can we try to follow them. God's Will is in the Owner's Manual, after all, and if we follow it we'll be okay.

I think there is a time when we're all like that, as indeed there should be. "Following the rules" is what lays our spiritual foundation, just as the Old Testament of the Law laid the foundation for the New Testament of Grace. If we keep on following the rules, and in the process develop a habit of prayer and Bible study, we will indeed be okay. Sooner or later, however, if we are faithful in these things, God will lead us to want more. The Holy Spirit will engender in us a desire for an immediate, intuitive relationship with God. Sooner or later—"later" is fine, it's all in God's time—we wind up here: listening for that Still, Small Voice.

"Here" can be a scary place. How prepared are we to actually say, "Father, not my will be done, but Yours?" The last time Jesus said that, He got crucified. (cf. Luke 22: 42)

Of course, Jesus was God the Son, and we're not. With us, there's a fresh onion to be peeled back with every step along the way.

Mercifully, we never really quite know where along the way we are. The beginner doesn't realize how far he still needs to go, develops some facility in the spiritual life, and soon sees himself as an elder. The elder sees Eternity, and knows himself to be a beginner. God leads us at our own speed. Wherever we are along the Path is just fine, as long as we stay on it.

Certainly, there are rules. But as they are internalized, they lose their "do this, don't do that" character. At the last, rules exist because the creation has structure. If the rules are Godly, they will mirror that structure, because God created it. Here, you might want to re-read the section on Prudence.

Trust

The key to developing a listening ear, as it is to Disponability itself, is trust. Practicing silence is not an easy thing, in the beginning. We are so used to noise, to distraction, to not really being alone with ourself and confronting our situation, that there may even be a mild panic reaction when we do it. But, remember, this is just another wheelbarrow we need to climb into.

We know that God is on our side, that He loves us and desires to fit us for Eternity in accordance with the fulfillment of the nature He gave us, our vocation, our "noetic self." With each step along the way there is a fresh metanoia, and a fresher, larger cast to the process of Theosis. We don't need to worry about our willingness to know and follow God, because if we persevere along the Path the Holy Spirit will increase that willingness within us. It is such a gentle process, we might not even feel it happening until one day we notice that our disponability has matured a little: yet another occasion to give thanks!

Father James Rosselli

Ego, ambition, deception and availability

The things that happen in our life in response to our desire to know God's Will are ever encumbered by our ego's interference. As we proceed along the path of Theosis, ever more freely and willingly seeking God's will, the plans we find ourselves formulating will proceed in a more orderly way. Our prayers, too, will bear more fruit, because we will be planning and praying more in accordance with God's Will and less in accordance with our own.

No matter where we are along the Path, if we are faithful and persevering we are in the right place. The deepening process is not ours, but God's. Our part is to continue to be available to Him.

God's response to our availability varies widely from person to person. Not many of us see visions or hear voices. In fact, things like visions and voices are among the enemy's favorite deceptions. Any such incident should be reviewed with our spiritual director or counselor. That's not to say that dreams, visions or voices should immediately be discounted, but they should definitely be subject to confirmation.

> *To one of the brethren appeared a devil, transformed into an angel of light, who said to him: I am the angel Gabriel, and I have been sent to thee. But the brother said: Think again—you must have been sent to somebody else. I haven't done anything to deserve an angel. Immediately the devil ceased to appear.*
>
> --From the *Verba Seniorum*

God ordinarily speaks to us by ordering the events of our life. We all want to serve God. We would all like to do "great things" for Him. God, however, does not need us to do anything for Him. He puts us here to do things for others, and what He wants from us may not be the same as what we want for ourselves.

For example, a priest who is a compelling speaker may never find himself addressing conference crowds, but may wind up preaching in a small, obscure parish, somewhere. It may not be what he expects of himself, but it's what they need and what the Lord wants for them. A gifted musician may not ever become a major Christian album and touring artist, but may simply find that his God-given niche is in his parish music ministry. It seems frustrating, like we "could be doing so much more," and we may even wonder "what we've done wrong." But neither of these is the point.

Ambition is natural to us. The question is, in what direction is my ambition pointed? "I could do so much good if I were (a billionaire / an in-demand conference speaker / a famous Contemporary Christian musician / etc.)" are certainly all true statements. And maybe that's even where the Lord wants us. But maybe it isn't.

> *For I say to you that God is able to raise up children*
> *for Abraham from these stones.*
> (Luke 3: 8c)

By the same token, He is able to raise up from the same stones billionaires, famous musicians and conference speakers. I might be one of them. Or I might not. Where my natural gifts, coupled with my ambition, might take me if I were striving for fame and fortune in the world, is not the issue. The issue is where God, Who equipped me with those gifts in the first place, wants me.

My ambition is properly directed to the Lord, Himself, that I might be and become ever more and more available to Him. As part of this, I should seek to put my own ambitions and strivings on hold, lest my ambition be a creature of vanity rather than Godliness. Believe me, it isn't all that easy to tell the difference! As my interior peace grows and I become more immersed in God and in availability to Him—as my listening ear becomes more acute—God's ambition for me will supplant my ambition for myself, and I will be guided by Him in the way He would have me go.

PART SIX: CONVERSION OF MANNERS

Custody of Mind, Custody of Eyes, Custody of Hearing, Custody of Speech, Custody of Self.

> *For if anyone is a hearer of the word and not a doer,*
> *he is like a man observing his natural face in a mirror;*
> *for he observes himself, goes away, and immediately*
> *forgets what kind of man he was. But he who looks*
> *into the perfect law of liberty and continues in it, and*
> *is not a forgetful hearer but a doer of the word, this one*
> *will be blessed in what he does.*
> (James 1: 23-25)

~ ~ ~

Our goal is to become a whole person, balanced in body, mind and spirit. Interior transformation produces exterior transformation. The two go hand in hand.

Our prayer life is not a flowering, but a planting. It flowers as God responds to our petitions and in the transformation of our behavior.

That's because our maturing interior life will reveal itself in a maturing exterior life. This will be most apparent to us in our attitude toward, and approach to, the behaviors to which sin has made us accustomed. This is another reason maintaining an active Church life is so vital: it keeps us grounded.

Any good self-improvement program can make me a nicer, more forthright, more confident person, but it is only the process of Theosis that can make me Godly. As we have discussed, the process of Theosis incorporates my willing co-operation with the changes God brings about in me. So, as my awareness and attitudes change, the Holy Spirit prompts—and helps--me to change my behavior.

The non-Scriptural quotes that follow are all from the Verba Seniorum, unless otherwise noted.

SIXTEEN: CUSTODY OF MIND

--*The Phronema. Spiritual ambition.*

...for as he thinketh in his heart, so is he.
(Proverbs 23: 7a, KJV)

The mind is where we encounter and evaluate everything; so much so that often, as in this verse, the Bible equates the "mind" and the "heart" when speaking of centrality.

The transformed life requires a stable mind. By this I mean a mind which is firmly rooted in sound doctrine, and focused on reality. To put it bluntly, there's a lot of nonsense out there. Some of it is the product of human vanity, some of it is the unvarnished product of hell. All of it can be misleading, even enticing, and can lead us, if we aren't careful, into unproductive and even counterproductive places.

The world has one way of thinking, the Kingdom another. Worldly thinking references myself, and Kingdom thinking references God. This sounds simple, but it really isn't. The most pestilent of heresies invoke the Name of God. The most obvious of temptations invoke His Grace. The first temptation in the Garden, to which we have so often referred in this discussion, presented itself as a high-minded, and even holy, opportunity to "be like God." Things like this lead us away from what God has actually said, and into suppositions based on the logic of mammon.

Misleading thinking involves a reversal of order: instead of applying the things of God to our personal logic, we apply our personal logic to the things of God. Thus, the things of God are present, but they have been placed in the wrong order of precedence.

For instance, I once knew of a churchman whose family had been among the founders of the very Christ-and-Scripture-loving Protestant congregation to which he belonged. This man was a pillar of his church and of his community, blessed with a loving and devoted wife and family and Christian business partners. In short, there was very little in this man's life that did not edify and support him. For all this, it came to light that he was having an affair with a woman in the same congregation, of equally good family and equally well-respected. She was even a friend of his family and a frequent visitor to their home.

These were the last two people one would ever suspect of carrying on an adulterous relationship. His logic: "This makes us happy, and God wants us to be happy." Her logic: "Since we have physically consummated our relationship, we have become one flesh. We have, therefore, married each other and have every right to be together."

Now, this may seem absurd, and even ridiculous. The thing is, they were absolutely serious. They had fallen prey to the logic of the enemy of our souls who, just as he did in the Garden, took a desire, pointed it in the wrong direction, and made the direction seem acceptable.

Before we scoff at these two (who have since, blessedly, repented), we need to think of all the times we ourselves have used a "convenient logic" to justify an action which we later regretted. Wasn't it easy? That's what makes it so dangerous.

We need to guard our mind, to "keep custody" of it, so that when we are tempted by the logic of mammon we will be able to recognize and reject it.

The Phronema

The Phronema, the "Orthodox mindset." is the means by which we discern Truth from falsehood; what is Godly from what is merely our own wishful thinking.

Here again, I'm going to stress the importance of ancient and sound doctrine, of immersing ourselves in the thinking of the Fathers and using that to guide our approach to the Scriptures and to life in general. You'll find a Recommended Reading list at the end of the book, and I hope you'll profit by it. Don't just limit yourself to my little list, however—use it as a guide to recognize sound writing and explore on your own from there.

As you read in the Fathers, you'll notice something surprising: They didn't always agree with each other. Sometimes. their disagreements were quite strenuous. Witness for instance, the tensions between the ancient Antiochian (predominantly Literalist) and Alexandrian (predominantly allegorical) schools of Biblical exegesis. The Church recognizes a symmetry and a symbiosis between the two approaches, but would never have had a chance to, without those arguments and discussions.

Or, regard the life of Abbot Arsenius of Scete, who was so penitential that he would fall on his face before visitors, considering himself unworthy to look upon them, since they were human and therefore icons of Christ. Compare this with the life of Abbot Joseph, also of Scete, a charismatic who uttered the famous verbum, "Why not simply become fire?" Different men, yes, with two radically different Rules of life—but with the same foundational mindset.

It is reported that there were fistfights at the Council of Nicaea!

With all this, then, where is the commonality from which we can discern the Phronema?

Believe it or not, it's right there, in those very incidents. The fact that the early Fathers argued is less important than the basis from which they argued. Reading them, one detects a constant thread, a consistent point of view, for all that that point of view was being applied differently to different specific matters. And while the arguments over specific matters are interesting, it is the point of view that we read the Fathers to absorb, not the arguments.

As we read the sayings and discourses of the Church through the Conciliar Period, the period of the seven great and holy ecumenical councils, we find our mind beginning to run along the same channels: we begin to acquire the Phronema. As we read further, in the writings of those who have steeped themselves in this Holy Tradition, we mature in the Orthodox Mindset. We may formulate arguments of our own—but we will find ourselves, like the Fathers, formulating them according to a certain sort of spiritual / epistemological pattern that draws us deeper into Christ and His Church, that makes Scripture come alive with greater clarity.

To absorb oneself in the Church is to absorb oneself in—and thus to absorb—the Theanthropic dealings of God with men. Our minds, after all, are formed by our studies. This, however, isn't even "study." Patristics scholarship is a noble undertaking, to be sure, but we aren't talking here about formal study, but about simply sitting comfortably and reading at leisure, absorbing as we go.

To clarify, the Phronema is not acquired by setting pen to paper and analyzing the statements of the Fathers, systematically seeking to isolate a common thread. Trying to do it that way will only make what you're looking for more elusive. Immersion in the Fathers is a matter of absorption, not analysis. You may never remember an exact quote, or even where the inexact one came from. It doesn't matter. What matters is that your spirit is transformed in the reading, and that your eyes are thereby opened to the expanded reality viewed by the Fathers—the Theanthropic Reality that is the living home of the Church.

Custody of the Mind is rooted in and grows with consistency with the Church and her legacy. This consistency is the way to a clear mind in Christ and is key to avoiding the waywardness that would distract us.

Spiritual ambition

One enemy of a clear mind is the temptation to strive after God in the flesh. This is easier than it would seem, particularly for clergy, monastics and ministering lay people. We can become so wrapped up in what we are doing that, gradually, we are not so much serving Him as serving our desire to "advance" in His service, much as we would "advance" in a worldly occupation.

We are told in Romans 8:7 that, *The mind that is set on the flesh cannot obey God*. The enemy, though, is ever eager to turn our minds back upon ourselves; to get us to strive in ourselves and to immerse ourselves, without even realizing it, in pride in our strivings; so that our "striving after God" becomes a matter of ambition, and gradually replaces God, Himself, as our focus.

Yet another elder said: If you see a young monk by his own will climbing up into heaven, take him by the foot and throw him to the ground, because what he is doing is not good for him.

Remember that *verbum* from before? Beware of spiritual ambition.

We are not fitted for Heaven by using the tools of the world. The "spiritually ambitious" wish to "advance" along the Path as quickly as possible, and strive for holiness before God as if they were, as we said, striving for a promotion at work.

This sort of approach forms itself subtly, seeking to import a worldly mindset into the Kingdom through its victims and to cloud our understanding of the difference between worldly advancement and Christian advancement.

Spiritual ambition is centered on self and on stuff: this guy over here sees visions, so I want to see visions. That guy over there talks in tongues, so I want to talk in tongues. This other guy brags about how he has just come off a forty-day fast, taking nothing but fruit juice. So, I want to run out and do a forty-day fast of my own. I want to "get somewhere" in the spiritual life, to compile a list of "accomplishments," to be as impressive as the people by whom I am impressed; to "prove myself."

What I should be trying to prove is what is that good and acceptable and perfect will of God , the way to which is to not be conformed to this world, but be transformed by the renewing of your mind. (See Romans 12: 2).

Spiritual ambition is antithetical to following the edifying examples of elders in the Faith under competent spiritual guidance. It's different, but it can look frighteningly similar, and can even look the same. It isn't the same. It's the exact opposite, and it can't produce a healthy spiritual life. It can only retard, rather than advance, our progress. In one instance we look at a spiritual elder and want to be like him, so we try to pretend we are like him already. In the other instance, we are where we are and take the advice of the elder about how to get where he is--or where we should be.

There's another consideration: Maybe where he is, is not where God wants us to be. A sound and mature spiritual counselor will give us sound guidance—but that guidance won't be about how to "become him." It will be about how to become the "me" God wants me to be.

So, we need to build up our mind with sound, solid nourishment. Custody of mind is a matter of being vigilant about what we let into our minds. It's about discernment, so we can tell the difference between the good and the simply good-looking.

We can take a clue from how Treasury agents learn to spot counterfeit currency. They don't study the counterfeits, they study the real thing. They study it so closely, and become so intimately familiar with it that a counterfeit stands out like a neon sign. In the same way, we need to study the Faith: to become so intimate with the Scriptures and the Fathers, to have our minds so well-formed in the content of the Faith, that the unsound and harmful will, despite its best deceptive efforts, be unconvincing.

SEVENTEEN: CUSTODY OF THE EYES

Making Choices, The Killjoy, The Art of Seeing, False Heroism, The Importance of Grace

> *I will not set before my eyes anything that is base.*
> (Psalm 101: 3)

~ ~ ~

There is an art of Godly seeing, a way of looking out upon the world God created and seeing it as iconic, and the things in it as icons. We've already discussed the iconic mindset, and its ability to see the Hand of God in all created things, and to see in them expressions of the Divine Character. Custody of the eyes is rooted in this art. In this regard, Mathew 6: 22-23 tells us:

> *The lamp of the body is the eye. If therefore your eye is good, your whole body will be full of light. But if your eye is bad, your whole body will be full of darkness.*
>
> *If therefore the light that is in you is darkness, how great is that darkness.*

The things we look upon form us. By this I mean the choices we make about what our gaze lingers on and about how we choose to think about what we see.

Making choices

We all like to look upon beauty: beautiful people, sunrises, paintings etc. We have a choice as to whether we will look upon them appreciatively, covetously, resentfully, even pornographically.

Say, for instance, someone parks a Maserati or some other beautifully-made car on my street. I can admire it as a thing of beauty and a marvel of engineering, and it will fill me with joy. It would also be entirely natural to dream about having one—but if I can't afford the car I would certainly not be able to afford the upkeep, and reality would soon intrude. This would not need to affect my frank appreciation of the vehicle, and my admiration of its designers, and its presence would edify me nonetheless.

Or—I might begin to let my admiration of the car lead me not into appreciation that someone was able to design such a car, but into dwelling on the fact that I do not, and can not, own one: the frustrated longing of covetousness. This might further morph into resentment, even hatred, of the person who does own the car—someone I don't know, have never met and who is probably a perfectly nice person.

In this latter case, my joy is stolen. It has been eclipsed by vanity, which may have led me, interiorly, into injustice toward someone I don't even know. Rather than being edified, I am depressed—and, moreover, depressed over nothing.

It's the same with, say, a beautiful woman. Looking at her can elevate the senses or degrade them. It's entirely my choice. I can allow God to form me as someone who is appreciative of her as iconic of the intrinsic beauty that lies within all women, as potential mothers, or as a person I might like to meet and get to know. Or I can interiorly "bracket out" her humanity and regard her as an object for my use. In the former case, my senses can be elevated to a heightened appreciation of everything around me. In the latter, I'm simply frustrated and depressed.

We are, in "the natural," prone toward the latter reactions. In fact, our society forms us to have just these reactions. Cars and women are waved before our eyes not as transportation and people, but as status symbols. The reality is removed from them and is replaced by a fantasy that can never be lived up to. Even if we are "successful" by these standards, the "success" sooner or later turns to ashes: we were trying to live up to something that never existed in the first place, and it fell apart—usually accompanied by disappointment and bitterness.

From these fantasies, it is best to avert our eyes. It is the fantasies that lead us into the attitudes that steal our joy and ruin our appreciation of people and things as they are.

Father James Rosselli

The killjoy

Have you ever spent any time around someone who was never satisfied with anything he looked at? That beautiful woman's hair was out of place. Picasso painted lopsidedly. That sunrise was okay, but the morning was cold. The restaurant's décor was expensive and okay, but there was that smudge on the baseboard on the way to the kitchen.

Wasn't that guy a pain in the neck? Didn't he make you want to leave wherever you were, early?

If that's what he was doing to you, imagine what he was doing to himself. Nothing he ever looked upon was good enough. Whatever he looked at, however beautiful, all he saw was some imperfection. As a result, he crippled his capacity for joy.

Not only does this sort of person "set before his eyes that which is base," he makes base, at least for himself, whatever comes before his eyes. This is a gross misuse of the gift of sight.

The temptation is to see the killjoy as a shallow and vapid man who delights in exalting himself above everything around him. And he might be so. But it takes quite a bit of insecurity to get to such a place, and the source of that insecurity is usually a "God-shaped hole" in the center of his being that needs to be filled. On the other hand, it may be the result of a misplaced "Christian" zealotry that seeks to avoid sin by labeling all that comes before the eye as undesirable.

The art of seeing

Just as God wishes us to think clearly, He wishes us to see clearly.

Acts 9: 1-22 tells the story of the conversion of Saul of Tarsus, the arch-persecutor of the Faith who became Saint Paul. In verses 8-18 we see that when he met the Lord on the road to Damascus, he was struck blind and had to be led the rest of the way by his companions. Upon coming into contact with the Church, in the form of Ananias and his house-church, his sight was restored. Immediately he was baptised and remained to be taught. He then went on to become an apostle, the Apostolic Era's greatest evangelist and the human author of almost half of the New Testament.

This passage is iconic of how God would have us see. Saul's blindness brings graphically home to us the condition he was in before meeting the Lord. The restoration of his vision happened when he entrusted himself to the Church, his physical blindness an icon of his spiritual blindness, his newly-restored physical vision an icon of his newly-awakened spiritual vision. Moreover, we see that the two are not separate, but one and the same.

Saul-become-Paul acquired a whole new way of seeing, an "inner vision" that worked hand in hand with his "outer," physical vision. And things looked different.

Before, Saul could only see the Law as viewed through the eyes of the Temple authorities. In their view, these followers of the executed Jesus were dangerous heretics, criminal agitators who threatened the stability of the Jewish society by claiming their leaders had murdered their Messiah! And to claim that this man was the Messiah, in the first place! He healed on the Sabbath, plucked grain on the Sabbath, put the honest merchants and money-changers in the Temple precincts to flight—men who had valid reason—and paid a tax—to be there, assaulting them into the bargain! He acted as if He owned the Temple, calling it "His Father's House," making Himself equal with God! He spoke charitably of Samaritans, of all people, and uncharitably of the very authorities of the religion! And all of this to parade before the people, even the common and unlearned people, some prattle about "newness of life!" Clearly, this movement had to be stopped!

Saul's eyes were blinded by ugliness, his vision hedged in by recrimination. Paul's eyes opened upon beauty, and the vast, wondrous limitlessness of Eternity-made-now. It all started when he beheld the vision of Christ.

This is how God would have us see, not as Saul but as Paul. It begins by beholding, and keeping our inner vision fixed on, Jesus.

Our outer vision has the power to either defer to or interfere with this inner beholding. To keep custody of the eyes is to bring the interior and exterior faculties into co-operation with each other in the higher purpose.

False heroism

Looking upon sin can be a thrilling experience. Exposing ourselves to temptation can cast us in a daring light to ourselves: Warriors of the Faith, fearlessly challenging the adversary. And if we lose one now and then, so be it. We'll overcome. Next time...

Face it, sin is fun. If it weren't, temptation wouldn't be tempting. I don't mean all sin, just the ones we find appealing. These are the sins that. when we encounter them, we tend to linger over. "What harm could it do?" I may ask myself, "I'm only looking."

This may be a legitimate enough question, but my need to ask it indicates my awareness of a need to justify what I'm doing.

The problem with "only looking" is that it reinforces less-than-worthy behavior. You see, the problem with sin in the first place is that it seeks to form alliances with us. It solicits our consent as it seeks to become part of our life. The more we have to do with it, the more consent we give it and the more firmly it establishes itself as part of us. Averting our eyes from sin, particularly from those sins that cast themselves before us on the largest billboards, denies them the consent they seek. Accordingly, their influence over us grows weaker.

The importance of Grace

Sin is our enemy. It draws our focus away from Christ, back to us and our vanity. Temptation is sin's deception, a lie authored by the father of lies that represents our enemy as a friend. A bottle of booze or a bag of drugs present themselves to our eyes as consolation in tough times. Pornography beckons as relief from a stressful day. An unlocked door speaks to us of things inside that "we deserve," that "no-one will miss." A highway casino billboard assails our eyes with visions of a sharp player, sexually attractive and personally powerful in his luck, a mountain of chips in front of him, and a steely, knowing look in his eye.

All of these are not simply offers of opportunities to "unwind." They are invitations to excess; to a focus on vanity that draws us away from God and throws us back upon ourself and our fallen nature.

The blandishments are not simply offers of particular things or opportunities: they are attacks on our character. They are invitations to habits—habits that, at best, waste our time and desensitize us to sin; and at worst, desensitize us to the business of harming others.

If we do not turn our eyes away, we give the enemy an avenue to cloud our interior vision and distract it from remaining focused on the things of God.

Genesis 19: 12-26 tells the story of the angelic rescue of Lot and his family from the destruction of Sodom and Gomorrah. The angels gave the family strict instructions not to look back upon the scene, but to head straight out for the town of Zo'ar. Lot's wife, however, looked back. Who knows why? Maybe she wanted to take one last look at the place that had been her home. Maybe she just wanted to see the show. At any rate, she hung back behind Lot and her family, looked back, and was turned into a pillar of salt.

This was not some petty retribution on God's part. People familiar with the Dead Sea area and its heavy salt content remark that, in the presumably high winds generated by the angelic act, it is entirely plausible that Lot's wife could have been encased in salt. She stands there, in fact, to this day: a pillar of solid halite salt, in the figure of a woman, standing on Mount Sodom, looking back at where the city would have been, her back turned to Zo'ar.

We learn from this that God's warnings are not spoken in vain, in theory or as some silly "test." The angels well knew what would happen to someone who stood there watching the city's destruction. Their warning was about natural consequences, not about some, "Let's see if ya can do this..." imposed by the loving God Who had sent them on the rescue mission in the first place.

When we leave our "old life," we need to leave it and not "look back" upon it. "Nostalgia" for our untransformed days will only slow us down, and might even freeze us up, on our progress along the Path.

Returning to Genesis Three, we return to those two critical words, *she saw*. Eve did not keep custody of her eyes, and so was led into the sin that cast her and her husband from a state of perfection into the state of a newly-fallen nature.

God does not desire similar destruction for us. We are already fallen. The only next step down from here is hell. The remedy is available to us, if we will have it: God's Grace.

As we have discussed earlier, Grace is not something God "does." It is not an activity, something He created to express a benevolent nature. Rather, it is part of His Nature: an uncreated Energy. God is Love. And, even as our vanity is the active expression of pride, God's Grace is the active expression of Love. It is how God deals with us, and in fact with and through His whole creation.

Reflect for a moment on what happened after the expulsion from the Garden: not only did our first parents not, in a final and physical sense, die, but God permitted the entire creation to fall with them, just so they could live in it. This was as much an act of Grace as was the creation, itself.

In the fifth chapter of Paul's letter to the Romans, we read of God's Grace and how, in Christ, we are justified by it. Where sin threatens us, Grace is there to rescue us. Yet,

> *What shall we say, then? Shall we continue in sin that grace may abound? Certainly not! How shall we who died to sin live any longer in it?*
> (Romans 6:1)

Does this mean we can just quit sinning? Obviously, not. But...

> *My little children, these things I write to you so that you may not sin. And if anyone sins, we have an Advocate with the Father, Jesus Christ the righteous.*
> (1 John 2: 1)

To stand in Grace is to, in effect, "take the pressure off." It is an acknowledgment that our enemy is stronger than we are, that he preys on our greatest vulnerability: the fact that, in the moment, in our fallenness, we really want to grab the shiny object he dangles before us.

Our most potent weapon is, rather than to fight a battle we can't win, to stand behind Christ and let Him fight for us—and co-operate in the effort by averting our eyes.

Father James Rosselli

EIGHTEEN: CUSTODY OF HEARING

Credulity

> *Let no one deceive you with empty words, for because of these things the wrath of God comes upon the sons of disobedience. Therefore do not be partakers with them.*
> (Ephesians 5: 6-7)

~ ~ ~

What do we let inside of ourselves? The Lord tells us, in Galatians 5:9, that "a little leaven leavens the whole lump." So, what are we leavening our life with?

When we add yeast to dough, it doesn't just stay in one place. It becomes part of the mix, and acts throughout the whole loaf. In the same way, the things we let into our lives become part of us.

What we let in through our eyes and ears helps to form us into the kind of people we are. If we wish to advance in holiness, we will safeguard these "gates" into our character: we will "keep custody" of them.

There is a tendency among humans to take a certain amount of satisfaction in trading in the shortcomings of others. "Celebrity gossip" magazines, all of which apparently stay prosperous, crowd the shelves of our supermarkets. Our ears itch to hear "the latest" about one or another of our acquaintances, particularly if he or she is "having problems."

What is it that prompts our fascination with other peoples' business? is it an attempt to take our minds off our own? Is it a competitive urge to measure our spiritual progress against that of others? Perhaps it's an exercise in self-exaltation, as we learn we are "better off" in some way than someone else, particularly someone who is better-known or more accomplished than we are. After all, if Bob or Betty, or some famous person "has done something like that," how bad can I be?

The question we need to ask ourself is, how does this help? We are Christians. God wants to bless the world through us. How can we equip ourselves to do that if we let ourselves become traders in the things that degrade us?

What a waste of the finite time we have on this earth! We are where we are along the Path. We aren't better because someone else is worse or worse because someone else is better. God sees us as who we are individually, not in relation to others.

Gossip is more than just a waste of time, though. It is spiritually unhealthy. Comparing ourselves to others can birth a judgmental spirit within us. After all, if we absorb ourselves in the sins of others, aren't we claiming, consciously or unconsciously, some sort of moral authority over them?

By the same token, we can lapse into spiritual pretense. How often, for instance, has someone come to you and shared, in a conspiratorial voice and with gleaming eyes, that "poor (whoever) needs prayer for...," followed by a rendition of the unfortunate person's supposed lapses? Interestingly, these "spiritual sharings" never seem to get around to actually praying for the person.

Gossip is poisonous. It damages reputations, disturbs our peace and panders to a purely worldly and sensual desire to be "one up" on others. It encourages dishonesty, diminishes, even destroys, others and has even brought down congregations. Yet, it's so...tempting.

The solution to being drawn into this sort of vain conversation is to follow the Lord's advice:

> *Moreover if your brother sins against you, go and tell him his fault between you and him alone. If he hears you, you have gained your brother. But if he will not hear, take with you one or two more, that 'by the mouth of two or three witnesses every word may be established.' And if he refuses to hear them, tell it to the church. But if he refuses even to hear the church, let him be to you like a heathen and a tax collector.*
> (Matthew 18: 15-17)

People who come to us with juicy news about what "poor Bob, who is in need of prayer," has done are ordinarily more in need of help than Bob is. For one thing, it's almost certain that the "information" is inaccurate—and the "juicier" it is, the less accurate it is sure to be, so they have either let themselves become liars or have let themselves become involved in a lie. Even if the poison they are peddling is true, it's still poison. The gossips have ignored, or discounted, the Word of God in the matter—and are the ones who really need our prayers, that they may be set free from the gossip habit. For our part, we need to turn away from the temptation they offer.

I find the best way to deal with this is simply to ask, "How long ago did you take this up with Bob?" or, "What did Bob have to say about this, when you approached him?"

The conversation will end, and the gossip-monger will, hopefully, have taken note. I know of one Protestant minister who, having been approached in this manner after the Service, took the person who approached him gently by the arm, saying, "That's terrible! Let's go talk with (Name) about it right now." The gossip reportedly made excuses and fled, hopefully chastened.

A word of counsel, here: if before you do this there is any hint in you of relishing being "one up" on the gossip, don't do it. The idea is not to "teach the gossip a lesson," but to place the matter before Christ the Teacher.

Custody of hearing is like custody of the eyes: what we allow into our mind and our life affects us. We need to be careful of what we allow in, and discerning about what comes in unbidden.

Credulity

Why discerning? frankly, because the air of our culture is filled with misinformation. Much of what passes for "information" can be anything from misunderstanding to misinterpretation to plain lying.

Sadly, it is our professional information-givers who are among the worst offenders in this. Time after time I have been to events which were covered by the media, the reports of which bore little, if any, resemblance to the event. I have heard "summaries" of speeches politicians have given. When I later accessed the speeches themselves on, say, You Tube, the speaker turned out to be saying something entirely different, even completely opposite, to what the reporter reported.

We need to be careful about what we give credence to. Custody of hearing concerns more than simply guarding what we let into our ears, it concerns what we do with the stuff that barges in unbidden.

We are caught in an ethical crossfire when it comes to discernment. On one hand, we live in a cynical society. We've been lied to so many times, by so many people, about so many things, many of us just don't believe anything, anymore. On the other hand, as Christians we want to be able to trust, to give people the benefit of the doubt. So what do we do?

The Lord's counsel to His Apostles is no less valid for us:

> *Behold, I send you out as sheep in the midst of wolves.*

> *Therefore be wise as serpents and harmless as doves.*
> (Matthew 10: 16)

We need to be realistic about the world—it's the world. It is not run on Godly principles, but on vying for advantage. There isn't anything wrong with giving people the benefit of the doubt, we should treat everyone as someone who will behave and deal honesty. We need to listen closely and carefully, however, and with a clear mind, and not simply let what we're hearing on the outside be the determinant: it is the interior ear, the one with which we hear the Still, Small Voice, that needs to be engaged. When we have acquired the habit of being recollected in our listening, so that our interior ear and exterior ear work together, we will have acquired the habit of custody of hearing.

NINETEEN: CUSTODY OF SPEECH

Gossip, Vain Speech, Vainglorious Speech

> *If anyone among you thinks he is religious and does not bridle his tongue but deceives his own heart, this one's religion is useless.*
> (James 1: 26)

~ ~ ~

The Lord tells us in Matthew 15:11 that it isn't what goes into a man's mouth that defiles him, but what comes out of his mouth. We don't want to be hearers of evil speech—much less do we wish to be purveyors of it.

Custody of speech is among the most critical of the elements of our spiritual growth. We think in terms of language, express ourselves in terms of language and can either uplift or destroy someone's (or, for that matter, our own) life by means of language. Also, we who wear the name, "Christian," need to remember that we represent the Lord. A nonbeliever's impression of us could bring him closer to Christ, or drive him farther away.

There are so many ways in which our speech can become a stumbling block to ourselves and others...

Gossip

Just as we don't want to be spiritually impeded by hearing gossip, we must avoid becoming an impediment to others by speaking it. On the purely pragmatic level, there are few sources of information less reliable than gossip. It tends to be second-third-or more-hand, viewed at each stop through an individual emotional agenda and edited accordingly. In fact, it is more probable than not that the thing being gossiped about never happened. In institutional settings it is all too often the product of a deliberate (or eagerly-received) misinterpretation aimed at someone who is seen as "in the way" of some agenda.

> Even so the tongue is a little member and boasts great things. See how great a forest a little fire kindles! And the tongue is a fire, a world of iniquity. The tongue is so set among our members that it defiles the whole body, and sets on fire the course of nature; and it is set on fire by hell.
> (James 3: 5-6)

Don't think churches are immune to this. Like any other institutional setting inhabited by fallen human beings, there are those who are quite pitiless in the pursuit of what they view as noble goals. Churches are in fact quite vulnerable, indeed, to this, because the perpetrators see themselves as acting selflessly, for the good of all, and may thus be quite blind to the sensual "power rush" they are experiencing as they see their victim's reputation crumble.

Perhaps most frightening is the cumulative effect of the process, as one made-up "fact," rooted in some innocent, but conveniently-interpreted circumstance, piles on another. Inferences are drawn from some previous falsehood (a "half-truth" is a falsehood, after all), and another "fact" is born. Before long, the web of misinformation is woven so tightly that total falsehoods are accepted as "common knowledge" and there remains no way out for the person targeted.

The pertinent things that normally come to mind are, say, the Inquisition of the late Middle Ages or the "show-trials" in totalitarian countries. But they are commonplace right here in our own, "socially enlightened" age and places. Gleeful character assassination by evil school-children regularly drives their victims to suicide—or, increasingly, to murder. Executives see honorable careers they have spent a lifetime building, vanish because they are "in the way." Pastors are driven from parishes by vengeful parishioners who prefer retaliation to repentance over some sin the pastor preached against. Someone who is simply doing a superb job, and is as a consequence popular, may be viewed as "getting too powerful" by an insecure superior.

What all these things have in common is that the perpetrators often see themselves as selflessly serving noble goals that are greater than themselves. This is indeed "a course of nature set on fire by hell" and pursued by perpetrators who are themselves victims.

The worst consequence is not what happens to the victim, but to the perpetrator. Someone who has invested his own reputation in a lie is unlikely to repent. Indeed, the greater the damage he has caused, the more likely he is to wall himself off from the truth, and even to cause more damage in defense of his position. Tragically, this does nothing but place his soul in even greater jeopardy as he denies himself the relief of confession.

In my time on earth I have seen this sort of thing happen over and over, in a variety of environments, to individuals great and small, who have found themselves on the wrong side of someone else's agenda.

Now, we all have agendas. We are human, and can't help it. Custody of speech is perhaps our most effective means of keeping our agendas constructive of their purpose, and not destructive of the lives of others.

Of course, not all gossip issues in the dramatic. One of hell's great advantages is that gossip at the "minor" level is slowly corrosive of the perpetrator's soul. This is because traffic in gossip is traffic in the unreliable. To trade in it damages both us and our hearers: us, because it lowers our standard of what is real and true and encourages us in sloppy thinking; our hearers, because we thus help form them away from Godliness and a sound mind.

If I approach someone with news about some third party, it should either be in a mood of celebration of something good done by or for the person. or out of genuine concern for his welfare. At any rate, I should have the person's permission before proceeding.

We always need to approach the individual in question, and not simply retail what we have heard to all and sundry. If we are hesitant to do that, it's a pretty good indication that what we are considering is for our own vanity, not for his (or her) benefit.

"Do you mind of I ask a few people to pray with me, for you?" is a question that always needs to be asked. This permits the individual to set the boundaries of what he wants disclosed. It also gets my ego out of the way, as there is now a context for prayer and perhaps counsel that was not established by me.

Gossip is a deadly thing. It situates us, our mind and our spirit firmly in the world of Mammon, and has no good effect where it is shared. It is bad fruit from a corrupt limb that needs to be cut off.

Vain speech

> *You shall not take the Name of the Lord your God in vain; for the Lord will not hold him guiltless who takes His Name in vain.*
> (Exodus 20: 7)

Regardless of what we may hear on the golf course, the bowling alley and while watching sports, God's last name is not "dammit." And regardless of the enthusiasms encountered in various movies, "God d- - - !" is not an expression of approval, regardless of how it's used.

Consider for a moment the implications of calling upon God to damn something.

Let's say I hit my thumb with a hammer, and exclaim, "God, damn it!" What, precisely, is it that I am asking God to damn, that is, to send to hell? the hammer? What if I am successful, and the hammer vanishes? what happens next time I need it? My thumb? If the thumb vanished to hell it is true it wouldn't be a target, anymore, but it's also true that I might need it for other things in the future. The situation in general? Well, I'm part of the situation, so that puts me in hell with my thumb and the hammer, and who-and-whatever was involved in the carpentry project.

This would probably not be what I had in mind.

This sort of mindlessness, this casual calling upon God to damn something or other, is serious business. We may say, "Oh, I don't mean it, of course!" But then, why say it? "God, damn it!" is as much a prayer as any other. To be in the habit of using the expression as just another phrase in my vocabulary is to degrade prayer in general, and to diminish the Name of God in particular, in my life.

Moreover, it is a direct act of defiance of my position as a Christian in the midst of a world without forgiveness or any sense of the sacredness of the human person. It is my job to be, insofar as I am called to be, the presence of Christ to my surroundings. As much as is possible, I am to be an uplifting influence, an encouraging influence that will recognize, and thus help others to recognize, their noble estate before God. So we are told...

> *Let no corrupt word proceed out of your mouth, but what is good for necessary edification, that it may impart grace to the hearers.*
> (Ephesians 4: 29)

How often do we exclaim, "God, damn it!" when what we really mean is, "God, please fix it!" Why don't we just say that?

Something else we commonly hear is, "I swear to God!" Now, why would I have to do that? If I am someone whose word is good, if my "yes" means yes, and my "no" means no (Matthew 5: 37), why do I need to exert myself beyond my integrity? The Lord tells us, in this same passage, "Anything else is from the evil one."

Paradoxically, the enemy of our souls would have us continually swearing to God. This seems strange, considering the fact that we invoke the Name of God every time we do it. But consider: we are God's people, His ambassadors on earth. We are supposed to be upright, honorable people. But when we "swear to God," what we are saying, in effect, is "My word isn't really all that good, so I need to do this." What kind of representative of the Kingdom does that make me?

So, we're told in James 5: 12...

> *But above all, my brethren, do not swear, either by heaven or by earth or with any other oath.*

Couple this with the fact that, most of the time, when we blurt, "I swear to God," it doesn't mean anything. All we're doing is projecting a meaningless phrase into the empty air, while at the same time diminishing our own reverence for the Divine Name.

Invoking God is serious business. When we do it, we should be doing it toward a purpose, not just as some bundle of words. Empty speech about God doesn't do anything but diminish us and impede our growth in Him...

> *Therefore whether you eat or drink, or whatever you do, do all to the glory of God.*
> (1 Corinthians 10: 31)

Vainglorious speech

Finally, I'd like to say some things about vainglorious speech; you know, the kind you get from the guy who exhorts you to "claim your blessing." There are two verses these people use to anchor their speeches: Matthew 18: 19, that goes, "Again I say to you that if two of you agree on earth concerning anything that they ask, it will be done for them by My Father in Heaven;" and Mark 11: 24, which reads, "Therefore I say to you, whatever things you ask for when you pray, believe that you receive them, and you will have them."

Now, this sounds pretty good, doesn't it? Lifted out of the context of the rest of the Faith—like the exhortations to humility and disponability—God becomes our own personal magic vending machine. Just say the right words (always include "in the Name of Jesus," because John 14: 13 says, in effect."whatever you ask for in My Name, you'll get...") and blessings will rain down from the heavens so hard you'll need an umbrella!

The thing is, it doesn't work. And it doesn't work for a very good reason: it's unholy. I heard one "word of faith" preacher (I wish I could remember his name) carry it to its logical conclusion, one night, on the radio, when he said something like, "Up to now we've prayed, 'Thy Will be done.' Now, though, in this time, God would have us pray, 'My will be done!'"

The technical term for that sort of thing is, "thaumaturgy:" an attempt to access the power of God's Name for my personal use, to enable me to project my own personal will onto events. I even heard one of these guys preach, at one time, "God has given you the power to command Him!"

If you've been around for a while, I'm sure you've heard these, or similar, things. They aren't as widespread, anymore, because sooner or later the lie caught up with the liars and the people who had been sending them "seed faith" money (after all, doesn't Luke 6:38 tell us that if we give it will be given back to us abundantly?) ran out of money to send them.

This is the ultimate vanity, the ultimate taking of the Lord's Name in vain: to presume that I might be able to command Him.

Are the promises cited above, true? Of course they are. But they need to be contextualized within the rest of Scripture and the teaching of the Church. The promises are made to those who are committed to the transformed life: to those whose desire it is to be caught up into the Will of God, so that they may become vessels to bring forth His Will in the service of the Church and of our beleaguered planet. They are made to encourage us, to let us know that our work in Him will bear fruit—not to raise up magicians who believe they can send forth their word and thereby compel God.

> *Keep your tongue from evil and your lips from speaking deceit.*
> (Psalm 34: 13, quoted in 1 Peter 3: 10)

Yes, God cares for and will provide for us. He will, however do this according to His Will for us, for the advancement of our salvation and our preparation for the greater world to which we are destined. Our goal must be to pray according to God's Will, to be available to Him, to be conduits of His Will here in the earthly dimension.

Ultimately, to "pray in the Name of Jesus" is to pray for the things He wants: as His ambassadors, to declare that we are acting in His Name.

As we have discussed, the way we use language forms us. It puts together the concepts that guide us and these concepts determine how we approach life in the world. Custody of speech makes us conscious of our interior dialogue, and guides it toward holiness, by teaching us to guard, and submit to God. our exterior dialogue.

The Lord put it this way, in Luke 6: 45...

> *A good man out of the good treasure of his heart beings forth good; and an evil man ut of the evil treasure of his heart brings forth evil. For out of the abundance of the heart his mouth speaks.*

TWENTY: CUSTODY OF SELF

The Error of Quietism, Co-operation with God

Custody of the senses brings stability to our lives, and stability provides a platform for Theosis. A life based on the vagaries of emotion, on "how we feel," is frankly too busy compensating for its own chaos to accomplish much in the way of genuine spiritual growth.

Growth in the transformed life brings about consistency between our interiority and our exteriority, between what we profess and how we behave. This is essential, if there is to be peace between our convictions and our emotions. Without this peace, we are at war within ourselves and are too distracted by the warfare between body and mind to cultivate the spirit.

The object of Theosis is outlined in Ephesians 4:

> to come to the unity of the faith and of the knowledge of the Son of God, to a perfect man, to the measure of the stature of the fullness of Christ. (v. 13)

The next verse frames for us the opposite of this, the immature condition we should seek to outgrow:

> That we should no longer be children, tossed to and fro and carried about by every wind of doctrine, by the trickery of men, in the cunning craftiness of deceitful plotting... (v. 14)

The passage tells us, first, that this is accomplished within the Church:

> but, speaking the truth in love, (we) may grow up in all things into Him who is the head—Christ—from whom

> *the whole body, joined and knit together by what every joint supplies, according to the effective working by which every part does its share, causes growth of the body for the edifying of itself in love.* (vv. 15-17)

There is an old monastic adage that applies universally throughout the transformed life: "Before you lay down your life, first have a life to lay down."

The error of Quietism.

The Quietist error assumes that we can give to Christ that which we have not yet taken. If, for instance, I have not made up my mind to reform my speech, I can say, "Lord, I give you custody of my speech" all day and I will make little, if any, progress.

Quietism, like most error, begins with a good intent and then overextends it. It is, after all, God the Holy Spirit Who effects change in me. If I try to take the process over, I will do nothing but get in His way. Some have concluded that the way to avoid this is to contribute little, if any, effort of my own and simply pray that I may be acted upon: that my free will would be, in effect, overridden.

Now, God will do lots of things with me, but He will not override my free will. He didn't do it in the beginning, in the Garden, and He won't do it now.

It sounds good. After all, I'm a fallen creature and everything I do is imperfect. Why, then, not simply stop inputting my imperfect efforts, and instead rely on the perfect work of God?

At the very beginning, when I am seeking the transformation of my desires, praying for God to override my free will makes sense. He won't, of course, but praying this way convicts me of just how much of an impediment my own will is. It opens me to the transforming work of the Holy Spirit, and makes me more aware of—and hence makes it easier for me to confess—sin. I need to move on from this very beginning place, however, or I will never grow.

God didn't make me a variety of plant, without volition. He made me in the Divine image, with a virtually unlimited scope of activity and a sovereign will. Yes, He wants that will to be submitted to Him, to be at His disposal. But I cannot submit it if I don't have a handle on it.

The moral and ethical language of Scripture is active, not passive. It tells us that if we do things a certain way, a certain kind of fruit will proceed from it. *Depart from evil and do good*, we read in Psalm 34: 14, *seek peace, and pursue it.*

This is written in the active voice. It is telling us to do something. Can we do it? Not perfectly, and not without God's transforming activity within us. But we can decide to *depart*. We can decide to *seek*. These decisions are whose solution to sin is, "just stop sinning," which of course is impossible.

We don't "mature" to the point of taking over the whole affair; or, in fact, of "taking over" any of it. To the contrary, it's a life-long process of putting God ever more and more in charge. As we do this, however, a curious thing happens: walking in the Spirit becomes more and more "natural" to us, and our experience is one of becoming progressively more "in charge" of our life.

The transformed life is full of seeming paradoxes: the more we abandon to God, the more "ourself" we become; the more we commit to God, the freer we become. Far from being a diminution of self and an abandonment of volition, it is an enlargement of self and a transformation of volition. We become, simply, more.

Father James Rosselli

As we become more, our desires change accordingly. Our will becomes more consistent with God's Will. We "clean up our act," so to speak: not because we feel we have to, or should do, but because we want to.

And we find ourselves moving closer to that blessed condition where our life becomes a prayer; where, unabashed and unintimidated, we offer all we have and do, the good and the bad, to God, that He might increase us in the one and free us from the other.

There is nothing that is not prayer—or at least nothing that cannot be made a prayer.

God has given us intelligence, and curiosity to know the nature of things. The ultimate knowledge is that God is All in all, that He is involved in every thought, every action, every speck of dust that skitters across the road. Wherever we go and whatever we do, we are in His Presence. That means we can use the activities and circumstances of our life as connecting points, as occasions to reflect on life and its vagaries. Before long, if we pursue this, we will come to see life and its vagaries in light of God's preparation of us for Eternity, and they will become occasions for prayer.

Since all prayer--petitionary, contemplative, Liturgical, praiseful or lamentational—engages us with God, all prayer is transformative. The more we see the occasions of life as occasions for prayer, the more we allow the Holy Spirit to transform us.

Custody of self—of our eyes, of our ears, of our speech, of our character and its growth--begins with a desire to change. This desire is the fruit of a conscious decision that we want to serve God and not mammon. There thus ensues a conscious and deliberate effort to be Godly and to conduct ourselves in a Godly manner. This in turn encourages a habit of consciously submitting our thoughts and actions to God. The habit matures, until we find it has become part of our nature. It is then that we begin to experience co-operation with God, and an ever-maturing custody of self. It's the stuff of Theosis, and of the transformed life.

PART SEVEN: MARY, THE MOTHER OF GOD

An Important Personage, Mary as Icon, Mary as Intercessor, Mary and Virginity

> *My soul magnifies the Lord, And my spirit has rejoiced in God my Savior.*
>
> *For He has regarded the lowly state of His maidservant; For behold, henceforth all generations will call me blessed.*
>
> *For He who is mighty has done great things for me, And holy is His name.*
>
> *And His mercy is on those who fear Him From generation to generation.*
>
> *He has shown strength with His arm; He has scattered the proud in the imagination of their hearts.*

> *He has put down the mighty from their thrones,*
> *And exalted the lowly.*
>
> *He has filled the hungry with good things,*
> *And the rich He has sent away empty.*
>
> *He has helped His servant Israel,*
> *In remembrance of His mercy,*
>
> *As He spoke to our fathers,*
> *to Abraham and his seed forever,*
> (Luke 1: 46-55)

~ ~ ~

There are some who read this who will say, "Wow, he saved the best for last!" Others will say, "Aww, why did he have to go and spoil it?"

Just to set minds at rest (and, admittedly, some teeth on edge), this is not going to be a defense of "Marianism," at least not as I understand it. I have been in environments where very little emphasis is placed on Jesus except for the fact that He's Mary's Son; where the first recourse in prayer is to Mary, and where prayer to Mary is considered equivalent, or even identical, to prayer to God; where no Marianist claim, however outrageous, is considered too extreme (there was even a movement a while back to claim that Mary was "co-redeemer" with Christ!). All of this, however well-meant or piously intended, is simply heterodox and nothing I say here is intended to support it.

That having been said, this isn't going to be a defense of the "anti-Marian" positions, either.

It is axiomatic within the Church that the Church in Heaven and the Church on earth are one. It is also axiomatic that we come to a deeper understanding of this as we enter into a relationship with the Mother of God.

First, why the "Mother of God?" Wasn't God around before Mary?

The appellation comes from the Third Ecumenical (full-Church) Council in 431. The Council convened in order to deal with certain heresies. Some of these held that Jesus was not Divine from birth, but had "grown into" His Divinity at one point or another (adoptionism); others held that, while Jesus was indeed the Son of God, He was not God the Son (Arianism).

So, her person being an important presence in the Church, the question of what Mary should be called arose. Should she be called *Christotokos* (Mother of Christ), or *Theotokos* (Mother of God)? The latter, which was already widespread in the Church, was chosen as a definite statement against heresy: Jesus was the very Incarnation of the Second Person of the Holy Trinity, "true God from true God," as the Creed states, and was so from the moment of His conception.

Thus, Mary's title, "Mother of God," doesn't reference her as much as it does her Divine Son.

Okay, fine. But why enter into a "relationship" with her? Isn't a relationship with Jesus, enough?

This is a little like asking, "Why do I need a knowledge of how waves break? Isn't being able to balance on the surfboard, enough?"

The logical answer to this is, it depends on how intimate you want to become with the wave. A relationship with Mary only enhances our relationship with her Son. Mary's example speaks to us of the highest order of human Godliness, a Godliness rooted in the simplicity to which the transformed life aspires. Mary's life and witness are all about relationship with Jesus, about intimacy with God. Why shouldn't we wish to befriend her, to learn from her example?

An important personage

There is an idea in some circles that regard for the Theotokos is some invention of the Middle Ages, that she was not all that honored by the Early Church. Luke 11: 27b–28 is often offered in support of this notion:

> ...a certain woman from the crowd raised her voice and said to Him, "Blessed is the womb that bore You, and the breasts which nursed You!" 28 But He said, "More than that, blessed are those who hear the word of God and keep it!"

In these cases, verse 29 is seen as a rebuke to the exultant statement in verse 27. This, however, is simply a misuse of language. The Lord didn't say something like, "Instead of that," or "Rather than that," He said "More than that..." . The statement wasn't a rebuke of the woman's praise of the Lord's mother, it was rather a statement about the importance of action over admiration. Moreover, it was an optimistic response, implying that the woman was, herself, capable of this superior action.

In fact, Mary was an important and highly revered member of the Early Church, and the notion that she was just another bereft woman in the care of a family friend (in this case the Apostle St. John) doesn't mesh with the accounts of the people who were actually there.

Typical is this letter from St. Dionysius the Areopagite (see Acts 17: 34), who was converted and mentored by St. Paul himself, and subsequently became Bishop of Athens, one of the Church's first bishops. St. Dionysius visited the Holy Mother in Jerusalem, and

Father James Rosselli

wrote to St. Paul–who had, apparently, arranged the meeting--about it:

> *It is impossible for the human mind to grasp what I have seen not only with the eyes of my soul, but with my bodily eyes, too. I have seen with my own eyes the most beautiful and holy Mother of Our Lord Jesus Christ...That time was for me a time of supreme happiness. I thank the most high and most gracious God and the Divine Virgin, the great Apostle John, and thee (St. Paul) for having mercifully granted me such a great blessing.*

Saint Ignatius, later called the God-bearer, was the successor of St. Peter as Bishop of Antioch and is numbered among the greatest of the Church Fathers. While he was still a neophyte (a catechumen), studying under the Apostle St. John, he wrote this letter to St. John:

> *If it is made possible, I intend to come to you in order to see the faithful gathered in Jerusalem, and especially the Mother of Jesus: they say of her that she is honorable, affable, and arouses wonder in all, and all wish to see her. But who would not wish to see the Virgin and to converse with her who bore the true God? ...With us she is glorified as the Mother of God and the Virgin full of grace and virtue. They say of her that she is joyful in troubles and persecutions, does not grieve in poverty and want, and not only does not get angry with those who offend her but does good to them still more...All who see her are delighted."*

There ensued a correspondence between him and the Theotokos, herself:

Her friend Ignatius to the Christ-bearing Mary.

> *Thou oughtest to have comforted and consoled me who am a neophyte, and a disciple of thy [beloved] John. For I have heard things wonderful to tell respecting thy [son] Jesus, and I am astonished by such a report. But I desire with my whole heart to obtain information concerning the things which I have heard from thee, who wast always intimate and allied with Him, and who wast acquainted with [all] His secrets. I have also written to thee at another time, and have asked thee concerning the same things. Fare thou well; and let the neophytes who are with me be comforted of thee, and by thee, and in thee. Amen.*

This was her reply:

> *The lowly handmaid of Christ Jesus to Ignatius, her beloved fellow-disciple.*
>
> *The things which thou hast heard and learned from John concerning Jesus are true. Believe them, cling to them, and hold fast the profession of that Christianity which thou hast embraced, and conform thy habits and life to thy profession. Now I will come in company with John to visit thee, and those that are with thee. Stand fast in the faith, and show thyself a man; nor let the fierceness of persecution move thee, but let thy spirit be strong and rejoice.*

The Early Church is not obscure, not hidden in some distant mist of the past. It was vital, and its members were living and breathing people who lived in a highly civilized, literate (if brutal) society. Much of their correspondence and pastoral writing has come down to us through the generations.

Witness this excerpt from *Against Heresies* (5:19), written by St. Irenaeus in 180 AD. Irenaeus had been a pupil of St. Polycarp, who had been a pupil of the Apostle St. John...

> *The Virgin Mary, being obedient to his word, received from an angel the glad tidings that she would bear God.*

...and, later, from St. Gregory the Wonderworker, who studied under the great (though in some areas misled) Biblical scholar and exegete, Origen:

> *For Luke, in the inspired Gospel narratives, delivers a testimony not to Joseph only, but also to Mary, the Mother of God, and gives this account with reference to the very family and house of David*
>
> Four Homilies 1 [A.D. 262])
>
> *It is our duty to present to God, like sacrifices, all the festivals and hymnal celebrations; and first of all, [the feast of] the Annunciation to the holy Mother of God, to wit, the salutation made to her by the angel, "Hail, full of grace!"* (ibid., 2).

So we see, in the very earliest days of the Church, the consistent high regard for the Mother of our Lord that continues to this day and is part of our legacy and mindset.

So, fine, one might fairly ask, say, but what does that have to do with anything we're talking about, here?

Mary as Icon

For one thing, the Theotokos is matter for reflection. Her life holds up a mirror to the Church, and to us who are part of it.

The most obvious and striking part, of course, is the fact that, impregnated with Christ by the Holy Spirit, she carried Him inside of her and then revealed Him to the world.

Isn't that what we're all about? Should we all not be "pregnant with Christ" as a result of the indwelling in us of the Holy Spirit? Should we not, then, render Him forth to the world?

Reflect for a moment that the "man" part of the God-man, Jesus, came from His mother. He inherited his body, His humanity, from her. The Theotokos's body was, literally, the body of Christ. This leads us into contemplation of what it really means for the Church to be the "Body of Christ." Does the Lord actually take on His earthly, physical presence, from us? The Scriptures teach us, most frankly in 1 Corinthians 12, that the Church is the Presence of Christ in the world:

> *Just as a body, though one, has many parts, but all its many parts form one body, so it is with Christ. 1 Corinthians* (v. 12)

> *Now you are the body of Christ, and each one of you is a part of it.* (v. 27)

Just as the Holy Spirit formed Christ within the Theotokos, so He forms Him within us:

> *For by one Spirit we were all baptized into one body—whether Jews or Greeks, whether slaves or free—and have all been made to drink into one Spirit. For in fact the body is not one member but many.* (vss. 13-14)

Mary is called, among other things, the "God-bearer." Isn't that what we're all about?

Reflection on Mary brings home to us—perhaps as never before, that His blood-inheritance as "Son of David" and "Root of Jesse," His royal inheritance as the rightful King of Israel, comes from Mary.

This brings home to us—with perhaps jarring impact—that our Baptism into the estate of "Prophet, Priest and King," is not just something "Theological" or "theoretical" but is actually real, and derives from our being part of the Body of Christ, the Church.

Meditation on icons being what it is, this could go on for much, much longer. But you get the idea: to reflect on the Mother of God is to reflect on the Church and to reflect on ourselves as members of it. It is to gain a deep—and if I may use the term, gut-level—appreciation of just how real and immediate this "mystery" business actually is.

Mary as Intercessor

It is axiomatic that the Church in Heaven and the Church on earth are one. The Saints in Heaven are where we are going to be one day, if we remain faithful, and we can cultivate friendships with them right now.

Intrinsic to the transformed life is, as we have seen, what amounts to "trans-dimensionality." Heaven is not some distant geographical location: it is right here, all around us, in a dimension of being that Christ, in His Ascension, made accessible to us. As we grow in Christ, we become "more comfortable with mystery:" with the increasing reality and palpability of the unseen in our lives.

And why not? The Creed we recite at every Divine Liturgy reminds us that God is the Creator of all things, "both visible and invisible." The "invisible" is just the other side of the coin, another part of the creation we inhabit. It makes sense, then, that as we learn more about the great ones who have gone before us and about their lives and personalities, we should ask them to pray with and for us, just as naturally as we would ask each other, here in the "visible," to do. It is entirely natural and appropriate that we should honor them, as we are used to honoring any other person of accomplishment.

Just for example, look around at all the people who wear sneakers, jerseys and hats that commemorate sports figures; or whose cars wear candidate bumper stickers. We have retirement parties for people who have stuck it out at our companies for twenty years, statues and portraits of generals and politicians in our public and private places. From Mount Rushmore to a portrait of an ancestor on our wall or the picture of a friend on our refrigerator door, we are always honoring people who have gained our respect and always, when we can, establishing relationships with them. It's just as natural to do this with the "great cloud of witnesses" (Hebrews 12: 1) whose prayers go up for us continually before God:

> *Then another angel, having a golden censer, came and stood at the altar. He was given much incense, that he should offer it with the prayers of all the saints upon the golden altar which was before the throne. And the smoke of the incense, with the prayers of the saints, ascended before God from the angel's hand.*
> (Revelation 8: 3-4)

At the head of the Saints stands the best among us, the Queen of Heaven (Revelation 12: 1), the Blessed Mother (Luke 1: 28) of our Lord, God and Savior Jesus Christ.

So where, you may ask, do they get the time? With thousands of prayer requests coming at them at once, how do they cope?

Even here on earth, we see "time" becoming nonlinear, and in fact even fluid, at light and near-light speeds. "Clock time," the "time" we experience, is only one—and is in fact the simplest—aspect of "time" as a category.

Heaven is not subject to our linearity.

So, reflecting on the Blessed Mother as intercessor leads us naturally to consideration of the whole of the Church in Heaven as intercessors and from there to appreciation of the timelessness of the Heavenly dimension. This in turn draws our attention to the timelessness of our own lives who are in Christ; of the Eternity of which this, here, is the beginning, which we touch by entering into the Now.

Reflecting on the Theotokos as intercessor not only helps to bring all this into focus but also helps us build a relationship with this elect lady (2 John 1:1), and with other Saints and angels to whom we feel drawn, all of whom, if we remain faithful, we will one day meet.

Mary and Virginity

Mary's virginity speaks volumes to a society obsessed with sex and self-indulgence.

Human sexuality is a holy thing. God gave it to us as His partners in bringing new images of Himself into the world. That's why the sexual experience is so ecstatic!

A sexuality submitted to God results in a stable life, physical and spiritual health and a stable, well-ordered and successful society.

Because it is ecstatic, sexuality is also volatile. As well as the power to create, it also has the power to destroy. A renegade sexuality produces instability, disease, personal and social disorder and cultural decadence.

The former serves Heaven, the latter serves hell.

Sexuality--the drive to reproduce—is, in the natural, our prime directive. As a result, it has been at the heart of the world's pagan religions, and has taken some horrendous forms. The demon-gods of the pagans demanded devotions rooted in the basest of our personal perceptions and vanities. They have foisted these upon culture after culture through the ages—based on expediency and driven by ecstatic sensuality and human sacrifice. As our society turns less and less to Christ and more and more to a mythification of "Self," this demonic religion is once again—albeit cloaked in secular and pseudo-scientific language—upon us.

Its fruits, as they have always been, have been tragic: over fifty million innocent infants murdered in the womb; an epidemic of unspeakable venereal diseases; pandemic drug dependency, and a self-centered, morally depraved and epistemologically degraded society that is on the brink of collapsing under the weight of its own sin.

It is a religion without comfort for its adherents. Just look at our contemporary "sexual freedom activists," for instance. Have you ever seen emptier, angrier, more unhappy people in your life? Their lives are spent attempting to force the rest of the world to conform to them, in the desperate but vain hope that approval, or at least capitulation, will bring them release from their interior prison. Tragically, they see God, Who loves them and wishes to see them healed, happy and free. as their enemy. They choose, instead, the idols their real enemy has placed before them; their inner torment relieved only by their stridency in trying to force us to join them in their empty worship as the bars of their interior prison grow stronger.

Mary's virginity gives the lie to mammon's folly. Here we see the humble maiden of Nazareth raised to the highest possible human estate by the God Who loves her and Whose Love she returns. Her fidelity to God speaks volumes to a culture made unhappy by devotion only to self. Her protection was provided by God through John—the most mystical of the Apostles, and the only Apostle who lived to an old age and died a natural death. It speaks to us of God's protection of us, through the Church, wherein we ourselves enter into the Borderland, where physical death can reach us but not end us.

The Theotokos is not a "substitute for" Jesus, She isn't a divinity or a semi-divinity, and we don't "pray to" her as we would pray to God. She is a human being, like us but not like us. Like us, because she is entirely human. Unlike us, because she has had an experience no-one else has ever, nor will anyone else have ever, had. She is the best among us, and has realized the pinnacle of what it is to be human. As a result, iconic meditation on her helps us grow into realization of just what an incredible thing it is to be human, an image of God, an icon of Christ. It helps us realize the immediacy and the living vitality of the Church. And just as getting to know someone's family enlarges our relationship with that person, getting to know Mary enlarges our relationship with her Divine Son.

The Blessed Mother helps us understand the connectedness between the Church in Heaven and the Church on earth, and so prepares us to be vulnerable to the experience of living in the Borderland, the dimension between the dimensions. Conversation with her and asking for her "backup" in our prayers, helps the rest of the Heavenly Host become more accessible to us, simply because we have become more accessible to them. So, we wind up with a host of reliable prayer partners.

In short, she helps us understand, and live joyfully and vitally as part of this unique and incredible Theanthropic organism that is the Church.

PART EIGHT: A PRACTICAL FAITH
The Anthropic Principle, Intelligent Design, A Life of Faith

> *For since the creation of the world His invisible attributes are clearly seen, being understood by the things that are made, even His eternal power and Godhead, so that they are without excuse.*
> (Romans 1: 20)

~ ~ ~

The transformed life begins and ends with a Personal relationship with Jesus, our Lord, God, Savior and Friend (John 15: 15). All the smells and the bells, the great panoply of the Divine Liturgy, the Great Councils and the teaching of holy men and women over two thousand years, all the spiritual disciplines, have one single purpose: to enhance that relationship.

Life with Christ is not "other-worldly" or "supernatural" in the way we might ordinarily see those words. The Christian's world isn't "other," it's just bigger. It encompasses all of creation, "visible and invisible." As a result, Christian spirituality doesn't "float off" anywhere. It doesn't have to, because Eternity is right here with us. Accordingly, the Christian mindset is quite orderly: it was the Church, remember, that founded the great universities and hospitals. The monasteries were the first "public schools," and also the repositors and preservers of the learning of the classical world that fell with the fall of Rome.

It was Christian thinkers who laid the foundations for modern civilization: people like Erasmus, Augustine, Aquinas, John Henry Newman, Thomas More, Isaac Newton and scores of others.

The Church has always had a great appreciation for the Creator Who speaks through His Creation, and has always had a very down-to-earth attitude toward life on earth. Accordingly, a mature Christian Faith is a practical Faith; not in terms of the demands of mammon, but of those of the dimensional interface between Heaven and earth.

God acts through the Church, speaking to us in language we can understand and providing a means for our response, because He desires our growth in that relationship. It is hard to fathom, but this God—Whom we fallen sinners, beset by vanity, offend constantly—not only loves us but actually likes us. He wants to be around us, and wants us to be around Him. In fact, this Love that He has for us is the only thing that holds our universe together.

Modern science is beginning to be able to see the effects of this dimensional interface at first hand. Luke 15: 17 tells us, *For nothing is secret that will not be revealed, nor anything hidden that will not be known and come to light.* Indeed, we are seeing this fulfilled every day. "Charmed quarks" pop in out of "nowhere" and just as abruptly disappear, perhaps back from whence they came, but who knows? Space and time have been revealed as a continuum, and both of them not fixed but fluid. The forces of the universe balance precisely, like a gyroscope on the point of a pyramid, in just the right order and proportion to support intelligent life.

We are beholding with our eyes the creating Hand of the Creator.

In 1546, a British Catholic playwright by the name of John Heywood paraphrased Jeremiah 5:21 with his famous,

> There are none so blind as those who will not see. The most deluded people are those who choose to ignore what they already know.

This is no less true today than it was then. Many, however, are seeing. And the more they see, more it is who join them. Increasingly, the vainly-created, artificial gap between the Creator and those who study His creation, is narrowing.

The Anthropic Principle

Science increasingly finds itself having to use language that comes close to being religious. The Anthropic Principle, for instance, maintains that the razor-fine exactness of the universe, which enables it to support life, exists precisely for the support of life—specifically, us.

This idea, while far from universally embraced, is universally seriously considered (to support, refute and / or further examine) by modern science, particularly in the rarefied fields of quantum and cosmological physics.

From Oxford University Professor Nick Bostrom (in *Was the Universe Made for Us?* at http://www.anthropic-principle.com):

> It appears that there is a set of fundamental physical constants that are such that had they been very slightly different, the universe would have been void of intelligent life. It's as if we're balancing on a knife's edge. Some philosophers and physicists take the 'fine-tuning' of these constants to be an

> *explanandum that cries out for an explanans, but is this the right way to think?*

There's an old joke that you've probably heard, about a band of scientists who had heard The Truth was to be discovered at the top of the highest mountain. So, setting out with food and gear, they climbed for days. They ran out of food. They ran out of water. They almost lost their gear, their resolve and their lives. Finally, exhausted and bleeding, they collapsed onto the peak—only to find a group of Theologians there, having a picnic and offering them a cheery welcome.

Daily, those most advanced in our sciences are beginning to view the creating Hand of God "up close and personal." Daily, more and more of them admit that the ultimate questions cannot be answered by their disciplines as they currently stand.

Intelligent Design

The science of Intelligent Design is pursued by people like Dr. Stephen C. Meyer (Ph.D Cambridge University, Philosophy of Science), a former geophysicist who now directs the Discovery Institute's Center for Science and Culture in Seattle WA. (See http://www.discovery.org/p/11).

Briefly, Intelligent Design Theory maintains that the complexity of the universe could not have come about by chance, that its elaborate, elegant design requires a Designer.

> *The idea of intelligent design has deep roots in the history of science. Indeed, the co-discoverer of the theory of evolution by natural selection—Alfred Wallace—strongly disagreed with Darwin and believed that nature exhibited evidence of intelligent design,*

> especially when it came to the development of the human mind.
>
> --Discovery Institute, Educator's Briefing Packet on Intelligent Design, Part One.

A look at the available literature demonstrates that proponents of Intelligent Design Theory tend to speak in terms of science, while opponents tend to use the language of insult and political correctness. See, for example, *Frequently Raised but Weak Arguments Against Intelligent Design*, at http://www.uncommondescent.com/faq/ .

It takes a lot to deny God. All of creation cries out to us that there is a Creator (Romans 1: 20). The evidence of our senses insists to us that there is meaning and purpose to a world which is not only exquisitely organized, but exquisitely beautiful.

To deny God is to oppose the fundamental principle of causality, which is actually one of the more desperate positions of Postmodernism. For more on this, I recommend Geisler and Turek's *I Don't Have Enough Faith to be an Atheist* (Crossway, Wheaton IL 2004).

So why all this "science talk," all of a sudden?

It's to show that the practical and pragmatic, the examinable and verifiable, are not the exclusive—or even the most responsibly-handled—property of mammon. C.S. Lewis once famously remarked that "Christianity is a religion for grownups," that we do not park our intelligence at the church door. The purpose of the transformed life is not to "bracket out" our mind, but to renew it (Romans 12: 2).

We have nothing to fear from the speculations and philosophies of the world. We even have much to learn from science rightly pursued or rightly viewed, because—far from militating against God, it increasingly brings us closer to Him as it more and more graphically looks in on Him at work.

A Life of Faith

For all of that, at the last the transformed life is a life of faith. It is possible to have all the evidence in the world at one's fingertips, and still to ignore it. Knowledge by itself is not trust, and trust is the key to the Christ-life.

The Christian walk is a matter of trusting a Person—Jesus Christ—absolutely: of trusting Him so much that I am willing to invest my life in Him and to entrust Him with my Eternity.

When I do this, an amazing thing happens: He responds!

To entrust our life to Christ is to be transformed in spirit and character. It is to leave behind our loyalty to the vanities and blandishments of a dying world that wants us to die with it, and to enter into an altogether different—and much, much fuller—life.

To be sure, life in Christ is far from problem-free. We still have to pay the bills, see the doctor, bear with disease, danger and bereavement. In fact, living in a world that is increasingly hostile to us, we might even face entirely new sets of problems.

The change, then, isn't so much outside of us, but inside. We find ourselves facing life differently, and because of this our attitude toward—and ability to cope with—the curve-balls life occasionally throws us becomes better and more effective. That's the thing about the transformed life: it's actually, and wonderfully, transforming.

THANKS

There are people without whose influence and friendship this book never could have been written. Some of them are Protestant, some Roman Catholic, some "non-canonical" Orthodox, some "canonical" Orthodox. It has, after all, been a forty-year journey up to now. They all have one thing in common: a fierce love for Christ, and an ability to impart wisdom from the wellsprings of that love. Some have gone to be with the Lord, and I miss them. Others I haven't seen in years, and I miss them, too. Others, I have the great privilege of continuing to know and continuing to learn from. Some have been teachers, some friends, even some I've done little more than argue with. All of them, some, without even knowing it, have been examples and have helped me grow.

First and foremost among these are my wife, Sue, a brilliant, wonderful, God-loving woman who is perfectly described in Proverbs 31, and our daughter, Alyssa, who has a heart as big as an Olympic-size swimming pool, a fiercely inquiring mind and a burning zeal for Christ and His work.

I would also like to mention our cat, Victoria, who almost never misses family prayer time and is thus a fine example for us...

All you beasts, wild and tame, praise the Lord!
(Daniel 3: 81a)

My humble thanks go, in alphabetical order, to...

Bishop +Andrei, who brought me into Orthodoxy, Dom. Anthony Bondi, former Pastoral Vicar of the ROCOR Western Rite; Mr. Bill Burgess, former co-ordinator of the Sacred Heart Prayer Group in New York, Sr. Mary Fidelis, my great friend and prayer partner in the earliest days of my walk; Bishop +James Fisher, my Bishop at the close of my days in the UAOC, Brother Giles, O.Pent, my prayer partner at undergraduate Seminary, H.E. Metropolitan +Hilarion, First Hierarch of ROCOR, my Bishop and most excellent example; H.G. Bishop +Jerome, Bishop Emeritus of the ROCOR Western Rite, my former Bishop and patient counselor; Fr. Barnabas Keck, OFM. Cap., my first spiritual director; Rev. Ray Lorthioir, AALC, Pastor of Trinity Lutheran Church in West Hempstead, New York, and my Senior Pastor during my days as a Lutheran Minister; Bob Parmley, a true renaissance man of humble and unassuming brilliance; Fr. Raphael Tadros, Hieromonk, Rector of St. George's Orthodox Church (ROCOR) in Michigan City, Indiana, a good friend and an example to me of what quiet competence actually looks like; Fr. John Whiteford of ROCOR, whom I finally met after years of admiring his writing, Metropolitan +Yaroslaw, my bishop in my early days in the UAOC, Fr. Boris Zabrodsky, UOC-KP, my Senior Priest at the fantastic St. Nicholas Parish in Homewood IL during my days on loan to the Kiev Patriarchate from the UAOC, and Fr. David Zercie, MSA, my spiritual director at Holy Apostles Seminary.

Whatever is right with me is in great measure attributable to their individual and collective influence. Whatever is wrong with me is my own darn fault.

BIBLIOGRAPHY AND SUGGESTED READING LIST

You'll find the books that have been directly cited, below. More, you'll find a wealth of books for which I am grateful, which have provided me insights and which have contributed to such progress as I may have made along the Path of the transformed life in Christ. Among them you may find books that do not contribute to your own vocation or Rule, and for these all I can say, in the words of one of my early anam chara friends and advisors is, "eat the meat, spit out the bones."

In your voyage of discovery, may you sail with a fair wind, upon still waters.

~ ~ ~

Unless otherwise indicated, New Testament Scripture quotes are from the New King James Version of the Bible, and Old Testament quotes are from the Revised Standard Version–Catholic Edition.

Quotes From the *Verba Seniorum* are taken from *Wisdom of the*

Desert, a slim volume of excerpts edited by Cistercian Father Thomas Merton.

ANONYMOUS: *The Cloud of Unknowing and The Book of Privy Counseling*, Image Books, New York, 1973.

ST. BEDE THE VENERABLE: *Commentary on the Seven Catholic Epistles*, Trans. Dom David Hurst, O.S.B., Cistercian Publications, Kalamazoo, 1985.

ST, BENEDICT OF NURSIA: *Saint Benedict's Rule for Monasteries*, Trans. Leonard J. Doyle, OblOSB, Liturgical Press, Collegeville MN, 1950.

SERGIUS BULGAKOV (Trans. Boris Jakim): *Churchly Joy*, Eerdmans, Grand Rapids, 2008.

G.K. CHESTERTON:
The Everlasting Man, Galilee Books (apparently defunct), 1974, *Orthodoxy*, Image, New York, 1991.

ST. COLUMBA OF IONA: *Rule*, Medieval Sourcebook, Fordham University, New York, Online: http://legacy.fordham.edu/halsall/source/columba-rule.asp.

ESTHER De WAAL: *Every Earthly Blessing*: Morehouse Publishing, Harrisburg, 1991.

CATHERINE DeHUECK DOHERTY *Poustinia*, Ave Maria Press, Notre Dame IN, 1975.

FR, EDDIE DOHERTY: *A Hermit Without A Permit*, Dimension Books (apparently defunct), 1977.

CARMELA VIRCILLO FRANKLIN, IVAN HAVENER, O.S.B., J. ALCUIN FRANCIS, O.S.B. (Trans.): *Early Monastic Rules*, The Liturgical Press, Collegeville MN, 1982.

GEISLER, NORMAN L, Ph.D. and TUREK, FRANK, D. Min.: *I Don't Have Enough Faith to be an Atheist*, Crossway, Wheaton IL, 2004

M. REV. +PETER GILLQUIST: *Becoming Orthodox (First Edition)*, Wolgemuth & Hyatt, Brentwood, TN, 1989.

ST. GREGORY THE GREAT (Anonymous Trans.): *On the Mystery of the Resurrection*, Pamphlet, Unattributed.

C.S. LEWIS
The Abolition of Man
The Chronicles of Narnia
The Four Loves
The Great Divorce
Letters to Malcolm
A Mind Awake
Miracles
Mere Christianity
The Pilgrim's Regress
The Screwtape Letters
The Space Trilogy: Out of the Silent Planet, Perelandra, That Hideous Strength
The Weight of Glory
(All of the above have been reissued and are available through www.cslewis.com).

REV. LIONEL SMITHETT LEWIS: *St. Joseph of Arimathea At Glastonbury*, James Clarke & Co.,London, 1955.

THOMAS MERTON, O.C.S.O.
No Man is an Island, Harcourt-Brace, New York, 1983.
Seeds of Contemplation (the original), Hollis & Carter, London, 1952.
The Seven Storey Mountain, Harvest/Harcourt-Brace, Fort Washington PA, 1978.
The Silent Life, Sheldon Press, London, 1975.
Wisdom of the Desert, New Directions, New York, 1979.

THE BLESSED THEOPHYLACT
"*The Explanations*" *of the Synoptic Gospels*, Chrysostom Press, House Springs MO, 1997.

The Explanation of the Epistle of Saint Paul to the Ephesians, with additional commentary by Saint Nicodemus of the Holy Mountain (Trans. Fr. Christopher Stade), Chrysostom Press, 2013.

+MAELRUAIN (Kristopher Dowling), Celi De (Trans; Ed: Deaconess Elizabeth, Celi De): *Lorrha-Stowe Missal and the Hours of Bangor*, Celtic Orthodox Christian Church, 1996.

BARBARA PAPPAS: *The Christian Life in the Early Church and Today*, according to St. Paul's Second Epistle to the Corinthians (Foreword by M. Rev. +Kallistos of Diokletia), Amnos Publications, Westchester IL, 1998.

FRANK SADOWSKI, S.S.P. (Ed.): *The Church Fathers on the Bible*, Alba House, New York, 1987.

ARCHIMANDRITE VASILEOS OF ATHOS: *Hymn of Entry*, St. Vladimir's Seminary Press, 1984.

I'd like to refer you to *The Orthodox Study Bible, New Testament and Psalms*, Thomas Nelson Publishers, Nashville, 1997, as a sound and reliable basic Scripture commentary and study aid, endorsed by the

Hierarchy of every major Orthodox jurisdiction, which is my source for NKJV quotes.

Old Testament citations are taken from *The Revised Standard Version – Catholic Edition*, Catholic Biblical Association of Great Britain, Liverpool, 1966.

I would also like to recommend the full *Orthodox Study Bible*, Thomas Nelson Publishing, Nashville, 2008. It has a wealth of Patristic commentary accompanying the text. The Old Testament is a direct translation from the Septuagint, in its ancient order.

An absolutely essential resource is the *Ethereal Library*, on the Internet at www.ccel.org. It contains a wealth of material, from the writings of virtually all the ancient Fathers to the texts of the Councils. It is a searchable database of which, to my mind, no serious seeker should be unaware.

Inquiries may be directed to:

Fr. James Rosselli
St. Joseph of Arimathea Orthodox Church
and House of Prayer
402 Niesen Street
La Porte IN 46350
(219) 324-8364
frjames@arimatheachurch.com

I'd love to hear from you!

PASCHA PRESS
Catalog

Apostle of the Highlands-An Illustrated Abridgement
The Life of St. Columba, the Apostle and Patron of the Ancient Scots and Picts and Joint Patron of the Irish
Foreword by V. Rev. Mark Rowe

This retelling of the life of St. Columba will be of interest not only for adult students of Orthodox hagiography, but also those who wish to learn more about Western saints, Celtic Christianity, Scottish history, or anyone who has visited Iona and wishes to reclaim that moment of peace having stood in a sacred, thin place so blessed by God.

When Mama Had Cancer
Foreword by Father Joseph Gleason
An uplifting book that helps children understand a cancer diagnosis from an Orthodox perspective. Gently explains what their loved one will experience, the changes when one undergoes chemotherapy, and most importantly how to rely on God during this trying time.

When My Baba Died
Foreword by Father Milos Vesin
A gentle introduction to the Slavic Eastern Orthodox funeral process for ages 4-8. Richly illustrates what a child will see as we visit the funeral home, church, and cemetery with a little girl and her family.

Written by an Orthodox Christian funeral director with twelve years of experience, she is also a mother who understands how difficult it is to talk about death with your child. This comforting book answers questions, alleviates fears, and affirms faith.

When My Yiayia Died
Foreword by Father Konstantinos Tsiolas
A gentle introduction to the Greek Orthodox funeral process for ages 4-8. Richly illustrates what a child will see as we visit the funeral home, church, and cemetery, told this time through the perspective of a little boy.

Activity Workbook for When My Baba ♥My Yiayia Died
This companion full-color workbook for both editions of the children's book by the same name. It gives advice on personalizing the funeral experience during the visitation and also provides meaningful ways to help children participate in saying goodbye. Includes reinforcement of concepts presented such as vocabulary review and word searches, open ended questions to get children talking about their feelings, icons to color, recipe for a traditional Orthodox funeral food children can help prepare, Bible verses to look up, and a comforting prayer families can recite together.

Written by a funeral director and Certified Funeral Celebrant who has served thousands of families, this title honors Church Tradition, cultural heritage, and evolving funerary practices.

Links to purchase our titles from Barnes and Noble or Amazon are here:
www.paschapress.com